How the Bible Destroyed My Religion

How the Bible Destroyed My Religion

Peter Erbacher

Published by Kelly & Sons Publishing
Cairns, Far North Queensland, Australia
bibledestroyedreligion@gmail.com

First published in 2023

Copyright © Peter Erbacher, 2023

The moral right of the author has been asserted.

All rights reserved. No part of this publication may be reproduced, distributed, stored or transmitted in any form or by any means, including photocopying, recording, or other electronic or mechanical methods, without the prior written permission of the publisher, except in the case of brief quotations embodied in critical reviews and certain other non-commercial uses permitted by copyright law.

Some names have been changed to protect the privacy of individuals.

DISCLAIMER:
All Scripture is from The King James Bible, KJB.
They are direct quotations, which are four hundred years old.
For this reason, they contain, what we would call, **spelling, capitalisation and punctuation errors.**

Scripture quotations from The Authorised (King James) Version. Rights in the Authorised Version in the United Kingdom are vested in the Crown.

Scripture from King James Bible—Public Domain, sourced from Biblegateway.com

Miscellaneous Scriptures also sourced from Biblegateway.com

'15 Questions for Evolutionists' by Don Batten
of Creation Ministries International

 A catalogue record for this book is available from the National Library of Australia

ISBN 978 0 6459684 0 8 (pbk)
ISBN 978 0 6459684 1 5 (hbk)
ISBN 978 0 6459684 2 2 (ebk)

Editing by Kristy Rackham
Proofreading by Small Planet Copyediting
Cover design by Antonio Cesar
Typeset in Australia

Thank you:
Mum and Dad, Peter Connolly, Isaac Erbacher, Dominic Erbacher, Natalie Erbacher, Patrick Erbacher, Veria Hoyle, Kristy Rackham, Antonio Cesar, Colleen Kaluza, Barry Campbell, Caleb Turner, Cameron Humphries, Travis Terry, Annette Morison, Christeena Middleton, Scott Andrews, Sandra Rhodes, Jake Shupe, Mike Anderson, Cate Turner, Kirsty Matthews, Don Batten, Tas Walker, Renise Judge, Terry Bale-Bethel, Darren Blake, Shayne Harris, Heather Williams, Craig Dawson, Ruth McLeod, Lisa Hersee, Beatrice Gestier, Kylie Maconachie, Gary Witt, Kerryn Kitchener, Bec Horseman, Brooke Morton, Bryan Winters, Kate Chisholm, Nina Hosemans, Kylie Russell, Danielle Mooney, Cassie Watson, Scott Senius, Alen Rogina, Shannon Porche, Paul Trevison, Mark Treston, Lawrence Ryan, Warren Robb, Gayle Robins, Jillian Patane, Chris McCoomb, Wayde Leard, Jason Carlin, Alista Miletic, Kate Francis, Diana Shield, Daniel Edmonds, Mitch Gilespie, Kristyn Werner, Tim Dick, Neda Guarrera, Steve Dooley, Marion Brown, Shirley Van Riel, Jason Hall, Jeff Murray, Aiden Pedler, Max Findlay, Ben Statham, Shane Mcgrath, Angus Byrnes, Ingie Maxwell, Shane Anthony.

Preface

GROWING up I asked questions that went unanswered or weren't answered satisfactorily. *Why are we here? Where did we come from? Were we apes? What about the dinosaurs? Is there a God? If so, where is He? Why is there so much suffering? Where do we go when we die?*

During my search for answers, I didn't have an axe to grind; I just wanted to find the truth, committing to follow it wherever it may lead. It became evident that a majority of Christian beliefs weren't Biblical. Subsequent studies revealed teachings of evolution were religious philosophies masquerading as science. Over the years, while interacting with others and being exposed to their fallacious beliefs, I'd often exclaimed in frustration, "I should write a book!" —that's if they hadn't suggested it first.

For your clarity, place me in the 'sinner' pigeonhole as 'Christian' is a vague term. We must remove all beliefs and biases to come to the truth with what the Bible teaches, rather than what we've been told to believe. Imagine you're an outsider. You've no concept of Earth's history, or where it came from. You've found a Bible and begun reading. Take it at its word. For example, you're reading about the creation of the first two humans, one male, and one female. If you're of the belief humans evolved from apes that were once fish, leave it aside for now, and keep reading.

Yes, Catholics get a bashing. Though after all, the Bible did destroy my religion. I don't have all the answers and I don't pretend to. Apart from personal testimonies, don't blindly believe a word I say. Neither hold fast to your particular belief, whether it's a Christian denomination, Judaism, Evolutionism, or any other religion. Read for yourself in the Bible, every single Scriptural reference; it's included for that reason. Test everything. It'll stand the scrutiny.

"These were more noble than those in Thessalonica, in that they received the word with all readiness of mind, and searched the scriptures daily, whether those things were so." Acts 17:11

This book uses Scripture, science, logic, and common sense to either make or destroy arguments.

So long as you're open-minded, with a desire to know the truth of where we came from, how we got here, where we're going and everything in between, this book is for you. Warning: truth lying dormant within these pages will enrage you, as it did me, if you choose to awaken it.

There are no rhetorical questions. Puns are everywhere; see how many you can find.

Question everything.

Contents

Part One: The Old 'Testimony'

Catholic School Indoctrination	3
A Saving Grace	11
Noah's Flood	16
I Drowned When I Was Thirteen	27
High School Hoaxes	31
Dabbling in the Occult	40
An Obsession for Truth	50
Ten Commandments	58
Sabbath Day	75
Sabbath Day Objections	79
Clean and Unclean Food	85
Holy Days or Holidays?	90
Counterfeit Christianity	105
Heaven and Hell	121
Easter Fairy Tale	132
Calvary Conspiracies	146
"Before Abraham Was, I Am"	155
Bible Versions	160
The Bible Was Written by Man?	184
Catholics	200
Non-Practising Messianic Jew	209

Fingerprints of God	217
Biblical Roots of Science	227
Tipping Point	230

Part Two: The New 'Testimony'

Everyone Is Religious	233
In the Beginning	240
Bait-and-Switch	249
Evolutionism	258
Atheism – a Hopeless Religion	280
What About the Fossils?	293
♪ Millions of Years ♪	304
Dragons or Dinosaurs?	309
Fool's Gold	317
I Can't Come to Bed Yet—Someone Is Wrong on the Internet	327
Evolutionism's High Priests	336
15 Questions for Evolutionists	349
Wanted Dead, in Israel	355
The Last Stand	359

Part One

The Old 'Testimony'

Catholic School Indoctrination

MY journey began in grade four, questioning contradictions between what I was taught and what the Bible actually says.

Growing up in Far North Queensland, I spent most of my primary schooling at St Therese's in Edmonton, which in the early eighties was a small sugar town just outside the tropical city of Cairns, where we lived.

Weekly church attendance was compulsory in our family. Since I loathed attending as it bored me to tears, I'd periodically ride my pushbike to a church service on a Saturday evening so as I could get it, 'out of the way'. By doing so, I could enjoy Sunday, fishing from the Marlin Jetty, without an awful dread feeling of having to attend 'Mass' later that day.

Catholic teachings were confusing. My grandmother informed me that if one family member became a priest, our whole family would essentially receive a 'ticket to Heaven'. This was illogical. *If what she was saying was true, and my brother became a priest, it wouldn't matter what I did; I could murder, steal, and still go to Heaven.*

The Old Testament

Weighing the Bible in my hand during our religion class, I asked my teacher why she never taught from the Old Testament. She said it was before the time of Jesus, with his birth rendering it obsolete. Her words made no sense. *How can it be obsolete? It comprises two-thirds of the Bible. Why do we have it if it's not needed—especially as there's so much of it? Besides, I have to lug that book home every day.* "Why don't we just tear it off and throw it away?"

Her eyes widened in horror, "You can't do that, that's the Bible!" Now, I was well and truly confused.

Fire and Brimstone

During grade five we learned how terrifying eternity in Hell would be—a real fire-and-brimstone story. I told the teacher this was in stark contrast to the very nature of the Bible. Even at such a young age, I couldn't believe anyone could be sadistic enough to torture someone for eternity. Although this incident occurred over forty years ago, I still remember the feeling of confusion in attempting to reconcile the two conflicting thoughts. It didn't make sense, because it's not true. Eternal torment isn't Biblical.

Jesus' Brothers and Sisters

We read from the Gospels with a substitute teacher during a grade five religion lesson.

"And it came to pass, that when Jesus had finished these parables, he departed thence. And when he was come into his own country, he taught them in their synagogue, insomuch that they were astonished, and said, Whence hath this man this wisdom, and these mighty works? Is not this the carpenter's son? Is not his mother called Mary? And **his brethren, James**, and **Joses**, and **Simon**, and **Judas**? And his **sisters**, are they not all with us?" Matt 13:53–56

Brothers and sisters? Jesus? Confused, I raised my hand. "Miss, wasn't Jesus an only child?"

"Yes, Peter."

"But it says he had brothers and sisters."

She came over, reading the verse over my shoulder. "Yes," this time with a hint of confusion in her eyes, uncertainty in her voice. The eyes of the other students were on us. Suddenly, she straightened up, "But everyone was Jesus' brother and sister."

Other students appeared satisfied with her explanation. I might've been nine or ten years old, but I wasn't an idiot. "Yes, but it seems as if they're specifically talking about real brothers and sisters. Look, "Is this not the Carpenter's son? Is not his mother called Mary?" I then repeated the rest of the verse.

Too bewildered by her refusal to see the obvious, I don't recall her response. My mind wandered, *Who were these brothers and sisters? Did He fight with them like I fought with mine? There would be descendants; I wonder who and where they are. Could I be directly related to one of His brothers or sisters?*

After being taught for years He was an only child, it seemed strange to imagine Him being a big brother to several siblings. Seemingly tainted too, as these were half-brothers and sisters. Further, He had a step-father. On the other hand, it also seemed to make Him more real to me; or perhaps more Human. Either way, it was early days for the Man of Sorrows.

Heaven's Waiting Room

At church, they'd talk about Heaven and Hell, and of course, as Catholics, 'purgatory'. Catholics allege purgatory is a 'waiting room'. To release souls into Heaven, the living had to offer prayers. *What happens if those praying for you die before you're released?* I remember my grandmother informing me my grandfather was in purgatory, so we had to pray to have him released. It made me wonder about my grandfather's father. *Who was praying for him? Does it mean he's stuck there, in the limbo of purgatory for eternity?*

Also, how could you be content in Heaven, gazing down on family members enduring suffering and hardship on Earth? Or worse, watching family members supposedly being relentlessly pursued around a fiery pit by a goateed, red-suited demon with horns, a tail and a pitchfork? This would be their experience, for eternity. Besides that widely accepted scenario being illogical, the Bible talked about a Resurrection and Judgement:

"And I saw the dead, small and great, stand before God; and the books were opened: and another book was opened, which is the book of life: and the dead were judged out of those things which were written in the books, according to their works. And the sea gave up the dead which were in it; and death and hell delivered up the dead which were in them: and they were judged every man according to their works. And death and hell were cast into the lake of fire. This is the second death. And whosoever was not found written in the book of life was cast into the lake of fire." Rev 20:12–15

How could we possibly be assigned to Heaven or Hell at death, and be supposedly living in either place, before we'd been sentenced on Judgement Day? This occurs in the future when Jesus returns. What's Heaven anyway? Us dressed in long white gowns, sitting on fluffy clouds, playing harps for eternity? Would it be a case of, in the future at the Judgement, Saint Peter comes knocking at your cloud, "G'day mate, court was today. There's been a mistake, you were supposed to go to the Lake of Fire, pack your things."

Good Friday–Easter Sunday Fairy Tale

In year seven, we were reading a verse which now, almost forty years later, I know only too well—Matthew 12:40. What was to follow would wreak the most havoc on my faith—an apparent and glaring contradiction, which destroyed the very foundation of Christianity:

"For as Jonas was three days and three nights in the whale's belly; so shall the Son of man be three days and three nights in the heart of the earth." Matt 12:40

Logic gnawed. Jesus was placed in the tomb near sunset, allegedly on Good Friday, rising at dawn, allegedly on Easter Sunday. As a twelve-year-old, it wasn't difficult to work out you simply cannot fit three days and three nights between sunset Friday and dawn Sunday. The problem was compounded by the two verses below, preceding the one mentioned above.

"Then certain of the scribes and of the Pharisees answered, saying, Master, we would see a sign from thee. But he answered and said unto them, An evil and adulterous generation seeketh after a sign; and there shall no sign be given to it, but the sign of the prophet Jonas: For as Jonas was **three days and three nights** in the whale's belly; so shall the Son of man be three days and three nights in the heart of the earth." Matt 12:38–40

Therein lays the problem. Religious leaders demanded a sign, proof He was indeed, God's Son. The proof Jesus gave was that He'd be in the heart of the earth for three days and three nights. Although they may not have known what He'd meant at the time, it was pretty obvious after His death.

It follows if He wasn't in the tomb for three days and three nights, He was a liar, a madman, or both, but He most certainly wasn't the Son of God, by His own admission. If Jesus was entombed from sunset Friday until dawn Sunday, that's only one full day, two part days, and two nights. If you factor in, Biblically, a day is calculated from sunset to sunset, then you have one full day, two nights, and one part of a day.

Putting it to Father Grundy, his excuse was, "When Jesus was on the cross and God turned His back, the sky went dark, which was the first night." *Did he think that was a satisfactory answer?* I was recounting this story to someone I'd met in Israel, who until that point in time, had believed the Good Friday–Easter Sunday fairy tale. She claimed the priest sounded like he was, 'clutching at straws'. I also reminded her, that when the sun darkened, Jesus hadn't yet died.

I'd then queried the priest over Easter eggs, and their relevance with Jesus' death. He stated eggs were symbolic of a tomb and new life. Although it seemed like a stretch, I was willing to concede the point, "But rabbits? Why not chickens? After all, chickens lay eggs, rabbits don't." He smiled, shrugged, and hobbled away.

Many years later, I'd encounter a plausible explanation for the meanings of those two Easter symbols. What's more, there'd be a time in the future when I'd unlock the mystery of the alleged three-day and three-night contradiction. All will be revealed in subsequent chapters. Ironically, although I wasn't aware of it at the time, the key to unlocking the mystery would be contained within my very next unanswered question, posed in my final year of primary school:

A Pivotal Point

"Since it was the day of Preparation, and so that the bodies would not remain on the cross on the Sabbath (for that Sabbath was a high day), the Jews asked Pilate that their legs might be broken and that they might be taken away." John 19:31

I questioned my substitute religion teacher, "Miss, what's a high day?"

Reading over my shoulder she was stumped, "It's not important."

What a stupid thing to say. It was obvious the Bible had an emphasis on brevity, "If it wasn't important, it wouldn't be in there." My words fell on deaf ears. Little did I know at the time, my unanswered question was significant, pivotal, the key to solving the three-days and three-nights conundrum. It'd be fifteen years before I'd discover what a High-day Sabbath was and be able to solve the riddle. During this period, I'd also encounter others who'd strayed from Christianity, due to no logical answer being provided for this alleged contradiction.

Inconsistencies with Bible teachings chipped away at my faith. During high school, Evolutionism dogma (Darwinian Evolution), would erode my faith at an alarming rate.

Local Flood?

We were reading the Genesis Flood account with Father Grundy. The class was split; half believing it was true, half believing it wasn't. The priest assured us, "It wasn't a worldwide flood, it was a local flood." *Why then, did Scripture say the whole earth was covered? Why bother to build an ark? Why not move?*

Glancing out the window, I gazed across the tops of swaying sugar cane fields at the towering heights of the rugged mountain range behind Cairns. It was difficult to believe floodwaters had once covered those escarpments. Still, the Bible claimed Earth was submerged—and I believed. The priest went on to say Genesis and the Book of Revelation weren't true—they were metaphoric. I told him the Bible couldn't be part true and part wrong, it could only be all true, or all false. Smiling patronisingly, he shrugged once more, turned, and shuffled away.

What right did he have, teaching something he didn't believe, which, by the nature of his occupation, he should believe? Jesus believed it as truth, as evidenced by His words below; so, what makes a random Catholic priest the final authority?

"And as it was in the days of Noe, so shall it be also in the days of the Son of man. They did eat, they drank, they married wives, they were given in marriage, until the day that Noah entered into the ark, and the flood came, and destroyed them all." Luke 17:26–27

I Became an Altar Boy

Attending St Monica's Cathedral one Sunday, I noticed an advert in the church bulletin, 'Altar Boys Wanted'. *Well, I wanted money and had to attend mass anyway, so why not get paid? Besides, it would give me something to do, thereby making time pass faster.*

I had absolutely no idea it wasn't a paid position, the thought hadn't occurred to me. Would you see a 'wanted' sign in a window and assume you'd work for free? Why should this be any different?

Nudging my mother, I pointed to the advertisement. Intrigued, she whispered, "Do you want to be an altar boy?" I nodded. Later, when I inquired as to the pay rate, she became angry, asking if that was my sole motivation. I had to lie. Yes, that's right, I broke the Ninth Commandment. I bared false witness. Now I had no recourse, I couldn't back out. Fortunately, I ended up getting sacked. During a service, the other altar boy, who is still a close friend today, and I, managed to lose the key to a cabinet containing the Eucharist.

A Saving Grace

PERHAPS I've been too critical of my religious education in primary school. As you'll see below, they did offer proof of the validity of Scripture.

Sweating Blood

My religion teacher spoke of the betrayal and arrest of Jesus in the Garden of Gethsemane before He was tortured and publicly executed the following day.

Luke, a medical doctor and historian, had this to say:

"And he was withdrawn from them about a stone's cast, and kneeled down, and prayed, saying, Father, if thou be willing, remove this cup from me: nevertheless not my will, but thine, be done. And there appeared an angel unto him from heaven, strengthening him. And being in an agony he prayed more earnestly: and his sweat was as it were great drops of blood falling down to the ground."

Luke 22:41–44

Some say this may be a simile, in that Jesus' sweat fell like drops of blood. Haematohidrosis is a rare medical condition that produces the symptoms described. Sweat glands are surrounded by tiny blood vessels that can rupture due to extreme anguish, causing blood to seep into sweat glands.

Scientific Crucifixion

The teacher mentioned Jesus being speared in the side:

"But one of the soldiers with a spear pierced his side, and forthwith came there out blood and water." John 19:34

It seemed odd water would spill out; though as the teacher explained, medical science disagrees. Jesus' brutal flogging would've led to hypovolemic shock, causing fluid to gather around the heart and lungs.

Betrayal

Another recollection concerned the betrayal of Jesus, by Judas, one of His Twelve Apostles. The betrayal was predicted by King David and recorded in Psalms, approximately 1,000 years before its fulfilment:

"Yea, mine own familiar friend, in whom I trusted, which did eat of my bread, hath lifted up his heel against me." Ps 41:9

However, my point doesn't relate to the betrayal so much, as to the sum of money prophesied. You could say, it's a prophecy within a prophecy. Namely, the fee Judas would be paid, to betray Jesus:

"And I said unto them, If ye think good, give me my price; and if not, forbear. So they weighed for my price thirty pieces of silver." Zech 11:12

The above Scripture was written 500 years before the events were recorded below:

"Then one of the twelve, called Judas Iscariot, went unto the chief priests, and said unto them, What will ye give me, and I will deliver him unto you? And they covenanted with him for thirty pieces of silver. And from that time he sought opportunity to betray him." Matt 26:14–16

That's remarkable. In fact, that's an understatement. As my teacher pointed out, this prophecy correctly prophesied an amount of thirty pieces of silver, despite the occurrence of 500 years' worth of inflation. My teacher proceeded to say Scripture accurately predicted what would become of those thirty pieces of silver:

"And the Lord said unto me, Cast it unto the potter: a goodly price that I was prised at of them. And I took the thirty pieces of silver, and cast them to the potter in the house of the Lord." Zech 11:13

Prophecy Fulfilled

"When the morning was come, all the chief priests and elders of the people took counsel against Jesus to put him to death: And when they had bound him, they led him away, and delivered him to Pontius Pilate the governor. Then Judas, which had betrayed him, when he saw that he was condemned, repented himself, and brought again the thirty pieces of silver to the chief priests and elders, saying, I have sinned in that I have betrayed the innocent blood. And they said, What is that to us? see thou to that. And he cast down the pieces of silver in the temple, and departed, and went and hanged himself. And the chief priests took the silver pieces, and said, It is not lawful for to put them into the treasury, because it is the price of blood. And they took counsel, and bought with them the potter's field, to bury strangers in. Wherefore that field was called, The field of blood, unto this day. Then was fulfilled that which was spoken by Jeremy the prophet, saying, And they took the thirty pieces of silver, the price of him that was valued, whom they of the children of Israel did value; And gave them for the potter's field, as the Lord appointed me." Matt 27:1–10

So, you could say, three prophecies in one:

1. Betrayal
2. Thirty pieces of silver
3. The Potter's Field

If you were to delve deeper, you'd uncover several more. Remember, these prophecies came from the Old Testament books, Psalms and Zechariah. These were written 500 years apart, yet they share an amazing symmetry. Jews divide the Old Testament into three segments—The Law, The Writings, and the Prophets. Of the prophet section, Jeremiah was often listed first. Any reference to the Prophets was occasionally referred to as, 'Jeremiah the Prophet'.

The betrayal prophecy was written 1,000 years before Jesus' birth. It mentions the eating of bread; so now we're at a total of four prophecies in one:

"Yea, mine own familiar friend, in whom I trusted, which did eat of my bread, hath lifted up his heel against me." Ps 41:9

The prophesied betrayal occurred immediately after Jesus passed Judas a hunk of bread, instantly fulfilling a new prophecy—exposing the betrayer:

"Jesus answered, He it is, to whom I shall give a sop, when I have dipped it. And when he had dipped the sop, he gave it to Judas Iscariot, the son of Simon. And after the sop Satan entered into him. Then said Jesus unto him, That thou doest, do quickly." John 13:26–27

We've already added the breaking of bread to the prophecy list. How about Jesus predicting the betrayer would be Judas? Now we're five prophecies in one:

1. Betrayal.
2. Thirty pieces of silver.
3. Potter's field. Even today, the term 'potter's field' is used to denote a place for the burial of unknown, unclaimed, or destitute people. It was called the potter's field, as that's where potters would obtain clay. Where Judas Iscariot died is called Akeldama, meaning Field of Blood. I visited it in 2023.
4. Breaking and sharing of bread.
5. Prophesying Judas would be the betrayer.

If you were to look further into it, you would uncover several more. For example:

6. Betrayal payment would be returned.
7. Returned payment wouldn't be accepted and would be thrown to the floor of the temple.

"And I took the thirty pieces of silver, and cast them to the potter in the house of the Lord." Zech 11:13

Here's the Old Testament prophecy coming to life in the New Testament, exactly as predicted:

"And he cast down the pieces of silver in the temple, and departed, and went and hanged himself." Matt 27:5

Still, there are more, if you were to do your research.

Matthew was an accountant/tax collector. Trust him to pick up on the price of the potter's field correlating with the prophecy of thirty pieces of silver. It's not mentioned by the other three Gospel writers.

The Bible consists of prophecy, criss-crossing prophecy, often written hundreds and even thousands of years apart; penned by men from three continents, from a diverse range of occupations. Need I mention, accurately fulfilled prophecies? Some are coming true now, thousands of years later. Some will occur in the future.

Based on these truths alone, and forgoing all other evidence, do you really believe the Bible was, 'written by men'? Pause until you've resolved this question logically. The discovery of the Dead Sea Scrolls alone, has proved the authenticity of the recordings of these prophecies, centuries before their fulfilment.

Noah's Flood

JESUS and Peter believed Noah's Flood was a historical event. Christians, you claim to believe in Jesus. While it's all very well to believe *in Him*, do you, *believe Him*? If not, why not?

"But as the days of Noah were, so shall also the coming of the Son of man be. For as in the days that were before the flood they were eating and drinking, marrying and giving in marriage, until the day that Noe entered into the ark, And knew not until the flood came, and took them all away; so shall also the coming of the Son of man be." Matt 24:37–39

"Whereby the world that then was, being overflowed with water, perished: but the heavens and the earth, which are now, by the same word are kept in store, reserved unto fire against the day of Judgment and perdition of ungodly men." 2 Peter 3:6–9

"Where did all of the water go?" you may ask.

"Go to the beach and see for yourself."

Seventy per cent of Earth's surface area is water. If you were to push every mountain range down and level the oceans' floors, water would cover Earth to a depth of three kilometres. Most of us are familiar with how it rained for forty days and forty nights. What most of us are ignorant of is, the majority of water emerged from the ground:

"In the six hundredth year of Noah's life, in the second month, the seventeenth day of the month, the same day were **all the fountains of the great deep broken up**, and the windows of heaven were opened. And the rain was upon the earth forty days and forty nights." Gen 7:11–12

Flood Evidence

'All the fountains of the great deep broken up', points to the tectonic rupturing of Earth's surface in numerous places, resulting in earthquakes, volcanoes, and tsunamis, creating immense sedimentary deposits. Rapidly receding floodwaters worldwide, carved geological formations from these sodden deposits.

Evidence of this flood is identified across the earth. I've witnessed numerous examples myself: Large-scale cross-bedding, flood plains, canyons, plateaus, and folded sediment layers. Not to mention, the depositing of these sediments in the first place. Massive conglomerate rock formations of the Olgas in Australia's Northern Territory are testimony to a catastrophic deluge. These sit upon eroded conglomerate rocks. There are flat-topped mountains and hills called 'mesas' or 'buttes' with 'rock aprons' at their base. Many of these formations are studded with marine fossils. Once you see it, you see it everywhere, it jumps out at you. Grand Canyon is a perfect example. So too is Monument Valley, both of which are in the US. Then there are the Blue Mountains of Australia, just for starters.

Noah entered the Ark in the second month (Hebrew calendar), exiting on the 27th day of the same month the following year. In other words, floodwater covered Earth for a year. Picture the Earth submerged for such a length of time. What normally happens when dirt is subjected to water? Sediments settle.

Floodwater sifted sediments out of solution into coloured layers 'strata', which later hardened into rock once floodwaters had retreated. Have you ever seen water and coloured sand contained between two sheets of glass within a wooden frame, which you'd shake? Notice how the layers form?

Immense beds of floating foliage, vegetation, and torn-off tree branches from violent floodwaters would in time sink into soft, pliable sediments. These have become the coal deposits we mine today.

Billions of decomposed marine organisms would later be mined as oil. Why do you think they're called fossil fuels? What else could've created worldwide, immense oil and coal beds, other than a watery catastrophe on the magnitude of Noah's Flood?

"And the flood was forty days upon the earth; and the waters increased, and bare up the ark, and it was lift up above the earth. And the waters prevailed, and were increased greatly upon the earth; and the ark went upon the face of the waters. And the waters prevailed exceedingly upon the earth; and all the high hills, that were under the whole heaven, were covered. Fifteen cubits upward did the waters prevail; and the mountains were covered." Gen 7:17–20

Following the flood, our Creator sent a wind to evaporate the water:

"And God remembered Noah, and every living thing, and all the cattle that was with him in the ark: and God made a wind to pass over the earth, and the waters assuaged; The fountains also of the deep and the windows of heaven were stopped, and the rain from heaven was restrained; And the waters returned from off the earth continually: and after the end of the hundred and fifty days the waters were abated." Gen 8:1–3

He also raised the land, while lowering what would become the seabed:

"Who laid the foundations of the earth, that it should not be removed for ever. Thou coveredst it with the deep as with a garment: the waters stood above the mountains. At thy rebuke they fled; at the voice of thy thunder they hasted away. They go up by the mountains; they go down by the valleys unto the place which thou hast founded for them. Thou hast set a bound that they may not pass over; that they turn not again to cover the earth." Ps 104:5–9

Grand Canyon Creation

We're taught it formed over 'millions of years', cut by the Colorado River. In other words, Evolutionism believers claim it was carved by a 'little bit of water, over a long time'. In reality, it was carved by 'a lot of water, over a short time'.

Most of the rock that makes up the Grand Canyon is sedimentary. Where did those sediments come from? They had to be deposited by one of two elements, either water or air. Leaving emotion out of it, using only logic and common sense, which depositor is more likely? Water is. Especially considering the vast area and depths a formation such as Grand Canyon encompasses. Remember, too, marine fossils are found within these layers.

Picture the land, submerged for a year. Suddenly, that sodden land is yanked upward. Natural dams are formed, before rupturing and carving a swathe through that water-logged mass as floodwaters desperately seek sea level. Eventually, they leave a trickle by comparison, at the bottom of these newly formed valleys and canyons.

Grand Canyon's colourful, distinct layers often run on a knife's edge, straight and true for kilometres. We're told 'millions of years' separate these layers. If this is true, why is there no evidence of erosion during these alleged spans of 'millions of years'? Some layers are slanted, intersecting with horizontal layers—'cross-bedding'.

Noah's Flood offers the most plausible explanation for Grand Canyon's creation. It explains the arrival of the fossil-bearing sediments, which would be later carved by the rapidly retreating floodwater, resulting in Grand Canyon.

Mount St Helens erupted in 1980. This small eruption carved a canyon complete with layers, over forty-five metres deep, all within twenty-four hours, on a scale of 1:40 to Grand Canyon. Further, unlike Grand Canyon, Mount St Helen's ground hadn't been softened by being submerged for a year. Imagine if it had.

If Mount St Helens had erupted before America was 'discovered', experts examining the strata would've dogmatically concluded the layers were individually formed over 'millions of years', saying each layer was deposited by 'shallow seas', as they always do, when presented with such layers.

Native Americans from the Grand Canyon area have oral traditions stating the canyon was carved by retreating waters of a great flood. Similarities with the Genesis account are depicted in their paintings.

If you were to cast your bias aside, eliminate emotion from your thinking, and contemplate this explanation, you'd have to be an idiot to conclude the 'millions of years' explanation is more plausible. Especially as the just-so story has no satisfactory explanation for the immense sedimentary deposits to begin with.

Polystrate Fossils

This is the name assigned to fossils which are found as a single object, cutting through several sediment layers. 'Poly', as in 'many', and 'strate', as in 'strata'. These are found across Earth and are a headache for Evolutionism believers.

Trees are often found as polystrate fossils. Or rather, tree trunks. They often have no branches or root systems. Noah's Flood provides an excellent explanation. Catastrophic conditions, breaking up of Earth's crust and accompanying volcanic eruptions and violent floodwaters, tore branches from trees, snapping trunks at ground level.

Years ago, an acquaintance tried to sell me on the mythical concept of 'millions of years'. I described the typical polystrate fossil of an upside-down tree trunk, devoid of branches and roots, running through several layers of sedimentary rock on an angle. Then I put forward a ridiculous scenario as a way of explanation, *if* the 'millions of years' mantra were true:

"So, you're telling me, a tree suddenly lost all of its branches and root system, then flipped over, with the top falling into a hole, and the rest of the trunk standing upside-down above the ground on an angle, as layer, after 'millions of years' layers, slowly built up around it?"

Staring at me through glassy eyes, he failed in his attempt to sound confident, "… Yeah …"

Noah Down Under?

Genesis seems to suggest Earth was one landmass in the beginning:

"And God said, Let the waters under the heaven be gathered together unto one place, and let the dry land appear: and it was so. And God called the dry land Earth; and the gathering together of the waters called he Seas." Gen 1:9–10

Ignoramuses ridicule the historical account of the Flood, asking how Noah could've gathered the animals to the Ark. The short answer is, "He didn't."

"How did Noah cross the oceans to Australia to get the kangaroos?" This ignorant question is reminiscent of sayings that are deemed, 'Fool's Gold'. You've already seen the Bible suggests Earth was one landmass before the Flood. It's likely catastrophic conditions at the Flood's commencement instigated the tearing up of Earth. Secondly, read and comprehend the following verse:

"Of fowls after their kind, and of cattle after their kind, of every creeping thing of the earth after his kind, **two of every sort shall come unto thee**, to keep them alive." Gen 6:20

Noah didn't have to gather animals. Are you familiar with salmon returning to the same section of stream in which they'd been birthed, after dwelling at sea for years? How about the remarkable abilities of homing pigeons? Animals could've been summoned to the Ark.

Here's another unscriptural belief most Christians hold. They believe two of all kinds of animals boarded the ark. This is true for unclean animals. Clean animals went as seven pairs:

"Of every clean beast thou shalt take to thee by sevens, the male and his female: and of beasts that are not clean by two, the male and his female. Of fowls also of the air by sevens, the male and the female; to keep seed alive upon the face of all the earth." Gen 7:2-3

Another argument is, "The animals wouldn't have fit aboard the Ark." There are 400 breeds of dogs. Noah wouldn't have had to take aboard every single breed we have today, just two, of the dog kind. They would've contained all of the genetic information required to produce the hundreds of modern varieties within the dog 'kind'.

It's the same for cats. Siamese, lions, tigers, tabbies, pumas, cougars, leopards—they're all a kind of cat.

Next, they bring up the matter of food for the animals. Who's to say animals didn't enter a state of hibernation? Many animals eat fish—They were surrounded by water …

While undertaking laborious work, workmates would say I ate a lot. They didn't see what I'd consume on weekends. Sometimes, it was next to nothing. There were days I'd take a large plate of food to work, though only eat half, as the work that day wasn't as physically demanding as usual. Animals aboard the Ark wouldn't have had much to do. As for pigs, they'll eat anything, including animal waste. All aboard the Ark were under our Creator's protection. If required, He could evoke miracles, or 'magic', as some may say. Has it occurred to you that if someone who lived centuries ago saw the modern world; their explanation for our technology would be 'magic'?

"Any sufficiently advanced technology is indistinguishable from magic." (Arthur C. Clarke)

Another revelation for me was that dinosaurs were aboard the Ark. At first, this seems ludicrous until you realise, they weren't required to be fully grown. Besides, many dinosaurs were the size of a sheep, some the size of a cat.

Regardless, we don't have to play semantics. As the Creator, He's not bound by the very laws He set in place to govern His physical Creation. He's independent of them.

Noah's Tankers

Korean Naval ship engineers conducted a test of a sea-going vessel using dimensions on a ratio of 1/50 to Noah's Ark. They found the vessel to be incredibly stable in rough seas. Their research led to tankers developing similar ratios, drastically reducing their tendency to capsize in violent seas. So, if not God-inspired, how could Noah have possibly devised plans for such a sturdy ship, appropriate for the task? Coincidence? (S.W. Hong et al., 'Safety investigation of Noah's Ark in a seaway,' *Creation*, 8(1):26–36, 1994, Creation.com)

Flood Legends

Following the human dispersion at the Tower of Babel, there are ancient stories worldwide linked to a past great deluge. Included are similar significant details, such as: a massive flood that destroyed everything; human transgression; a divine warning issued; a floating vessel; all were saved in a vessel; a rainbow; a favoured family; amassing of animals; God's wrath; few survivors; animals saved; bird or other creature sent out; vessel finally came to rest on a mountain; sacrificial offering; etc. While many may recognise the similarity with Noah's Flood, some may not be familiar with the relevance of birds:

"And he sent forth a raven, which went forth to and fro, until the waters were dried up from off the earth. Also he sent forth a dove from him, to see if the waters were abated from off the face of the ground." Gen 8:7–8

Atheists love to bring up the 'Gilgamesh flood'. They claim that Noah's Flood is derived from it. This is an absurd claim. Blind Freddy himself can see that it's a bastardisation of the true event.

When missionaries first came to Northern Queensland and Aborigines heard the history of Noah, they were adamant Genesis was their Creation story, The Rainbow Serpent. Anyone who's read it would be familiar with the Aboriginal man and woman who sinned, the great flood, the rainbow, the serpent, and their 'creator', the Rainbow Serpent. This serpent is credited with creating the sun, land, animals, mountains, valleys, rivers, and even knowledge itself. Other Australian Aboriginal tribes have flood legends similar to the Genesis account.

Chinese Characters

These have strong links within their construction to the events of Genesis. 'Garden' comprises characters for 'two', 'dust', and 'breath'. 'Boat' comprises characters for 'eight', 'mouth' (as in the eight mouths/people aboard the Ark), and vessel. The character for 'eight', also shows up in their character for 'flood'. What's the likelihood this was a coincidence? There are numerous other examples of Chinese Characters being grounded in Genesis. (James J. S. Johnson, J.D., Th.D., 'Genesis in Chinese Pictographs,' 2015, Institute for Creation Research, icr.org)

What's often overlooked, not only is there a universal flood legend, there's also a worldwide remembrance of its dead. What's more, you've likely participated in this annual ritual, unaware.

Halloween, Flood Memorial

"In the six hundredth year of Noah's life, in the second month, the seventeenth day of the month, the same day were all the fountains of the great deep broken up, and the windows of heaven were opened." Gen 7:11

This date coincides with the end of October/beginning of November in our modern Gregorian calendar, the 31st of October, or 'Halloween'. It's also known as 'All Saints Day'. Almost all who partake in this ritual are oblivious to the fact they're paying homage to Noah's Flood. It's symbolic of the day the deluge commenced and all of those souls perished.

During that time of year, Australian Aborigines would paint white stripes on their chests, legs, and arms to resemble skeletons — similar to the way modern people dress for Halloween, during their unconscious ritualistic homage to the death and destruction of the worldwide Flood.

Mexico has its 'Day of the Dead'. Other countries have similar festivals at the same time of year, marked by the remembrance of the dead and the offering of burnt sacrifices, as Noah had done:

"And Noah built an altar unto the LORD; and took of every clean beast, and of every clean fowl, and offered burnt offerings on the altar." Gen 8:20

Outback Crabs

As a child, I'd go camping with Dad in the outback, west of Cairns, at a place called Mt. Surprise. The name was derived from when a loud pioneer party surprised a group of Aboriginal people who were resting at the mountain's base in 1864. Dad would fossick for topaz, a semi-precious stone. Digging in sand, high in the hills, was a most unexpected sight—sea shells and a live crab. The nearest ocean was 300 kilometres away. As my mind did somersaults, the crab took advantage of the ensuing confusion, successfully burrowing to safety. Initially intrigued, Dad shrugged it off, "Well, this used to be under the sea, millions of years ago." Even then, I was struggling to understand how these creatures had managed to survive, generation after generation, supposedly, for 'millions of years'.

I Drowned When I Was Thirteen

HAVING no luck fishing from a Cairns wharf in 1986, my friends and I built a raft from a discarded wooden pallet. Finding anything that could float, be it small plastic drums or even plastic milk cartons, we lashed them to the pallet.

Somehow, I had a premonition of impending danger. While my friends horsed about with our raft, I was terrified! Worse, I had no idea why.

I was the one who'd venture into the deepest parts of crocodile-inhabited waters whenever drag-netting, or accepting a dare to swim across creeks known to contain crocodiles. So why was I fearful? Terrified, the question baffled me. It didn't make sense … yet …

Finally, my mates were ready for another round on our raft. Amongst themselves, they attempted to discern whose turn it was. Suddenly, "Hey, Erbie hasn't had a turn yet!" They called for me. Attempting to protest, my mouth was dry. Peer group pressure is real. Next thing I knew, I was down on all fours aboard the raft, petrified.

My best friend 'Ebo' ran alongside the wharf grinning, before leaping, headed for the raft. Horrified, I thrust my arm up, "Nnooo!" His feet struck the raft, launching me like a catapult. As I hit the water, the raft came down on top.

Drowning

What I remember next was an incredible feeling of peace, like nothing I'd ever experienced before, or since. Although I was underwater, it was as though I was in a black void. I felt free, unconfined to my body. In fact, I didn't have a body, as such. I didn't have arms—though it felt like I did. Floating, relaxed, somewhat contained within an oval shape, it was as if I was, 'my mind'.

Waving my 'arms' while looking from side to side, marvelling at the sensation, a peculiar movement ten metres distant caught my eye. A shadowy shape thrashed and struggled. Perplexed, I said, (it seemed more like, thought), "What is that thing?" Overcome by the amazing feeling, I reverted to moving my weightless 'arms' once more.

"That's You, You're Drowning"

Continuing to look from side to side, the annoying distraction caught my eye once more. Putting my 'hands' on my 'hips', I said/thought again, "Man, what *is* that thing!?"

It was then I heard a voice, "That's you, you're drowning." The realisation hit me! The horror of realisation didn't last. I felt incredible.

Growing up as an avid reader, one of the literary series I'd read was the boys' adventure series, 'The Hardy Boys'. One of them had been tied to an anchor and thrown overboard, conjuring an awful image in my mind at the time. I'd imagined the horror of realising that the next time I'd open my mouth for air, it would instead fill with water. Because of this, I'd always thought drowning was the worst possible way to die. Not anymore! I'd never felt better.

In the distance to my right, I spied a tiny, brilliant light, accelerating as it traversed from one side of my field of vision to the other. Passing in front, it paused, before expanding as an enormous picture of me wrestling with my dog at the bottom of a slippery slide. There's a photo of us in a family photo album, capturing this very moment.

'Devil' had died when I was seven, grieving me immensely. I'd vowed to never laugh again. Remembering him with sorrow, I felt a sharp stab of guilt. My actions had killed him. Or should I say, my lack of action …

Our family had travelled to Cooktown for the day. Upon our return, Devil was missing. A week later I was atop a bunk bed, playing with older siblings. There was a knock at the door. Cautiously, Dad entered the room. There was no easy way to say it, "Pete, Devvy is dead." Laughter ceased. Once the initial shock wore off, I scrambled down the ladder, running outside into the garage, crying uncontrollably.

Mum later told me I'd neglected to leave water for Devil. When he'd wandered in search of it, he'd been fatally struck by a car and buried at a house down the street. Until now, I've never told anyone of the part I played in the death of my dog. As they did close to forty-five years before, tears now flow freely. I'd always wondered if I'd ever see Devil again. Owing to this experience, I came to believe that somehow, somewhere, we'd be reunited.

"You Just Saw Your Whole Life"

Zoom! The light vanished. Dazed, I asked myself, *What was that?*

Once more the unearthly voice returned, "That was you, you just saw your whole life."

Suddenly, I realised I'd viewed every second of my whole life, from conception until that very point in time! In that instantaneous moment I'd heard every conversation, thought every thought. It was as though time ceased to exist, a lifetime in a fraction of a second.

'Leardy' was at the end of the wharf, pointing at me, laughing hysterically. It was as if I was now a camera lens, which zoomed in until he was all I could see. Bemused, I watched him in his hysterics. To him, it probably looked as though it wasn't a life-or-death situation.

Smiling, I contemplated my funeral, feeling sorrow knowing my parents would be upset, though looking forward to having the last laugh at Leardy. He'd probably be in the front row! In fact, he may be one of the pallbearers! Visualising tears in his eyes as he'd remember laughing at me, not knowing how dire my predicament was, I was grinning like a Cheshire cat, *Yeah, I've got you now mate!*

Next, it was as if I was a camera lens half submerged. All was silent, tranquil, still. Water lazily lapped the lens, seemingly forever.

Suddenly, the serenity shattered. Frantically I was grabbing a pylon on the side of the wharf. Ebo was laughing beside me in the water. He said he'd been trying to free me from under the raft the whole time and asked, "Why didn't I dive down and just swim out from under it?" Unfortunately, he would die thirteen years later.

I didn't tell my friends what I'd experienced, for a couple of weeks, as I didn't think they'd believe me. Besides, I didn't believe it myself. In reality, it probably lasted for a few seconds, but it felt like a lifetime.

I've been asked, "While you were drowning, who was talking to you? Was it your inner thoughts, God, or a deceased family member?"

I don't believe it was God. As for a deceased family member, I was thirteen, so most of those I knew were still alive. Inner thoughts? Good question, but no. I seemed to perceive the orator as simply a messenger. Devil was my dog's name, it's not a metaphor. In Cairns a few weeks ago, I visited his grave, over forty years since his death.

High School Hoaxes

IN 1986 I attended St Augustine's Marist Brothers College, 'Saints', in Cairns. Our science teacher told us life had been created in a test tube. That troubled me as it undermined the Bible's validity. Intuitively I knew the Bible was true. My teacher had been referring to the flawed Stanley Millar Experiment. It had failed to create life. We'd been lied to.

Simple Cell?

During grade eight we were learning about the cell, or so we thought. Ebo and I diligently copied the alleged cell diagram from the blackboard into our workbooks. This consisted of a shape similar to a lopsided three-leaf clover. The outline was labelled 'cell membrane'. A large black dot was placed in the centre and labelled 'nucleus'. Dots were added all over, 'cytoplasm'.

Our teacher explained cells were like jelly; and, grouped together, made up our bodies. Staring hard at my drawing, I was struggling to accept what I was being told. It seemed too simple. *Surely, we were more than walking jelly blobs? How could jelly be the sole building blocks of teeth, hair, bones, fingernails, and muscles?*

Science proved my reservations to be valid. Cells are complex. There are over 100 trillion cells in our bodies, each comprising a control room, power stations, transport systems, protein manufacturing compartments, storage compartments, information storage, laboratories, repair systems, waste treatment facilities, waste disposal, chemical treatment areas, maintenance workshops, shipping and landing docks, order pickers, quality control, assembly lines, supply pipelines, conveyor belts, workers, managers, engineers, and cleaners. These cells communicate and interact with other cells. They also have reproduction capabilities.

Do you believe this occurred by chance?

Cells are molecular machines. Some have the microscopic equivalent of an outboard motor, one-millionth of the size of a grain of sand, comprised of a flagella (propeller), hook (flexible joint), inner and outer membranes, cell wall, rings, bushings, rotor, stator, motor, clutch, switches, and gears.

"Harvard biophysicist, Howard Berg, has publicly described the bacterial flagellum as 'the most efficient machine in the universe'." (J. Warner Wallace, 'Is God Real? The Bacterial Flagellum and The Divine Design Inference,' 2019, coldcasechristianity.com)

Rotating five times faster than a Formula One engine, the bacterial flagellar motor has revolutions of 1,000 revolutions per minute, though is capable of 17,000rpm. It can stop mid-spin, instantly reversing in the opposite direction. Remarkably, the motor also self-assembles. How many engines, which are purposefully and intelligently designed by humans, are you aware of that can do the same?

"Without a doubt, the modern machinery of the cell, the replication of DNA and protein synthesis, it has all the characteristics of a highly advanced, specially designed equipment." (Richard Dawkins, Evolutionism High Priest and militant Atheist, *The Blind Watchmaker*)

Who was the Designer?

"What About the Fossils?"

Later that year I was speaking with Mum concerning the truth of Genesis. Her response, "Yeah, but what about the fossils?" I was stumped. We'd been taught they'd formed over 'millions of years'. If that were true, Genesis, and therefore the Bible, couldn't be. Dinosaurs were also a stumbling block. *Where did they fit?*

Years later, I was telling my parents the truth of Creation. My father's voice rose as he stated both Evolutionism and Genesis could be true. *My father was logical, so how could he not see his claim was illogical?* Either, it was bacteria-worms-fish-apes-humans over 'millions of years', or; a male and female human pair were designed and created six to ten thousand years ago.

During the writing process, I told Dad about Evolutionism's creation story, from the alleged explosion/expansion of 'nothing', to the magical pond scum evolving into worms, fish, dinosaurs, humans, and giraffes. It was amusing seeing the pained expression on his face as he heard the absurdity that so many have wilfully swallowed.

Nebraska Man

There was a drawing of Nebraska Man and his wife, half-ape, half-human in our social studies textbook in year nine. Wonderment echoed around the class at this drawing of the 'Ape of the Western world'. Despair, denial, and shock swept over me. This drawing in my textbook seemed so real, so factual. I remember frantically thinking, *This doesn't mean the Bible isn't true, maybe it's one of Adam's descendants.* I knew I was trying to justify it.

Nebraska Man and his wife were drawn by an artist after being shown a tooth, which was later discovered to be from an extinct pig. Confirmed to be an elaborate hoax in 1927, it was in my textbook sixty years later.

"During the famous Scopes evolution trial in Dayton, Tennessee, William Jennings Bryan was ridiculed by lawyer Clarence Darrow because Bryan had not heard of the tooth and other facts of evolution by a delegation of authorities, led by Professor H. H. Newman of the University of Chicago. In 1927, to the supreme embarrassment of many, the tooth was discovered to be that of an extinct pig." ('Question: Have we found the missing link?' *Missing Link*, allaboutscience.org)

'Science' Class

Grade ten, 1988, science class textbook, 'Towards 2000'. Inside was the Big Bang Theory—The explosion of 'nothing', for 'no reason', out of which came 'everything'. Mind you, as years passed, believers corrected me, telling me it's no longer an 'explosion', of 'nothing', but an 'expansion' of 'nothing'. Not only that, science would later prove the Big Bang Theory wasn't possible, admitting if it had occurred, the universe would've collapsed in on itself by now.

The law of cause and effect is one of several scientific laws detrimental to Evolutionism: "Everything that becomes or changes must do so owing to some cause; for nothing can come to be without a cause." (Plato, *Timaeus*, p. 28)

So, then, what 'caused' the Big Bang/Bloat? Remember, Evolutionism dogma states their creation story is as follows: An explosion/expansion of 'nothing', caused by 'nothing', for 'no reason', produced 'everything', including space, time, matter, energy, a finely tuned universe, natural laws, consciousness, intelligence, knowledge, truth, logic, emotions, morality, and 'life', itself.

You cannot get 'something' from 'nothing'.

'Global Warming'

Semantics in Evolutionism, changing 'explosion' to 'expansion', reminds me of global warming nonsense. As a child, I was terrified of 'global warming'. Newspapers warned Cairns' northern beaches would be underwater in ten years. Well, here we are, over forty years later. Not only are those beaches not underwater, they have major developments on them.

Science discovered Earth was cooling, the opposite of what 'science' had said the day before; so, they changed their propaganda slogan from 'global warming', to 'climate change'.

Embryonic Fraud

Here we were, fifteen-year-olds, being fed another lie that had been known to be fraudulent for 120 years.

Ernst Haeckel, a German professor of Zoology read *On the Origin of Species* by Charles Darwin and loved it. The problem was, there was no evidence—so he decided to create some. His goal was to promote Darwinian Evolution in Germany. This is the belief we were once apes, before losing our fur and tails, becoming progressively whiter as we evolved from an inferior black, sub-human ape ancestor. Do you remember Hitler's desire for a superior white race? Where do you think his racist ideas originated?

Haeckel published a book in 1912, *The Evolution of Man* with the laughable sub-title, 'A Popular Scientific Study'. Keep this in mind with some of his chapter headings: 'Our Worm-Like Ancestors' and, 'Our Fish-Like Ancestors'. In 'Our Five-Toed Ancestors' he rabbits on about how he wants us to believe humans were once amphibians.

The Princess and the Frog

Do you believe a princess kissed a frog, which instantly evolved into a prince? If not, why not? After all, Evolutionism stipulates frogs evolved into humans, the only difference being it took 'millions of years'.

Richard Dawkins reveals the reason for his incredible devotion to his faith, "I think looking back to my own childhood, the fact that so many of the stories I read allowed the possibility of frogs turning into princes; whether that has a sort of insidious effect on rationality, I'm not sure."

… What do you think …?

It's little wonder Evolutionism believers have an affinity for science fiction and fantasy. It's probably why they also have a predisposition to Evolutionism—pure fantasy is at its core. Those who fail to be swayed to the religion of Evolutionism are told it's because they lack imagination:

"You know, the problem with those who are unable to see evolution, I think, is they don't have imaginations." (Gail E. Kennedy, PhD, Associate Professor, Anthropology, UCLA, from the video, *Evolution vs God*, Living Waters Publication)

Haeckel redrew animal drawings from embryonic scientists in 1868, making them appear similar to human embryos, to fabricate evidence for Evolutionism. Human irregularities were erased to make them appear similar to animal embryos. What he claimed were 'gill slits' on human embryos, were neck folds that would become the bones of the outer and middle ear, nerves, and glands.

My Mother was involved with Right to Life. Looking at the alleged gill slits of the alleged human embryo, I was desperately trying to discover a major difference to point out to everyone. As with the alleged Nebraska Man, a collective sound of wonderment erupted from the class. A friend turned to me, saying knowledgeably, "See Erbie? There's nothing wrong with abortion."

Vestigial Organs

These were in the same textbook. It's believed there are parts of our anatomy that are useless, left over from an alleged animal ancestry. The claim was there were 100 of these organs. Science has since refuted all. There are no vestigial organs. Humans were designed; we're not rearranged pond scum that had been zapped by lightning. Only a fool could believe such nonsense.

"The fool hath said in his heart, There is no God." Ps 14:1

The appendix is revered as one such vestigial organ. It's important for our immune system. Tonsils and adenoids are also branded as vestigial. They're not. They're important in the development of our immune system. Here's another favourite of Evolutionism believers—the coccyx, colloquially known as 'tail bone'. Yes, the ridiculous claim we used to have tails. Tailbones are an insertion and anchor site for muscles, ligaments, and tendons, enabling us to walk and sit upright.

Apes or Monkeys?

Evolutionism believers deny we descended from monkeys. They claim we descended from apes. "What's the difference?" you ask. Well, they believe humans used to have a tail, mistakenly pointing to the coccyx (tailbone), as proof. Most monkeys have tails, whereas apes do not. This is a defining difference between the two.

So, which is it? Are we descended from tail-less, ape-like ancestors, or did we once have a tail, with a portion remaining, called a tailbone? If you believe we once had a tail, that should imply we were monkeys, not apes.

Over time, Evolutionism believers said we were no longer evolved from apes. Instead, we'd evolved from an 'ape-like ancestor'. They do this to 'muddy the water'. Their goal is to be as vague as possible. In the same way, 'global warming' advocates had their slogan changed to 'climate change'. The objective is the same, avoid scrutiny.

A 'Dog's Breakfast'

Once you begin looking into this, it quickly becomes a 'dog's breakfast'. Apart from the major contradiction surrounding the monkey/ape conundrum, consider this, as mentioned briefly before: According to Evolutionism, we were once fish, with tails, and gills. Why don't humans and all animals have vestigial gills?

After all, Evolutionism states all creatures with vertebrae evolved from the primordial soup. We left the ocean and our gills magically evolved into lungs and we walked around the Earth. Then, we decided we wanted to swing from trees, so we magically evolved tails. 'Millions of years' drift by. We've grown weary of swinging from trees, so we de-evolve our tails.

The problem is further compounded by believers insisting when the earliest apes appeared twenty million years ago, they had no tail. There are no apes, then or now, which have tails. Yet they assert we evolved from apes, but had tails. Tails shouldn't become vestigial, as they'd be useful. They could open the door when your hands are full of shopping, or hold your phone while you're driving.

Peppered Moths

These were the last alleged proof of Evolutionism in this textbook. Dark and light-coloured moths resting on the bark of light-coloured trees were studied. The story claims as darker moths were more visible to birds against a light-coloured background, they were eaten more. In time, no dark-coloured moths were left.

Peppered moths don't rest on tree trunks during the day. They conceal themselves under leaves and branches, or only on the tree trunk while amongst the canopy. For the so-called study, peppered moths were pinned or glued to the tree trunk, near the ground.

Even if their revered peppered moth story was true, it most certainly doesn't prove Evolutionism is true. It was still a moth, and a peppered moth, at that. It hadn't evolved into a butterfly, bird, or ladybug. That's a common example of an Evolutionism believers' bait-and-switch technique. They seem to think that moths changing colours, proves one kind of animal can evolve into another kind of animal. In other words, dinosaurs could evolve into birds, and bears could evolve into whales. All that was proven was Genesis, creatures producing after their kind. If anything, it disproved Evolutionism. No new genetic information was generated. Eventually, the moth would lose all DNA for light colour from its gene pool. Let's assume the study wasn't faked. How would that prove humans are descended from lightning-zapped pond scum?

So, there you have it, more proof for Evolutionism and all of it was hoaxes, lies, and just-so stories—I just didn't know it at the time. Do you think it should be inside a textbook as proof of Evolutionism, at a Christian school, no less? If there really was evidence for Evolutionism, why do they exhibit frauds and hoaxes to perpetuate their myth?

Understandably, I was becoming increasingly confused. *Surely the Bible is true, isn't it?* There were a couple of Charles Darwin books in our school library, *On the Origin of Species by Means of Natural Selection, or the Preservation of Favoured Races in the Struggle for Life*. The cover looked convincing—an ape gradually morphing into a human. Reluctantly, I took it home to read. Now that was confusing. It seemed to say a lot, without saying anything at all, a bit like listening to a politician waffle on.

Dabbling in the Occult

THE occult is any practice that leverages supernatural power or knowledge apart from God. Numerous times I've had people tell me God spoke to them. I know He didn't. If what they say doesn't align with Scripture, it was birthed from a demonic spirit, or their imaginations. Regardless of how fervently they believe their words to be true.

For a time, I became caught up in the occult, participating in séances. Although I never did, others allowed themselves to become possessed, causing us to witness many unnerving experiences. One possessed friend was picked up and slammed backwards into a wall. We'd have someone recording the developments with pen and paper, usually me.

All lights in the house would be off, with a few candles flickering in the kitchen. Ironically, this house was directly opposite the Cairns Pioneer Cemetery. Before being possessed, the entity explained the procedure via the Ouija board. One requirement was the use of a blindfold. Maybe there's something in the saying, 'The eyes are the window to the soul'.

This particular night, David volunteered to be possessed by an entity claiming it was from the 1500s. The setting was a naval battle between the British and Spanish. Once David was possessed, I began recording everything he said and did. At one point, he dived under the table, face down. His feet were kicking, as if swimming. One of his hands was moving, as if doing breaststroke. "He's swimming," my pen recorded the words as I spoke them.

My observation didn't sit well with another in attendance, "No he's not, he's scrubbing the deck."

I peered under the table once more, "Then why are his feet kicking?"

While David was doing this, we had turned the light on because the camera flash wasn't working and we wanted to take a photo. Some in the group expressed concern over turning on a light, though I didn't think it would be a problem. Events later that night would prove just how wrong I was.

After two minutes David began screaming and thrashing about on the floor. We struggled to subdue him as he frantically grabbed hold of one of our friends' legs, tugging desperately, pleading, "Don't, don't!" Terrified screams from his girlfriend added to the pandemonium as she pushed back from the table and cowered in a corner. Although of slim build, a photo was taken of three pairs of hands holding David's arm attempting to restrain him. Everyone was concerned. Imagine it—dark room, candlelight, a man possessed, inhuman strength. We immediately commenced the procedure to bring him out of possession.

David clutched at his eyes, screaming in pain as he came out of possession, demanding for the light to be turned off and wanting to know who'd turned it on. Once everything calmed down, although his eyes still hurt, he commenced to tell us what he saw. He'd been standing on the deck of a British naval ship; alongside the person whose spirit was allegedly the entity we'd made contact with. As they'd talked, this person dived overboard. David shrugged, "I didn't know what to do, so I dived overboard, following him."

While recounting his story he mentioned he'd been swimming under water using one hand, holding a knife in the other. He was confused when I interrupted him with my triumphant proclamation, "See, he was swimming!" Owing to the perplexed expression on

David's face, I then explained how everyone else thought he'd been scrubbing the deck.

He'd also mentioned when he'd suddenly seen a light appear. Immediately the person he'd been following turned to him, "Why did they do that? They didn't have to do that. You will be in great pain because of them." At the time, those words hadn't made sense to him.

Near the culmination of his story, he described being aboard the ship and the person he'd been following had wounded someone and was about to finish him off. At that point David leaped forward grasping the assailant, pleading with him not to do it. This was the precise moment at which we'd intervened.

After relating his story, David, still complaining about his eyes, retired to the lounge room. The makeshift blindfold, a tea towel, still hung around his neck. We continued using the Ouija board.

Spontaneous Possession

Time passed. Cameron was concerned. He'd checked on David who was now repeatedly muttering a strange phrase, in some unknown language. More alarming was, the blindfold was back over his eyes. Cameron offered to become possessed, to try to find out what had happened. I objected. Things were bad enough now; this seemed like a definite way to exacerbate the problem. In the end, I reluctantly conceded.

"A Strange Light, not of a Flame"

A number of strange happenings, enactments and utterances were performed by Cameron following his possession in our tiny, dimly lit lounge room. During his recount, Cameron had informed us there'd been a mutiny. He related how he'd been jumped, killed and his body rolled overboard. As he spoke, the rest of us exchanged knowing smiles, as we'd managed to work most of that out ourselves, due to his actions and words.

Dabbling in the Occult

He'd been walking to and fro, before stopping abruptly, shaking his head. Sighing, he placed his hands on his hips—it's just that, they weren't on top of his hips, they were on top of his thighs. I've never seen anyone stand like that, before, or since. Bending down, his hands cupped from below, an imaginary object. Groaning and straining, he straightened, pivoting his hips, placing the object to the side. Much to our bewilderment, he repeated this action numerous times. Amongst ourselves, in vain, we wondered what could possibly be occurring.

Abruptly, he halted. His blindfolded face showed terror as he cried, "Mutiny!" It was unnerving watching him manoeuvre around in what was obviously a sword fight. He thrusted downward, "Down, ribcage!"

At one point he was standing a metre from the wall, head lowered. Suddenly glancing up, he caught his breath. Before our very eyes, he was picked up and slammed backwards against the wall, falling in a crumpled heap at the bottom—His knees hadn't bent …

After a moment he began twitching, before rolling along the floor like a log, until obstructed by the lounge. Even so, he attempted to continue rolling. Glancing at the others and shrugging, I dragged him back to the opposite wall. It happened a few more times. Eventually, he was done and lay peacefully with his back on the carpet, silence punctured by David's repetitive, soft chanting from the corner of the lounge. We were all of the belief there'd been a mutiny, Cameron had been killed and rolled off the plank. He would later explain his perplexing behaviour, "I was walking along and noticed cannonballs had been stacked incorrectly. As I restacked them, I was jumped."

As the back of Cameron's head rested on the floor, with his blindfolded eyes staring toward the ceiling, he gestured for me to come to him. There was no way, on God's green Earth, I was going to do anything of the sort. Friends stated the obvious, "He's talking to you Erbie."

"I know."

"He wants you to go to him." They were glad it wasn't them being summoned.

"I'm not getting down there!"

Cameron persisted gesturing. Everyone was uneasy. I was feeling the heat. David continued his monotonous chant in that strange, unknown tongue.

"Get down there Erbie!" Others murmured their agreement.

Gingerly, I knelt beside him. He gestured for me to move closer still. There was no way I was doing that, especially in light of everything that had occurred and was still unfolding.

"He wants you to get closer!"

Giving a definite shake of my head, the gesturing abruptly ceased. Tense moments ticked by. Cameron's hand suddenly shot out, grabbing the front of my shirt, wrenching me close. Instinctively, my clenched fist, cocked and ready, sat under my chin. I was prepared to smash my friend's face, if need be.

Cameron's voice was calm, soft, reflective, "What is the god's year?"

My friends and I exchanged puzzled glances, "I don't know what you mean. It's nineteen ninety-three." He didn't seem to fathom this and after a few more questions, gave up.

An accusing voice rang out, directed at Cameron, "What happened to David? What's wrong with his eyes?"

Stroking what appeared to be an imaginary goatee, "Hmm, it is very strange. A light, not of a flame, from your land, was instantly turned on." Cameron never spoke like this. I don't know anyone who did.

In the end, somehow, some way, everything worked out. We had several inexplicable outcomes, on other nights. A few even revealing somewhat accurate, prophetic occurrences, many others were false.

Another night David had gone to bed in protest as he didn't like the way the night was progressing and complained about the requirement to be up for an early shift in the morning. Sometime later, an entity who regularly communicated with us made contact. Slowly, the disc indicated letters, 'd,h,e,r,e'. Someone turned to me, "What does it say?"

Peering at the letters I'd scribbled, I screwed my face up in frustration, "It doesn't say anything."

Someone suggested, "Maybe it means, David here."

Another leant forward, "Do you mean, David here?" The disc shot to 'Yes', accompanied by a terrifying scream piercing the night from the opposite side of the house, in the direction of David's bedroom.

We observed each other in stunned silence through the flickering candlelight, trying not to glance at the shadows on the wall, lest they move. To give you an idea as to what the scream sounded like, imagine the sound you'd make, awakening to a horrifying beast standing over you, clasping an axe dripping with blood, raised over its head, commencing a downward trajectory.

Gingerly, we began to investigate, turning on lights, creeping towards David's door. Cameron turned the knob, though could barely get the door ajar. Calling David to no avail, our concern mounted.

David, unconscious on the ground, blocked the door. He came to, remaining in his room, refusing to communicate. Finally, he agreed to speak with Cameron, who then proceeded to enter David's room. The rest of us sat on the lounge, deep in our own thoughts. Cameron and David emerged.

Someone asked the question all of us were thinking, "What happened?"

Cameron's face was contorted with concern, "He doesn't want to talk about it!"

David held up a weary palm in surrender, "No, it's okay, I'll tell them." Cameron's mouth opened in protest. David repeated his words. Cameron bit his tongue.

David laughed in a resigned, shell-shocked sort of a way, "You know that feeling when you know you're just about to drop off into a really long, deep sleep?" As one, we leant forward, nodding. "Well, that's what happened to me. Then I woke up with the sensation of being lifted and turned over. As I opened my eyes, I saw the bed six feet below me. That's when I screamed."

It was a light-bulb moment for me, "Ahhh, that's when it said, d-here."

"What!?" David stared at me as if I was an idiot. It turned out Cameron hadn't disclosed that detail. It's probably just as well he hadn't, at the time. It may have been a case of too much, too soon. We then told him of our version of events.

Suddenly, an awful thought struck me, "Hey, imagine if the door wasn't shut. Do you think he'd have been flown out to us?" Horror was written across our faces as the realisation of the likely occurrence dawned on us.

I'm only including the barest of details of our experiences. The least said, the better. I never wanted to disclose these stories. However, the nature of this book requires it, especially relating to what the Bible has to say about an after-life and also with regards to the concept of reincarnation. I dislike talking about our experiences, as do the others. Years ago, I brought up the subject with Cameron and was quickly shut down, with the admonishment he never wanted to talk about it again.

There is a spiritual realm. Working within it are supernatural forces of good and evil. Forces of evil may appear as forces of light:

"And no marvel; for Satan himself is transformed into an angel of light. Therefore it is no great thing if his ministers also be transformed as the ministers of righteousness." 2 Cor 11:14–15

Some may manifest, imitating a deceased family member. The dead are 'resting in peace' until the Resurrection. They're not haunting houses:

"As the cloud is consumed and vanisheth away: so he that goeth down to the grave shall come up no more. He shall return no more to his house, neither shall his place know him any more." Job 7:9–19

If your house has supernatural activity, it's not from the deceased, but from demons impersonating the deceased.

I'd hate for anyone to be influenced into delving into the occult. Many people who do end up in mental institutions. We were lucky. I believe a saving grace was never allowing myself to be possessed. It's not a game. It's evil, dangerous. This includes satanic symbolism, such as upside-down crosses, five-pointed stars and some music genres. They're all a window, a portal to the occult.

"When thou art come into the land which the Lord thy God giveth thee, thou shalt not learn to do after the abominations of those nations. There shall not be found among you any one that maketh his son or his daughter to pass through the fire, or that useth divination, or an observer of times, or an enchanter, or a witch. Or a charmer, or a consulter with familiar spirits, or a wizard, or a necromancer." Deut 18:9–11

Do you believe in the dogma and doctrines of Evolutionism? If so, you're about to be presented with another uncomfortable truth.

Sixth Sense

We're told by science we only have five senses: sight, taste, touch, hearing and smell. Our eyes, tongue, skin, ears and nose collect information about our environment which is then analysed by the brain. Science does not accept a sixth sense, (extra sensory perception—ESP), as that is immaterial. Deep down you know they're wrong. You've heard the powerful voice inside which speaks to you without words. There've been numerous occasions where your intuition has imparted pertinent information or guidance. Premonitions of sudden catastrophes or imminent death are examples. How about someone whose presence gives you an inexplicable, uncomfortable sensation within the pit of your stomach? Only to find out later, such intuitive warnings and guidance were prophetic.

Science only deals with the material world, natural phenomena and explanations. It demands testable and repeatable evidence. There is no place in science for the supernatural.

Star Wars

An Atheist friend from high school tried telling me once that aliens were real. I told him that if his concept was of 'little green men from distant planets', then he was wrong. However, if his concept of aliens was from the angle of being outside of our material realm, in another plane, yet capable of interacting with us and having far greater intellectual prowess than us; then yes, aliens did exist. I then pointed out that God, angels and demonic beings fall under this description.

Interestingly, a few years later, I was crushing another believer's fantasy about aliens. This same friend had interrupted the conversation, thinking he was tripping me up by claiming God falls into the alien category. Staring at him in disbelief, "Yeah, I know, I'm the one who told you that years ago, but that's not what he's thinking. He's implying from a 'little green men' perspective."

While scientists believe in the brain, they don't necessarily believe in the concept of a mind (soul). They believe once you're dead, that's it, the end. No scientific theory can satisfactorily explain consciousness, as consciousness (mind and soul), and your conscience (instinctive sense of right and wrong), are inextricably linked. Both are from our Creator.

Anything outside the natural world is immaterial. Therefore, it falls into the supernatural. By definition, this includes God, gods, souls, Heaven, Hell, reincarnation, prayer, miracles, 'magic', ghosts/spirits, devils, demonic possession, angels, witches, astrology, alchemy, palmistry, mind-reading, telekinesis, or anything related to ESP. The list also includes aliens, since extra-terrestrial life has never been proven, let alone, discovered. Supernatural events and concepts are accepted through faith. Therefore, belief in aliens is religious, as it's based on faith.

If you're an Atheist, you simply cannot accept belief in any concepts listed above. You cannot have your cake and eat it, too. Your worldview only permits natural phenomena, not supernatural ones. If you subscribe to even just one of the aforementioned, you are, at best, an agnostic. If the shoe fits, I implore you to be honest with yourself and denounce your religion.

An Obsession for Truth

HERE it is, the turning point in my quest for truth. The learning I was about to undergo would be astounding. Surprisingly, the process also included discarding previous beliefs of mine which I discovered were erroneous.

My wife and I had mentorship with Shayne, a businessman, who used to host a Bible study on Sunday nights. He'd never intended to and didn't want to, but felt compelled to, maybe in the same way I've come to writing this book. My wife had to drag me along kicking and screaming. Occasionally, I went, since following the Bible study, he'd talk business.

This was in Melbourne, Australia. Bible study participants were representative of agnostics, various denominations of Christians, and a few Jews. Debate raged one night in a room of about fifteen people. Time ticked by. There was a continual back-and-forth between two people. At this rate there wouldn't be time to talk business at the end of the night—I had to put a stop to the nonsense.

"Okay, listen," I turned to one of them, "I can see your point." Turning to the other, "And I can see your point, but I can also see that we could be here all night and both of you will never see each other's point, so let's just all agree to disagree."

You could've heard a pin drop. I looked at the leader. I knew I was in trouble. As someone said later, he 'saw the crosshairs' come up over me from Shayne's eyes.

One thing that ticked me off about this 'study' was that there was often an American pastor in attendance. For this reason, he was constantly deferred to as an ultimate authority. *So what? For every pastor who agreed with him, I could find another who didn't. Scripture is the authority, not man.*

Line in the Sand

Driving home, my logic meter was exploding. *It was one book! How could there be so many different interpretations!?* Then and there I resolved to discover the truth. I didn't have an axe to grind, all I wanted was the truth and I would follow the truth wherever it led.

Over the next three months, I undertook an independent and extensive study. Material was sourced from all denominations. Then as soon as I arrived home from work, with ruler and red pen in hand, doctrines were scrutinised against the Bible.

Reading some doctrines, I thought sarcastically, *Yeah, right.* Yet when I checked with the Bible, I was wrong. It went the other way too, *Well derrr, everyone knows that*, but to be consistent, I'd check it against the Bible anyway. It turned out that I'd been wrong. Each time, I changed my beliefs accordingly.

I recall reading a doctrine, thinking, *That sounds pivotal*, especially as there was a scripture reference provided. Unfortunately, referenced Scriptures often appeared to have no relevance to the claim their point was making. This happened far more times than I care to remember. Another annoying observation was they didn't stick with one Bible version. It was as if they'd combed through all versions to find the Scripture that most aligned with their claims. Often, the Scriptural reference was weak or ambiguous.

Many church organisations received phone calls from me, advising they'd referenced the wrong Scripture. Not because they were clutching at straws or trying to make a square peg fit into a round hole, but because they'd simply made a mistake. One Pastor summed it up, comparing me to the Bereans:

"These were more noble than those in Thessalonica, in that they received the word with all readiness of mind, and searched the scriptures daily, whether those things were so." Acts 17:11

That is exactly what I did.

I wanted the truth.

Far too many people listen to a pastor, friend, radio, idiot box or sensational new book, but don't study the Bible carefully for themselves. Don't be like the others. Be like the Bereans, question everything. Today, Berea in Greece is called Veria. Fittingly, it's also known as, 'Little Jerusalem'.

Intensity of my study waned after three months as I'd found the truth. Of course, I had yet to learn about Creation, dinosaurs, Bible versions, etc. Though I'd learnt many doctrinal truths. I'd also unlearnt, what I'd believed to be truths.

One of many truths that caught me off guard was—God has a name! This was a shock. All my life I'd thought Him to be just, 'God'.

Jehovah Witnesses

"Because he hath set his love upon me, therefore will I deliver him: I will set him on high, because he hath known my name." Ps 91:14

Understandably, the fact I call God by His name extends from studying Jehovah's Witness material. I have several thoughts regarding JWs. Insults levelled at them for preaching door-to-door are legendary. I have a lot of respect for them doing this. It takes a lot of courage; especially in light of the negative attitude society has towards their custom. Whenever I think of the ridicule and abuse they're subjected to, this comes to mind:

"Blessed are ye, when men shall revile you, and persecute you, and shall say all manner of evil against you falsely, for my sake. Rejoice, and be exceeding glad: for great is your reward in heaven: for so persecuted they the prophets which were before you." Matt 5:11–12

I'm not insinuating JWs will find favour in the Resurrection. Mormons follow similar customs too, but that's a whole other can of worms. While we mock and laugh at JWs, keep in mind, they're following the example of the apostles and disciples:

"And daily in the temple, and in every house, they ceased not to teach and preach Jesus Christ." Acts 5:42

Paul also says this:

"And how I kept back nothing that was profitable unto you, but have shewed you, and have taught you publicly, and from house to house, testifying both to the Jews, and also to the Greeks, repentance toward God, and faith toward our Lord Jesus Christ." Acts 20:21

Read Luke 10. Regardless of what you believe of their doctrines, at least they're showing great courage in their evangelism. JWs also believe the truth of Creation.

I remember being impressed as a kid when some JWs came to our house and engaged with Dad, a Catholic. It started quite cordial, but as time progressed, became somewhat heated, while still respectful. Dad was going toe-to-toe with them, using Scripture and countering with Scripture. Looking back, knowing what I know now, I wish I could go back in time and listen again.

After my studies, I loved it when they came to my door. Like Dad, I would go toe-to-toe with them too. Respectfully, like he did. While many of you silently pray they don't knock on your door, I'm hoping to God they do.

One day they were milling near the corner I lived on, as I eagerly peered out, concealed by curtains—I didn't want to spook them. Two started making their way towards my house. Just then, another called out to them and said something I couldn't hear. All three then looked at my house. The two hesitated, before bypassing. Previously, I'd engaged with JWs at my door. No doubt, I'd since been black-listed.

Jehovah or Yahweh?

As for the business of calling God by name, I thought it was rude and ridiculous—until I started looking into it. Jehovah? Yahweh? There appears to be no definitive answer. From what I remember in my study, there's no way of knowing how the four letters are pronounced. I may be wrong.

The Tetragrammaton, or Tetragram, is the four-letter Hebrew word YHWH, or Yahweh. JWs believe the pronunciation to be Jehovah. As a kid, I liked the hymn 'Strong and Constant'. You have to hand it to the Catholics on this one, their music is good. The opening line is, "I will be Yahweh who walks with you." It resonates with me, so I prefer to use the name Yahweh. Besides, if I were to use 'Jehovah', I'd be incorrectly pigeonholed as a JW and dismissed as such. Also, 'Jesus' is an English word for 'Yahshua'. Yahshua came from His Father, Yahweh. The similarity in their names makes sense.

"I am the LORD: that is my name." Isa 42:8

It doesn't sound like much of a name, does it? I'd prefer it if the King James Bible would've used Yahweh, instead of LORD. When 'Lord' is written in capital letters, the Hebrew origin of this word is the name of God, YHWH.

Therefore, we may read it as, "I am Yahweh, that is my name." Isa 42:8

It makes sense now, doesn't it? Why bother telling someone your name, unless you intend for them to use it?

Do Your Own Research

Question everything. Not only everything I say, but also your long-held beliefs. Below is a sample of people and resources that brought me to the truth. It never ceases to amaze me that outspoken opponents, rather than attacking the arguments of those listed, attempt to attack the character of those listed instead.

Worldwide Church of God

My quest for truth finally brought me to the United Church of God, a faction of the Worldwide Church of God, not to be confused with the Uniting Church of God. Herbert W. Armstrong (1892–1986) led the Worldwide Church of God.

This organisation produced a magazine called 'Tomorrow's World'. Funnily enough, years ago when my uncle visited Cairns from Melbourne or Perth, he'd leave them at his mother's house. Then, as a child when I stayed with my grandmother, I'd read them. From an early age, this magazine encouraged me to think independently and showed me the Bible was a historical resource, containing the fulfilment of ancient prophecies.

While living in Brisbane during my thirties, I attended a Church of God service. While there, I mentioned to the pastor how I had literature from other denominations and was scrutinising their doctrines. He was horrified, "Don't do that, it will confuse you."

Gob-smacked, I explained how ridiculous his advice was, "If I didn't do that, I'd never have found this church."

Creation Ministries International

I'm indebted to the team behind this ministry. Staffed by several scientists from varied and diverse scientific backgrounds, Creation Ministries has a comprehensive wealth of information available on their website. There you'll find a plethora of books, videos, pamphlets, children's comics, peer-reviewed scientific papers and studies.

Creation Magazine is their flagship publication, available in either printed or digital format. It's packed with relevant, interesting articles affirming humans, Earth, and all that's in it, were purposefully and intelligently designed and created. These are relatively cheap compared to similar publications. Generous donations from grateful readers have offset costs. Their staff continually tour the world, speaking at churches, schools and universities.

Toward the end of this publication, you'll find an article from CMI—'15 Questions for Evolutionists', copied by permission.

Ray Comfort

Ray runs Living Waters Ministries. He has a unique and effective style of evangelising, achieved by using simple basic truths, common sense, logic, and our instinctive trait for discerning between right and wrong, good and evil. Whenever we judge between these standards, we're affirming our Creator's existence. In this manner, Ray doesn't have to tell them the truth, their conscience tells them. It convicts them.

Kent Hovind

He has a way of articulating truth using basic scientific laws and principles, combined with logic and common sense. Reducing arguments down to their rawest details, his style is similar to Ray Comfort's method. Both men are formidable opponents against Evolutionism, and as such, are hated within Atheist circles.

Ken Ham

Born in Cairns Australia and living in the United States, Ken is the founder of another powerful truth ministry, Answers in Genesis. Forget taking your family to Disneyland. Instead, take them to Ken's 'Ark Encounter' in Williamstown Kentucky, where they can visit a life-sized replica of Noah's ark.

Lee Strobel

He's a former award-winning investigative journalist who set out to prove Christianity, especially the Resurrection, was false. Similar to many others before him with the same agenda, his search led him to the truth. Lee founded Lee Strobel Ministries.

All four men mentioned have numerous published resources on Christianity and the truth of Genesis.

Ten Commandments

"All his commandments are sure. They stand fast for ever and ever." Ps 111:7–8

WHEN I saw the Ten Commandments written in the Bible, it felt strange. Until then, I'd assumed they were someone's ideas of ten things that were considered important, incorporating a Biblical theme.

They were written by the very finger of our Creator on two tablets of stone. This fact alone demonstrates they carry much weight, pun intended.

"And he gave unto Moses, when he had made an end of communing with him upon Mount Sinai, two tables of testimony, tables of stone, written with the finger of God." Ex 31:18

Despite this, most Christian denominations deny we're required to follow these rules. This subject will be covered in greater detail in the chapter, 'Christian Counterfeits'.

"He that hath my commandments, and keepeth them, he it is that loveth me: and he that loveth me shall be loved of my Father, and I will love him, and will manifest myself to him." John 14:21

Ten Commandments

I. Thou shalt have no other gods before me.
II. Thou shalt not make unto thee any graven image, or any likeness of any thing that is in heaven above, or that is in the earth beneath, or that is in the water under the earth. Thou shalt not bow down thyself to them, nor serve them: for I the Lord thy God am a jealous God, visiting the iniquity of the fathers upon the children unto the third and fourth generation of them that hate me; And shewing mercy unto thousands of them that love me, and keep my commandments.
III. Thou shalt not take the name of the Lord thy God in vain; for the Lord will not hold him guiltless that taketh his name in vain.
IV. Remember the Sabbath day, to keep it holy. Six days shalt thou labour, and do all thy work: But the seventh day is the Sabbath of the Lord thy God: in it thou shalt not do any work, thou, nor thy son, nor thy daughter, thy manservant, nor thy maidservant, nor thy cattle, nor thy stranger that is within thy gates: For in six days the Lord made heaven and earth, the sea, and all that in them is, and rested the seventh day: wherefore the Lord blessed the Sabbath day, and hallowed it.
V. Honour thy father and thy mother: that thy days may be long upon the land which the Lord thy God giveth thee.
VI. Thou shalt not kill.
VII. Thou shalt not commit adultery.
VIII. Thou shalt not steal.
IX. Thou shalt not bear false witness against thy neighbour.
X. Thou shalt not covet thy neighbour's house, thou shalt not covet thy neighbour's wife, nor his manservant, nor his maidservant, nor his ox, nor his ass, nor any thing that is thy neighbour's. Ex 20:3–17

It's strange how, with a church upbringing, I'd never been exposed to the Ten Commandments as being recorded in the Bible. They're also listed in Deuteronomy 5.

Catholic Commandment Corruption

As you were reading through these, I'm sure various questions came to mind and also some confusion, especially with the Second Commandment which forbids graven images (statues).

This commandment didn't sit well with Catholics, so they got rid of it. I know what you're thinking, *Wouldn't it be obvious they only had nine commandments, instead of ten?* No, since Catholics aren't encouraged to read Bibles. Here's how they get around it. They took the Tenth Commandment ...

"Thou shalt not covet thy neighbour's house, thou shalt not covet thy neighbour's wife, nor his manservant, nor his maidservant, nor his ox, nor his ass, nor any thing that is thy neighbour's." Ex 20:17

... And split it into two, disguising the missing Second Commandment. This is the Catholic's new 'Ninth Commandment': "You shall not covet your neighbour's wife." This is their new 'Tenth Commandment': "You shall not covet your neighbour's goods."

There's no excuse for doing this.

"And he shall speak great words against the most High, and shall wear out the saints of the most High, and think to change times and laws:" Dan 7:25

After discarding the Second Commandment, the second-longest commandment, Catholics turned their attention towards the longest commandment, the Fourth Commandment. They changed the Sabbath day from Saturday, to Sunday.

Don't Break the Law

Here's Yahshua's advice if you don't want to be cast into the Lake of Fire:

"If thou wilt enter into life, keep the commandments." Matt 19:17

They're called the Ten Commandments, not the 'Ten Suggestions'. If you have a problem, take it up with Him, not me. They're His rules, not mine.

"Think not that I am come to destroy the law, or the prophets: I am not come to destroy, but to fulfil. For verily I say unto you, Till heaven and earth pass, one jot or one tittle shall in no wise pass from the law, till all be fulfilled. Whosoever therefore shall break one of these least commandments, and shall teach men so, he shall be called the least in the kingdom of heaven: but whosoever shall do and teach them, the same shall be called great in the kingdom of heaven." Matt 5:17–19

Yahshua then continues two verses later:

"Ye have heard that it was said of them of old time, Thou shalt not kill; and whosoever shall kill shall be in danger of the judgment: But I say unto you, That whosoever is angry with his brother without a cause shall be in danger of the judgment: and whosoever shall say to his brother, Raca, shall be in danger of the council: but whosoever shall say, Thou fool, shall be in danger of hell fire." Matt 5:21–22

Not only is Yahshua adamant the Ten Commandments aren't 'done away with' or 'nailed to the cross', as many 'Christians' claim, He instead makes them more binding.

"Ye have heard that it was said by them of old time, Thou shalt not commit adultery: But I say unto you, That whosoever looketh on a woman to lust after her hath committed adultery with her already in his heart." Matt 5:27–28

And:

"It hath been said, Whosoever shall put away his wife, let him give her a writing of divorcement: But I say unto you, That whosoever shall put away his wife, saving for the cause of fornication, causeth her to commit adultery: and whosoever shall marry her that is divorced committeth adultery." Matt 5:31–32

James, one of Yahshua's half-brothers, delivers a straightforward rendition of the subject matter:

"For whosoever shall keep the whole law, and yet offend in one point, he is guilty of all. For he that said, Do not commit adultery, said also, Do not kill. Now if thou commit no adultery, yet if thou kill, thou art become a transgressor of the law." James 2:10–11

Here's another uncomfortable truth. While it's all very well for us to sit on our high horses and judge child molesters, serial killers, and the like; all sinners, regardless of sin, are deserving of death. It's a case of the pot calling the kettle 'black'. There was a woman caught in the act of adultery. The religious leaders were set on stoning her to death:

Woman Caught in Adultery

"And the scribes and Pharisees brought unto him a woman taken in adultery; and when they had set her in the midst, They say unto him, Master, this woman was taken in adultery, in the very act. Now Moses in the law commanded us, that such should be stoned: but what sayest thou? This they said, tempting him, that they might have to accuse him. But Jesus stooped down, and with his finger wrote on the ground, as though he heard them not." John 8:3–6

Calm under pressure. Do you remember how he resolved the issue? He used their God-given conscience against them:

"So when they continued asking him, he lifted up himself, and said unto them, He that is without sin among you, let him first cast a stone at her." John 8:7

Such a wise response. How do you think it played out?

"And they which heard it, being convicted by their own conscience, went out one by one, beginning at the eldest, even unto the last: and Jesus was left alone, and the woman standing in the midst." John 8:9

Awkward. This woman stood before her Creator. She'd broken the Law which His own finger had carved in stone. This will be explained in the 'Before Abraham Was, I Am' chapter. It was for selfish reasons like hers that would lead to His horrible execution. How do you think He dealt with her?

"When Jesus had lifted up himself, and saw none but the woman, he said unto her, Woman, where are those thine accusers? hath no man condemned thee? She said, No man, Lord. And Jesus said unto her, Neither do I condemn thee: go, and sin no more." John 8:10–11

Think long and hard about that scenario. Don't worry about what others are doing wrong, have a good look in the mirror first:

"Judge not, that ye be not judged. For with what judgment ye judge, ye shall be judged: and with what measure ye mete, it shall be measured to you again. And why beholdest thou the mote that is in thy brother's eye, but considerest not the beam that is in thine own eye? Or how wilt thou say to thy brother, Let me pull out the mote out of thine eye; and, behold, a beam is in thine own eye? Thou hypocrite, first cast out the beam out of thine own eye; and then shalt thou see clearly to cast out the mote out of thy brother's eye." Matt 7:1–5

Pay attention, we're getting to the crux of the matter. It's pretty straightforward. If you miss it, it's because you want to miss it, whether consciously, or unconsciously.

"Even so faith, if it hath not works, is dead, being alone." James 2:17

If we believe Yahshua's death was atonement for our sin, yet our actions fail to convey our belief, then our belief is empty, worthless. It's just words.

"Yea, a man may say, Thou hast faith, and I have works: shew me thy faith without thy works, and I will shew thee my faith by my works." James 2:18

Now do you, see? Jesus' half-brother demonstrates his faith by endeavouring to keep the commandments—all of them.

Another way to say the above verse is, "You say you believe the gospel, so show me you believe in the gospel, without any actions. On the other hand, I will show you, and others, I believe in the gospel, by my actions." Sinners would rather see a sermon, than hear one. If you were arrested for believing the gospel, what evidence would they have against you? Or, in other words, listen to Yahshua Himself:

"Wherefore by their fruits ye shall know them." Matt 7:20

And His half-brother:

"For as the body without the spirit is dead, so faith without works is dead also." James 2:26

We'll use an algebra analogy for the verse above: *Faith* (belief in the gospel), without *works* (observing the Ten Commandments), is *dead* (futile, worthless). Or, in equation form: $F - W = \emptyset$

Yahshua's half-brother is saying it, not me. I'm not happy about it either. That said, standing back and removing all emotion, you can see it'd be a better world to live in—if we did follow the commandments. Life would be more fulfilling and less complicated. The difference is, just because I don't want to be bound by rules, I'm not running around saying we're no longer obliged to. We have free will, the freedom to choose between observing them, or breaking them. By choosing to break them, we must be willing to face the consequences.

What Is Sin?

"By the law is the knowledge of sin." Rom 3:20

What do you say sin is? Formulate an answer in your mind. Do you know how Scripture defines sin?

"Whosoever committeth sin transgresseth also the law: for sin is the transgression of the law." 1 John 3:4

If there's no Law, there's no transgression of the Law. If there's no transgression of the Law, there's no sin. If there's no sin, there's no punishment (soul death). If there's no punishment, what the hell was the point of Yahshua's sacrificial death?

Stop reading until you've comprehended what you've just read.

In the beliefs, words and actions of modern Christianity, we're no longer required to obey the Law. If this was the case, there'd no longer be a concept of sin. It stands to reason that if there's no sin, we do not require Yahshua's sacrificial death.

Sin is the breaking of the Ten Commandments. If we're no longer required to obey the Law, then there's no longer a concept of sin. If there's no sin, what do we need Yahshua for?

We may believe Yahshua died for our sins, (breaking the commandments), but if we're not endeavouring to keep from breaking them, our proclamation of faith is dead. It has no meaning; it's nothing but hollow words. Born from original sin, humans have a sinful nature. However, that doesn't mean we get to throw our hands in the air and say, "What the hell?" and do as we please.

"If ye love me, keep my commandments." John 14:15

To be clear, I'm not saying we can work our way into Heaven. Scripture is saying, even if you profess to believe in the truth of the gospel, it means nothing if you're not endeavouring to live by the commandments. If we don't try, we're no better than the demons:

"Thou believest that there is one God; thou doest well: the devils also believe, and tremble." James 2:19

Those who profess to believe in the Resurrection, yet refuse to believe we're required to observe God's Law:

"Many will say to me in that day, Lord, Lord, have we not prophesied in thy name? and in thy name have cast out devils?

and in thy name done many wonderful works? And then will I profess unto them, I never knew you: depart from me, ye that work iniquity." Matt 7:22–23

We're told we'll be judged at our future court appearance according to our works:

"And I saw a great white throne, and him that sat on it, from whose face the earth and the heaven fled away; and there was found no place for them. And I saw the dead, small and great, stand before God; and the books were opened: and another book was opened, which is the book of life: and the dead were **judged** out of those things which were written in the books, **according to their works**. And the sea gave up the dead which were in it; and death and hell delivered up the dead which were in them: and they were **judged** every man **according to their works**." Rev 20:11–13

WWAD?

Are you familiar with WWJD?—What Would Jesus Do? Well, WWAD stands for—What Would the Apostles Do?

"Here is the patience of the saints: here are they that keep the commandments of God, and the faith of Jesus." Rev 14:12

I'll take it a step further—What *did* the apostles do? They kept the Ten Commandments, including the fourth one, keeping the Sabbath day—on the seventh day. They also continued to observe the holy days and food laws, as commanded by our Creator, years after Yahshua had died and risen. They never observed Pagan holidays, which alleged Christians observe. Namely, Christmas and Easter.

A Loving God Wouldn't Allow Suffering?

"God shall wipe away all tears from their eyes." Rev 7:17

Suffering is because of evil. Evil, is because of sin.

People attempting to rubbish the Bible, claim we have no free will and a real God wouldn't allow suffering. Removing our free will is the only way our Creator could prevent evil and suffering, by making us robotic, unable to violate the Ten Commandments. Another way to destroy evil, would be to destroy every single one of us, as we're all evil. Which would you prefer?

1. Become a robot?
2. Be destroyed?
3. Continue living as is?

We're not forced to obey the commandments—we have free will. However, if we break the rules, there are repercussions. All fathers have rules for their children; ones who love them do, anyway. These are for their protection, such as holding hands and looking both ways before crossing a road.

Here's an experiment. Grab a newspaper. Circle any stories related to suffering. You'll find most, if not all, are due to a direct violation of the Ten Commandments. The rest, indirectly. As darkness is the absence of light, so too, is evil the absence of God's law.

Atheists and the like seem to think they have a monopoly on suffering. They don't. Every single one of us has endured suffering. It's synonymous with living in a sin-saturated world. Suffering can also bring us to truth, knowledge of a Creator, providing a path to the gift of salvation.

Sin, by any other name, is still sin. Don't whitewash it, repent of it. It's not an affair, it's adultery. It's not sex, it's fornication. It's not homosexuality, it's sodomy. It's not obsession, it's idolatry. It's not abortion, it's murder. They're not gaming machines, they're gambling machines. Suffering is a by-product of sin. Do you want to be part of the problem, or part of the solution? If you want to eradicate suffering, follow the Ten Commandments and encourage others to follow suit.

"If ye keep my commandments, ye shall abide in my love; even as I have kept my Father's commandments, and abide in his love."
John 15:10

Drug taking can produce several avenues of suffering in your life, as well as producing physical and mental deformities in offspring. Mutations are also caused by the Original Sin. This degenerative condition, affecting everything within the Creation, is called 'entropy'.

Forgiveness is reserved for those who repent of sin, not those who defend, promote, deny, justify or celebrate it. Sin is like a credit card—enjoy now, pay later. You'll pay with your life. The penalty for sin is death; and it is death, *not* eternity, in the Lake of Fire.

Typically, those living comfortable lives have no interest in a Greater Power. It's often suffering that tosses the haughty from their high horse, causing scales to fall from their eyes, awakening them from their slumber to the reality of our Creator. Suffering is the litmus test, the equaliser.

Fair-weather Christians are capsized when the dark storms of life gather, unleashing their unbridled fury. Mistakenly, they conclude there isn't a God. Fleeing the light, they cross over the abyss to the dark side. Joining the ranks of Atheists, they spread their dismal message of apathy and hopelessness.

Unanswered Prayer

This is often cited as an excuse for not believing the Bible. It's like an adult's version of throwing a tantrum, exclaiming, "It's not fair!" Just because you didn't get your way, doesn't mean the Bible isn't true. Unanswered prayers are like asking your dad for lollies when you were a child. If he said "No," by your logic, that would be proof your dad isn't real. While we may not understand why our dads may refuse a request, there's likely a valid reason.

Besides, how many of us are living wilfully sinful lives while demanding our requests are granted? There's only one man who lived a sinless life, yet at least one of His prayers went unanswered. As it turns out, every single one of us should be thankful it did.

"And he was withdrawn from them about a stone's cast, and kneeled down, and prayed, Saying, Father, if thou be willing, remove this cup from me: nevertheless not my will, but thine, be done. And there appeared an angel unto him from heaven, strengthening him. And being in an agony he prayed more earnestly: and his sweat was as it were great drops of blood falling down to the ground."
Luke 22:41–44

Without this unanswered prayer request from a sinless man, there would be no forgiveness for our sins.

Knuckle Sandwiches

The 'Holy Days or Holidays?' chapter describes how I almost had a punch-up with a 'Christian' during dinner with our wives at his house. He, like many Christians, was trying to force down my throat the idea we're not required to obey the commandments. Trying in vain to change the subject, he wasn't having a bar of it. So be it.

I don't recall his name, so he shall be called Jason, for personal reasons. I proceeded to place Jason in a Scriptural headlock, "If Yahshua was here and you asked Him what we had to do to go to Heaven, what would He say?" Jason said we could never know, then rabbited on about doing good to others.

"We can know," I corrected Jason, "because someone asked Him while He was here." After Jason was told to fetch his Bible and turn to the relevant Scripture, he stared quietly at the page.

I stirred him to life, "What does it say?"

Jason pointed to a passage on the page, "He said to sell everything and give it to the poor." Confused, I looked over his shoulder at where his finger pointed. He was right. I was bewildered.

"Sell all that thou hast, and distribute unto the poor, and thou shalt have treasure in heaven: and come, follow me." Luke 18:22

I asked for context, looking to where he pointed. Sure enough, there it was.

"And a certain ruler asked him, saying, Good Master, what shall I do to inherit eternal life?" Luke 18:18

My mind was doing cartwheels. Do my eyes deceive me? Taking the Bible from him, my eyes were drawn to subsequent verses.

"Thou knowest the commandments, Do not commit adultery, Do not kill, Do not steal, Do not bear false witness, Honour thy father and thy mother." Luke 18:20

He was deliberately lying, skipping over an extremely pertinent piece of Scripture, 'cherry-picking', as they say. Ironically, he was violating the Ninth Commandment—Thou shalt not bear false witness. It was akin to throwing holy water on the Devil when I pointed this out.

Here's the passage of the relevant Scripture, unadulterated, in its entirety:

"And a certain ruler asked him, saying, Good Master, what shall I do to inherit eternal life? And Jesus said unto him, Why callest thou me good? none is good, save one, that is, God. Thou knowest the commandments, Do not commit adultery, Do not kill, Do not steal, Do not bear false witness, Honour thy father and thy mother. And he said, All these have I kept from my youth up. Now when Jesus heard these things, he said unto him, Yet lackest thou one thing: sell all that thou hast, and distribute unto the poor, and thou shalt have treasure in heaven: and come, follow me. And when he heard this, he was very sorrowful: for he was very rich." Luke 18:18–23

Yahshua tells us we must obey the commandments. Jason attempted to make a weak argument, saying Yahshua wasn't referencing the commandments, as He didn't mention all. That's a common argument, a pathetic one, at that. Just because He doesn't reference all ten, doesn't mean He isn't referencing all.

"By this we know that we love the children of God, when we love God, and keep his commandments. For this is the love of God, that we keep his commandments." 1 John 5:2–3

Lawyer Trap

The following story entails an exchange between Yahshua and religious leaders. The Sadducees had failed to trap him so the Pharisees tried their hand:

"Then went the Pharisees, and took counsel how they might entangle him in his talk." Matt 22:15

They devised a number of schemes to ensnare Him, without success. In frustration, they sought the skills of a lawyer:

"When the Pharisees had heard that he had put the Sadducees to silence, they were gathered together. Then one of them, who was a lawyer, asked him a question, tempting him, and saying, Master, which is the great commandment in the law?" Matt 22:34–36

This was a brilliant question. After all, each commandment bears equal weight; break one, you're guilty of breaking all:

"For whosoever shall keep the whole law, and yet offend in one point, he is guilty of all." James 2:10–11

How did Yahshua respond when they asked Him which of the Ten Commandments was the greatest?

"Thou shalt love the Lord thy God with all thy heart, and with all thy soul, and with all thy mind. This is the first and great commandment. And the second is like unto it, Thou shalt love thy neighbour as thyself. On these two commandments hang all the law and the prophets." Matt 22:37–40

This passage of Scripture highlights the significance of every commandment. Jason referenced it as proof of not having to obey the commandments, arguing, "You only had to love Yahweh and your neighbour as yourself."

"Yahshua's reply was a summary of all Ten Commandments," I explained. Showing him the first four commandments, I pointed out they centred on loving God, while the remaining six are centred on loving your neighbour.

Works

'Works' refers to actions you do that are Biblical. Non-Christians don't read Bibles, they read Christians. Feeding the poor, taking care of orphans and visiting prisoners is works-based. Where a lot of people fall, is when their actions (works), are cross-examined with Scriptures such as:

"Take heed that ye do not your alms before men, to be seen of them: otherwise ye have no reward of your Father which is in heaven. Therefore when thou doest thine alms, do not sound a trumpet before thee, as the hypocrites do in the synagogues and in the streets, that they may have glory of men. Verily I say unto you, They have their reward. But when thou doest alms, let not thy left hand know what thy right hand doeth: That thine alms may be in secret: and thy Father which seeth in secret himself shall reward thee openly." Matt 6:1-4

It extends to prayer also. As you read the following verses, see if any denominations come to mind:

"But thou, when thou prayest, enter into thy closet, and when thou hast shut thy door, pray to thy Father which is in secret; and thy Father which seeth in secret shall reward thee openly. But when ye pray, use not vain repetitions, as the heathen do: for they think that they shall be heard for their much speaking. Be not ye therefore like unto them." Matt 6:6-8

"Moreover when ye fast, be not, as the hypocrites, of a sad countenance: for they disfigure their faces, that they may appear unto men to fast. Verily I say unto you, They have their reward. But thou, when thou fastest, anoint thine head, and wash thy face; That thou appear not unto men to fast, but unto thy Father which is in secret: and thy Father, which seeth in secret, shall reward thee openly." Matt 6:16–18

Works never atones for sin. Forgiveness of sins only comes by accepting Yahshua's death as atonement for every single commandment violation. However, and this is what so many seem to miss, we show our faith, by our works.

Under the Old Testament, remission of sins was granted through an animal blood sacrifice. In the New Testament, it's granted through the shedding of Yahshua's blood:

"By the which will we are sanctified through the offering of the body of Jesus Christ once for all. And every priest standeth daily ministering and offering oftentimes the same sacrifices, which can never take away sins: But this man, after he had offered one sacrifice for sins for ever, sat down on the right hand of God." Heb 10:10–12

Rather than declaring the Ten Commandments obsolete, Yahshua wrote them into everyone's heart:

"I will put my laws into their hearts, and in their minds will I write them." Heb 10:16

Yahshua's words are also reminiscent of the prophet Jeremiah:

"But this shall be the covenant that I will make with the house of Israel; After those days, saith the Lord, I will put my law in their inward parts, and write it in their hearts; and will be their God, and they shall be my people." Jer 31:33

"And hereby we do know that we know him, if we keep his commandments. He that saith, I know him, and keepeth not his commandments, is a liar, and the truth is not in him. But whoso keepeth his word, in him verily is the love of God perfected: hereby know we that we are in him. He that saith he abideth in him ought himself also so to walk, even as he walked." 1 John 2:3–6

Hanged for Murder

Ronald Ryan was convicted of murdering a prison guard while escaping. He was the last person executed in Australia—only if you were to exclude 100,000 unborn boys and girls, every year. Ronald made a profound statement before his hanging, "It is an oft-repeated thought of mine, that we could each do with two lifetimes … on this Earth. Then we could benefit from our mistakes and live closer to the Ten Commandments."

Ryan was hanged at Pentridge Prison in 1967. His last words were to the hangman; "God bless you, please make it quick." Does anyone else see a parallel with the thief on the cross, in that he appeared repentant?

We're required to keep the Ten Commandments, all of them. The below passage is taken from the last book of the Bible, set during the End of Days:

"And the dragon was wroth with the woman, and went to make war with the remnant of her seed, which keep the commandments of God, and have the testimony of Jesus Christ." Rev 12:17

From the man Himself:

"If ye love me, keep my commandments." John 14:15

Notice how He says *my* commandments, not *the* commandments.

Sabbath Day

BACK to Shayne's Bible study group. Our next topic was the Sabbath Day. It hadn't seemed like a big deal at the time. *This was going to be easy, almost all churches recognised Sunday.* My Catholic upbringing had explained it was 'Son'day, in honour of Yahweh's Son allegedly rising from the dead on a Sunday. In reality, it was 'Sun'day, worship of the created light source which rules the day.

Monday to Friday were work days, occasionally Saturdays were too. Sport was played on Saturdays, while Sunday was a day of relaxation before returning to work. It was also the day of church attendance, except for Jews and a fringe group of Christians—Seventh Day Adventists (SDAs).

Fourth Commandment

It's the longest and only commandment beginning with 'remember'. That is pertinent, as it's the one that has been forgotten:

"Remember the Sabbath day, to keep it holy. Six days shalt thou labour, and do all thy work: But the seventh day is the Sabbath of the Lord thy God: in it thou shalt not do any work, thou, nor thy son, nor thy daughter, thy manservant, nor thy maidservant, nor thy cattle, nor thy stranger that is within thy gates: For in six days the Lord made heaven and earth, the sea, and all that in them is, and rested the seventh day: wherefore the Lord blessed the Sabbath day, and hallowed it." Ex 20:8–11

Our Creator worked for six days, resting on the last day of the week, the seventh day. Well, this was no surprise to me, everyone knew the last day of the week was Sunday. The problem was, the material I was reading insisted Saturday was the last day of the week. Unable to get my head around it, I explained my frustration to my wife. She said Sunday was the first day of the week, not the last, showing me a calendar and diary.

'Pick a Day'

During the Bible study, participants argued over whether the Sabbath had to be observed. A few argued for Saturday, most for Sunday. Even so, the majority said it wasn't important. Others said there was no set day and to, 'just pick a day'.

From my research, it became clear the Sabbath was Saturday and humanity is required to observe it. The Biblical Sabbath is from sunset Friday, until sunset Saturday. The alleged Christian 'Sunday sabbath' is from midnight Saturday, until midnight Sunday. The Sabbath day isn't intended for Jews only, as many Christians claim. If you don't believe the Biblical sacrament of Marriage pertains to Jews only, why insist the Sabbath does?

One argument put forward is that the Sabbath was changed to Sunday because Yahshua allegedly rose from the dead on a Sunday. He didn't. Scriptures show the disciples continued to attend synagogues/church on the seventh day of the week, not the first day.

Throughout the New Testament, the first day of the week is called, 'the first day of the week' and the seventh day of the week is called, 'the Sabbath day'.

"When the Jews were gone out of the synagogue, the Gentiles besought that these words might be preached to them the next sabbath. Now when the congregation was broken up, many of the

Jews and religious proselytes followed Paul and Barnabas: who, speaking to them, persuaded them to continue in the grace of God. And the next sabbath day came almost the whole city together to hear the word of God." Acts 13:42–44

If you have a basic grasp of reading comprehension and a sprinkling of common sense and logic, you'll see the seventh day is the Sabbath. It's been said the apostles only preached on the Sabbath to reach the Jews. If that was the case, when the Gentiles were imploring them to preach to them next Sabbath, the apostles could've said, "Tomorrow is Sunday, the Christian Sabbath, so you don't have to wait until the seventh day," but they didn't. Why not? This isn't a rhetorical question. Attempt to answer it logically. Any discomfort you're feeling is cognitive dissonance.

"And he reasoned in the synagogue every sabbath, and persuaded the Jews and the Greeks." Acts 18:4

The verse above is saying Paul preached in the Greek Synagogue every Sabbath, to Jews and Greeks. There's no mention of Sunday worship. Greek Gentiles had to attend the Jewish Synagogue, on the Sabbath. There's no mention of preaching to Gentiles the following day.

Sabbath comes from the Hebrew word 'shavat', meaning, 'to rest'. It's a sign to our Creator that by resting on the seventh day, we acknowledge His six days of Creation, and the day He rested afterwards.

Catholics changed it to Sunday, to commemorate the sun. They allege following Yahshua's death, disciples held services on Sunday, in direct violation of the Fourth Commandment carved in stone by the finger of our Creator.

Christians point to the breaking of bread on Sunday:

"Upon the first day of the week, when the disciples came together to break bread, Paul preached unto them, ready to depart on the morrow; and continued his speech until midnight." Acts 20:7

Yeah, so? They broke bread daily. According to their logic, every day becomes the Sabbath.

"And they, continuing daily with one accord in the temple, and breaking bread from house to house, did eat their meat with gladness and singleness of heart." Acts 2:46

Catholics and Christians alike seemed to have missed the fact that verse 6, which is before the one they claim changes the Fourth Commandment, verse 7, alludes to the keeping of the Passover and the subsequent Days of Unleavened Bread. So why don't they stipulate the observance of those holy days?

"And we sailed away from Philippi after the days of unleavened bread, and came unto them to Troas in five days; where we abode seven days." Acts 20:6

Rhetorical questions aren't reserved for Evolutionism believers alone. Were you able to answer the question rationally? Perhaps you may believe you have. If so, reconsider your answer after reading the 'Holy Days or Holidays?' chapter.

Here's another verse to consider, below. Not only does it apply to the weekly Sabbath as commanded by the Fourth Commandment, it also applies to the seven feast days commanded by our Creator:

"And he shall speak great words against the most High, and shall wear out the saints of the most High, and think to change times and laws:" Dan 7:25

Sabbath Day Objections

FAR too often, what's encountered is an obscure verse to try and force the change of a major doctrinal belief. Usually, it's like having a few verses on one side of a scale, a mountain of opposing verses on the other, yet still concluding the former is the correct interpretation.

Below are a number of Scriptures commonly put forward by those who refuse to observe the day commanded by our Creator:

Colossians 2:16

Paul was preaching in the city of Colossae, in modern-day Turkey. The Colossians had been influenced by Gnostics, a religious philosophical group, similar to modern people who define themselves as 'spiritual' or 'New Age'.

"Let no man therefore judge you in meat, or in drink, or in respect of an holyday, or of the new moon, or of the Sabbath days. Which are a shadow of things to come; but the body is of Christ." Col 2:16–17

You could be forgiven for thinking it's implying you can do as you please, concerning the Sabbath. This couldn't be further from the truth. After hearing the gospel, Gnostic converts were pestered by Gnostic groups who didn't like their former companions observing a Sabbath day of rest. Or, the other holy days commanded by God, as well as with how they behaved on these days.

Notice how Paul says, "Which are a shadow of things to come." He doesn't say, "Which are shadows of things passed."

Paul was speaking directly to the newly-converted Colossians, warning them not to be swayed by their Pagan companions' judgement for observing the Sabbath. Food references had nothing to do with food laws observed by the apostles. They were directed at the celebratory feasting on the associated feast days. Keep in mind, he said, "Let no one judge you" as opposed to, "Don't keep the Sabbath."

Examine it logically. When Yahshua rose from the dead, which group would most likely be opposed to Sabbath day worship? The Jews? No, Jews were already worshipping on the Sabbath. The apostles and disciples? No, they were Jews too. The Gentile converts? Why should they care? They had no set day, they were converting. So then, which group was contentious over Sabbath day observance? It was the philosophical Gnostics, angered by the conversion of their former companions.

"Beware lest any man spoil you through philosophy and vain deceit, after the tradition of men, after the rudiments of the world, and not after Christ." Col 2:8

As with Paul's encounter with the Gnostics, Yahshua had similar interactions with pedantic Jewish religious leaders judging Him. Not against Scripture, but against their ceremonial traditions. He admonishes them for chastising Him for not washing His hands before eating:

"For laying aside the commandment of God, ye hold the tradition of men, as the washing of pots and cups: and many other such like things ye do. And he said unto them, Full well ye reject the commandment of God, that ye may keep your own tradition." Mark 7:8–9

That's what's occurring with Sunday worship. You're rejecting the commandment of your Creator, so as you may keep your tradition of Sunday worship.

Following 'Sunday worship', you could also add, 'Easter and Christmas'.

Romans 14:5

"One man esteemeth one day above another: another esteemeth every day alike. Let every man be fully persuaded in his own mind." Rom 14:5

If you were to look at the chapter, you'd see the discussion is centred around food, whether eating meat or plants only. Paul goes on to say:

"He that regardeth the day, regardeth it unto the Lord; and he that regardeth not the day, to the Lord he doth not regard it. He that eateth, eateth to the Lord, for he giveth God thanks; and he that eateth not, to the Lord he eateth not, and giveth God thanks." Rom 14:6

The context is centred around fasting in general, or fasting on the commanded holy days, such as the Day of Atonement, *not* Sabbath day observance. There's no mention of the word 'Sabbath'. Besides, earlier in the same letter, Paul had said:

"Wherefore the law is holy, and the commandment holy, and just, and good." Rom 7:12

Galatians 4:10

"Ye observe days, and months, and times, and years." Gal 4:10

Paul isn't implying the weekly Sabbath and holy days are no longer required to be observed. He observed them himself, as did the apostles and disciples. He's condemning Pagan superstitions. Here's one example of him observing a holy day:

"But bade them farewell, saying, I must by all means keep this feast that cometh in Jerusalem: but I will return again unto you, if God will. And he sailed from Ephesus." Acts 18:21

Hebrews 4:3–10

How anyone could read this and think it's abolishing or even altering the Fourth Commandment is beyond me. After all, look at the sentence in bold, below. If you still can't see it, read the one directly following it.

"For we which have believed do enter into rest, as he said, As I have sworn in my wrath, if they shall enter into my rest: although the works were finished from the foundation of the world. For he spake in a certain place of the seventh day on this wise, And God did rest the seventh day from all his works. And in this place again, If they shall enter into my rest. Seeing therefore it remaineth that some must enter therein, and they to whom it was first preached entered not in because of unbelief: Again, he limiteth a certain day, saying in David, To day, after so long a time; as it is said, To day if ye will hear his voice, harden not your hearts. For **if Jesus had given them rest, then would he not afterward have spoken of another day**. There remaineth therefore a rest to the people of God. For he that is entered into his rest, he also hath ceased from his own works, as God did from his." Heb 4:3–10

Sunday Resurrection

A common objection is, "Yahshua rose from the dead on a Sunday, the first day of the week." Most believe it because that's what they were told. The remainder believe, due to this verse:

"And very early in the morning the first day of the week, they came unto the sepulchre at the rising of the sun." Mark 16:2

It doesn't say Yahshua rose at dawn, only that it's when they discovered the empty tomb. He rose on the Sabbath day, at sunset. If you want to worship on 'Resurrection day', do so on the Sabbath. You'll have the added benefit of keeping the Law, as commanded.

Jews Only

It's claimed the Sabbath day was for Jews only, using verses such as the one below, saying it isn't intended for Christians:

"Speak thou also unto the children of Israel, saying, Verily my sabbaths ye shall keep: for it is a sign between me and you throughout your generations; that ye may know that I am the Lord that doth sanctify you. Ye shall keep the sabbath therefore; for it is holy unto you: Wherefore the children of Israel shall keep the sabbath, to observe the sabbath throughout their generations, for a perpetual covenant. It is a sign between me and the children of Israel for ever: for in six days the Lord made heaven and earth, and on the seventh day he rested, and was refreshed." Ex 13:13-17

Sabbath was established for mankind, not just the Jews:

"The sabbath was made for man." Mark 2:27

Yahshua and His followers were Jewish. Scriptures foreshadowed His birth, life, death and Resurrection. Gentiles converted to Judaism. All Jewish converts did was accept Yahshua as Messiah. Consider Christianity advanced Judaism, if you will. 'Christianity' should be an extension of Judaism, not an obliteration of it. Rest assured, pun intended, if Jews were told they must now worship on the first day of the week, as opposed to the seventh-day Sabbath, the New Testament would be filled with fiery exchanges. If Yahshua walked the earth today, He wouldn't recognise His Church. The closest resemblance would be the Jewish synagogues.

Sabbath Day Rabbit Holes

We can go down all sorts of rabbit holes, chasing one obscure verse after another. I don't have the time, nor the patience for that. Further, it's not necessary. Throughout the Bible we see the apostles, before and after Yahshua's death, observing dietary laws, commandments and holy days.

While there's contention surrounding the requirement of whether or not to observe the Sabbath, or which day of the week is involved, it doesn't flow on towards the subject of food laws. They tend to fly under the radar.

Clean and Unclean Food

CHRISTIANS think food laws don't apply to them. If they're open-minded and honest, they'll soon find they have another 'think' coming.

All animals designated by the Bible as clean, are herbivores. They chew the cud and have split hoofs:

"Of all the animals that live on land, these are the ones you may eat: You may eat any animal that has a split hoof completely divided and that chews the cud." Lev 11:2–3

Conversely:

"Every animal that has a split hoof not completely divided or that does not chew the cud is unclean for you." Lev 11:26

This was a tough one. While I didn't care for oysters, I loved shellfish. Roast pork, ham, salami—couldn't get enough of it. Reading a denomination's claim that we had to abstain from various meat and seafood didn't make sense. *After all, that was back in the day. Unlike us, they didn't have refrigeration. Therefore, that Scripture is irrelevant, it no longer applies.*

Further study revealed I'd been wrong on this point too. The lack of refrigeration is often used as a reason to discount food laws. If this was the case, why not rule out all meat eating? Another excuse Christians are inclined to spout is, 'It was nailed to the cross'.

Scavengers

The majority of creatures listed as unclean are scavengers. Typically, they don't hunt their food and they eat excrement and dead, decaying flesh. As a result, they're more likely to contain parasites and toxins. Catfish and yabbies clean the bottoms of ponds and streams. Catfish always show the highest levels of contamination in chemically polluted water.

Sewage laden with toxins, chemicals, harmful bacteria, viruses, and parasites becomes concentrated within shellfish. They can be placed into a tank contaminated with cholera bacteria, and they'll purify the water. Lobsters, prawns and crabs are the oceans' cockroaches, cleaning their floors. Oysters filter the water. Eating them is akin to eating filters.

Vultures, almost by definition, are notorious scavengers. Regardless, animals don't have to be scavengers to be classified as unclean. Rabbits and horses are deemed unclean as they don't have split hooves.

Fins and Scales

Years ago, the US Navy undertook a study to find a simple rule of thumb that stranded sailors could utilise, to know whether a fish was safe to eat or not. After spending millions of dollars over a couple of years, their conclusion: "If it has fins and scales, it's safe enough to eat."

Instead of spending all that money and investing all that time, they could've just read a copy of the Manufacturer's Handbook:

"These ye shall eat of all that are in the waters: all that have fins and scales shall ye eat: And whatsoever hath not fins and scales ye may not eat; it is unclean unto you." Deut 14:9–10

Filthy Pig

Pigs are filthy, eating garbage, faeces and decaying flesh. Everything consumed becomes part of the pig's flesh. Toxins in pork are stored in fat, dispersed throughout the meat, unlike lean beef. When stacked in cages on top of each other, pigs thrive, even if only the pig in the top cage is fed. Pigs below survive by eating waste from the pig above. Farmers can save money by feeding free raw sewage to pigs.

Christmas and its associated traditions are unbiblical. Contemplate, in light of the truth regarding clean and unclean meat, the role of the coveted Christmas ham. Prophet Isaiah mentions a Messianic prophecy concerning the eating of pork during the return of Yahshua in the last days:

"They that sanctify themselves, and purify themselves in the gardens behind one tree in the midst, eating swine's flesh, and the abomination, and the mouse, shall be consumed together, saith the Lord." Isa 66:17

"And the swine, because it divideth the hoof, yet cheweth not the cud, it is unclean unto you: ye shall not eat of their flesh, nor touch their dead carcase." Deut 14:8

"I am sought of them that asked not for me; I am found of them that sought me not: I said, Behold me, behold me, unto a nation that was not called by my name. I have spread out my hands all the day unto a rebellious people, which walketh in a way that was not good, after their own thoughts; A people that provoketh me to anger continually to my face; that sacrificeth in gardens, and burneth incense upon altars of brick; Which remain among the graves, and lodge in the monuments, which eat swine's flesh, and broth of abominable things is in their vessels; Which say, Stand by thyself, come not near to me; for I am holier than thou." Isa 65:1-5

Deuteronomy and Leviticus address food laws, and other health and hygiene matters, such as precautions following childbirth. There are procedures to identify and eliminate the spread of communicable diseases, such as washing an infected person in running water:

"And bathe his flesh in running water." Lev 15:13

Discarded wound dressings had to be burned. Water found to contain a dead animal couldn't be drunk; and let's not forget all directives concerning sexual practices. These were recorded thousands of years before germ theory was understood. As late as the mid 1800s, doctors moved from patient to patient, without washing their hands. Those who did, used standing water in a basin, as opposed to running water.

After adopting Biblical health guidelines, mortality rates in hospitals plummeted. Despite Moses recording hundreds of health regulations, he never recorded a single medical error.

Quarantining of the Sick

"All the days wherein the plague shall be in him he shall be defiled; he is unclean: he shall dwell alone; without the camp shall his habitation be." Lev 13:46

Decimated by the black plague, other populations blamed it on the Jews as they weren't affected. They were just following laws commanded by God. Such as, quarantining the sick, burying human waste away from living areas, and washing hands after handling the dead, or after using the toilet.

George Washington

There was a time when people were bled, as a form of medical treatment. George Washington is a well-known example. The method is believed to have killed him. If only they'd adhered to the truth of the Bible, they wouldn't have drained his life from him:

"The life of all flesh is the blood." Lev 17:14

Upholding food laws commanded by our Creator isn't a cause of contention among the vast majority of Christians—they consider it a non-issue. As with holy day observance also commanded by our Creator, they erroneously believe since these were given in the Old Testament, the New Testament overrides it. They'll dismiss these commands with a wave of the hand while spouting nonsense, such as, "It was nailed to the cross."

It wasn't.

You shall see in subsequent chapters that Yahshua and His followers observed food laws and holy days. His followers continued to do so, long after His death and Resurrection. You'll also see, holy days will be observed in Heaven.

Holy Days or Holidays?

AS with food laws, holy days also fly under the radar. I certainly wasn't aware of them, falsely believing Christian holy days were Christmas, Easter and Lent—whatever that was. Of these, I despised Easter most, as the return on investment was horrendous. With Christmas, you only had to attend mass once and you'd receive presents. With Easter, we had to attend three times, one of which was midnight mass. During the service we had to go outside the church and turn to face east, the direction of the rising sun, as Easter is sun worship. So too, is *Sun*day worship. On top of that, we had to line up and kiss the feet of a statue of a graven image of a man on a cross, a direct violation of the Second Commandment. For all of this, we were only compensated with chocolate eggs and rabbits.

I Cooked for the Jews

Living in Melbourne, I'd become familiar with Jews as we'd lived in suburbs populated by them. You'd often see them walking around on Saturday with their black coats, black hats or small caps, and hair curls hanging about their ears.

As a chef, I worked for a Jewish catering company. It was peculiar, having Friday nights and Saturdays off, and yet, always working Sundays. We often cooked inside government buildings and prestigious homes. I'd cook for members of Parliament, and on one occasion, cooked for the Israeli Prime Minister, Benjamin Netanyahu, inside the home of Richard Pratt, who at one time, was the richest man in Australia. He had a personal chef, though it was his day off.

Unfortunately, it didn't stop him from showing up and putting in his five cents worth. At one point we were in the garage, setting up entrée plates on trestle tables, moving around the cramped conditions, dressing plates with ease. That was until the uninvited chef expressed caution, advising the plates were worth $500 each, as the gold edging was in fact, gold. From that point on, there were a few near misses. Thankfully, the main course was prepared from within a secret chamber in a wall inside the mansion and the troublesome chef wasn't party to it.

A Rabbi had to be present whenever we prepared food, so as to ensure dietary laws were followed. Pork and shellfish weren't allowed. There was a 'milk kitchen' where certain duties would be carried out. Under no circumstances could cooking utensils be transferred between it and the 'meat kitchen'. I remember them saying, "Thou shalt not cook the kid in its mother's milk." In other words, do not use beef in a cream sauce, for example.

"Thou shalt not seethe a kid in his mother's milk." Ex 23:19

Knowing what I know now, I wish I'd paid more attention, and asked more questions while I worked there.

Seven Holy Days

There are seven holy days/feasts, separate from the weekly seventh-day Sabbath, commanded by our Creator—Passover, Feast of Unleavened Bread, Feast of Firstfruits, Feast of Weeks or Pentecost, Feast of Trumpets, Day of Atonement, Feast of Tabernacles or Booths.

1. Passover

"In the fourteenth day of the first month at even is the Lord's passover. And on the fifteenth day of the same month is the feast of unleavened bread unto the Lord: seven days ye must eat unleavened bread. In the first day ye shall have an holy convocation: ye shall do no servile work therein. But ye shall offer an offering made by fire unto the Lord seven days: in the seventh day is an holy convocation: ye shall do no servile work therein." Lev 23:5–8

Passover is a memorial to the last plague in Egypt, when the angel of death 'passed over' the children of Israel who had applied the blood of a lamb to their doors:

"For I will pass through the land of Egypt this night, and will smite all the firstborn in the land of Egypt, both man and beast; and against all the gods of Egypt I will execute judgment: I am the Lord. And the blood shall be to you for a token upon the houses where ye are: and when I see the blood, I will pass over you, and the plague shall not be upon you to destroy you, when I smite the land of Egypt." Ex 12:12–13

Read all of Exodus 12. Not only did it point back to the deliverance from Egypt, but it also foreshadowed the Messiah, fulfilled by Yahshua. He'd become the Passover sacrifice.

"Your lamb shall be without blemish, a male of the first year: ye shall take it out from the sheep, or from the goats: And ye shall keep it up until the fourteenth day of the same month: and the whole assembly of the congregation of Israel shall kill it in the evening. And they shall take of the blood, and strike it on the two side posts and on the upper door post of the houses, wherein they shall eat it." Ex 12:5–7

They were instructed to place blood from the sacrificial lamb on their doorposts. Symbolically, the cross would also be covered with blood from Yahshua, the sacrificial male lamb, free from blemish (sin). The atonement for our sins/crimes is by the shedding of His blood. His death is a substitute for our death. Not only was the prophecy of Exodus a prophecy of deliverance for the time at hand, it was also a combination of detailed, specific prophecies for the sacrificial death of Yahshua, 1,500 years later.

We're not done yet. It's also a prophecy for the End of Days, the Resurrection and subsequent judging and sentencing at The Great White Throne Judgement. If we've chosen to believe Yahweh's son died as atonement for our sins, and have lived accordingly, then we too, shall be spared from eternal damnation—soul extinction in the Lake of Fire.

Here He likens himself to a door:

"Verily, verily, I say unto you, I am the door of the sheep. All that ever came before me are thieves and robbers: but the sheep did not hear them. I am the door: by me if any man enter in, he shall be saved." John 10:7–9

With this claim, you could liken Him to a gatekeeper:

"Enter ye in at the strait gate: for wide is the gate, and broad is the way, that leadeth to destruction, and many there be which go in thereat: Because strait is the gate, and narrow is the way, which leadeth unto life, and few there be that find it." Matt 7:13–14

Passover is a meal eaten within proximity to when Romans would celebrate Easter. It commemorated the children of Israel's deliverance from death by the blood of an unblemished male lamb. Passover initiated the week-long observance of the Feast of Unleavened Bread.

I've visited the traditional site, the 'upper room' of the house, where Yahshua ate the Last Supper. From here, it's just a hop, skip and jump to other sites, such as where Yahshua prayed, was arrested and jailed, and where Peter denied Him three times. Visiting Israel allows you to better understand events in the Bible.

2. Unleavened Bread

"And on the fifteenth day of the same month is the feast of unleavened bread unto the Lord: seven days ye must eat unleavened bread." Lev 23:6

Occasionally, the whole week of the Feast of Unleavened Bread is loosely referred to as Passover. The first day and the last day of the feast are High-day Sabbaths. These may fall on any day of the week.

Leaven, a raising agent in food, is symbolic of sin. We're instructed to remove it and anything containing it, from our houses for seven days as a symbolic remembrance to remove sin from our lives. A small amount of yeast expands an entire loaf of bread. It's symbolic of how suffering in our lives will flourish, after initially only allowing in a small amount of sin.

"Seven days shall there be no leaven found in your houses: for whosoever eateth that which is leavened, even that soul shall be cut off from the congregation of Israel, whether he be a stranger, or born in the land. Ye shall eat nothing leavened; in all your habitations shall ye eat unleavened bread." Ex 12:19–20

If you think we don't have to keep this holy day, see what Paul has to say about it in a letter he wrote to the people in Corinth. Keep in mind, this is after Yahshua's death:

"Purge out therefore the old leaven, that ye may be a new lump, as ye are unleavened. For even Christ our passover is sacrificed for us: Therefore **let us keep the feast**, not with old leaven, neither with the leaven of malice and wickedness; but with the unleavened bread of sincerity and truth." 1 Cor 5:7–8

"Let us keep the feast." How many of you are saying not to? Something else for you to ponder—Many mistakenly believe the New Testament was written several decades after Yahshua's death. It's logical Paul's aforementioned instructional letter to the Corinthians, would be written months or even a few years following His conversion, rather than several decades after.

3. First Fruits

"And the feast of harvest, the firstfruits of thy labours, which thou hast sown in the field: and the feast of ingathering, which is in the end of the year, when thou hast gathered in thy labours out of the field." Ex 23:16

"Speak unto the children of Israel, and say unto them, When ye be come into the land which I give unto you, and shall reap the harvest thereof, then ye shall bring a sheaf of the first fruits of your harvest unto the priest." Lev 23:10

The feast is the offering of the first of your labours. Fruit trees often sprout a few fruits early. This seems to occur everywhere in nature. Even when popping popcorn, a few kernels will pop before the others explode. With foreshadowing, the timing of Yahshua's Resurrection indicates He is the first fruits of the Resurrection to eternal life. You say you want to celebrate the Resurrection? Why don't you? Yahshua was the first fruits of the Resurrection. The Resurrection of the Dead is yet to occur. It's in the future, casting its shadow back to us. That's why Scripture often refers to these prophetic feasts as, 'shadows of things to come'.

4. Feast of Weeks or Pentecost

"Even unto the morrow after the seventh sabbath shall ye number fifty days; and ye shall offer a new meat offering unto the Lord." Lev 23:16

This feast begins seven weeks, exactly fifty days, or seven Sabbaths after the Feast of First Fruits. It's also known as Pentecost, meaning fifty. For this reason, it will always be a Sunday, the day following the Sabbath day sunset Resurrection.

Jews believe our Creator gave Moses the Torah (Pentateuch) at Mt Sinai on this feast. It comprises the first five books of the Hebrew Bible (Old Testament): Genesis, Exodus, Leviticus, Numbers, and Deuteronomy. Jews consider this the single most important event in Israel's history.

Fire was associated with the giving of Scripture on Mount Sinai:

"The angel of the Lord appeared unto him in a flame of fire out of the midst of a bush: and he looked, and, behold, the bush burned with fire, and the bush was not consumed." Ex 3:2

Fire is also associated with Pentecost in the New Testament, where apostles were gifted with the ability to preach the gospel of Messiah in 'tongues' (languages), of other nations:

"And there appeared unto them cloven tongues like as of fire, and it sat upon each of them. And they were all filled with the Holy Ghost, and began to speak with other tongues, as the Spirit gave them utterance." Acts 2:3–4

5. Feast of Trumpets

"Speak unto the children of Israel, saying, In the seventh month, in the first day of the month, shall ye have a sabbath, a memorial of blowing of trumpets, an holy convocation." Lev 23:24

This is celebrated on the first day of the seventh month, in the Hebrew calendar. In Scripture, the number seven is associated with holiness, completion and perfection. It's to remind us to stop and prepare for what is to come—Judgement. God manifests His presence in the Old Testament with the sound of a trumpet:

"And Moses brought forth the people out of the camp to meet with God; and they stood at the nether part of the mount. And mount Sinai was altogether on a smoke, because the Lord descended upon it in fire: and the smoke thereof ascended as the smoke of a furnace, and the whole mount quaked greatly. And when the voice of the trumpet sounded long, and waxed louder and louder, Moses spake, and God answered him by a voice." Ex 19:17–19

This foreshadows the return of Yahshua, who will alight on top of a mountain, the Mount of Olives in Jerusalem.

"For the Lord himself shall descend from heaven with a shout, with the voice of the archangel, and with the trump of God: and the dead in Christ shall rise first." 1 Thess 4:16

Here's another verse where the sound of a trumpet is associated with God:

"After this I looked, and, behold, a door was opened in heaven: and the first voice which I heard was as it were of a trumpet talking with me; which said, Come up hither, and I will shew thee things which must be hereafter." Rev 4:4

The day is coming when all of us will have to stand before a higher court and give an accounting of our lives at the Great White Throne Judgement.

Ned Kelly

The Australian Bushranger understood this. In court before his hanging, he continued to show his fighting spirit, admonishing Judge Redmond Barry, "A day will come, at a bigger court than this, when we shall see which is right and which is wrong. No matter how a man lives he is bound to come to judgment somewhere."

Sentencing Kelly to death, Barry concluded with the traditional, "May God have mercy on your soul."

Kelly countered, "I will go a little further than that, and say I will see you there where I go." Strangely enough, twelve days after Kelly was hanged, Barry himself died, of natural causes.

6. Day of Atonement

"And this shall be a statute for ever unto you: that in the seventh month, on the tenth day of the month, ye shall afflict your souls, and do no work at all, whether it be one of your own country, or a stranger that sojourneth among you: For on that day shall the priest make an atonement for you, to cleanse you, that ye may be clean from all your sins before the Lord. It shall be a sabbath of rest unto you, and ye shall afflict your souls, by a statute **for ever**." Lev 16:29–31

Take note, the last words are 'for ever'. What do you think God meant when He said, 'for ever'?

It's the most solemn of all holy days, being a foreshadow of Messiah's crucifixion, and a foreshadow of Yahshua's atonement for sin on Judgement Day. His atonement, if we are deserving, is the only thing saving us from the second death, soul death, in the Lake of Fire.

"I will remove the iniquity of that land in one day." Zech 3.9

On this day from sunset, to sunset on the following day, not only is it a Sabbath rest, consumption of food or water is forbidden. Abstinence reminds us of our mortal nature.

7. Feast of Tabernacles or Booths

"Speak unto the children of Israel, saying, The fifteenth day of this seventh month shall be the feast of tabernacles for seven days unto the Lord." Lev 23:34

Heaven won't consist of us sitting on fluffy white clouds, wearing white gowns and playing harps for eternity. It will be Heaven, on Earth, literally:

"Thy kingdom come, Thy will be done in earth, as it is in heaven." Matt 6:10

"And I saw a new heaven and a new earth: for the first heaven and the first earth were passed away; and there was no more sea." Rev 21:1

Earth will be restored to its original Creation:

"And I John saw the holy city, New Jerusalem, coming down from God out of heaven, prepared as a bride adorned for her husband. And I heard a great voice out of heaven saying, Behold, the tabernacle of God is with men, and he will dwell with them, and they shall be his people, and God himself shall be with them, and be their God. And God shall wipe away all tears from their eyes; and there shall be no more death, neither sorrow, nor crying, neither shall there be any more pain: for the former things are passed away. And he that sat upon the throne said, Behold, I make all things new." Rev 21:2–5

This feast also occurs in the seventh month of the Hebrew calendar. During the seven days, we're to abode in temporary accommodation. 'Tabernacle' is derived from a Latin word meaning 'tent', or 'hut'. It's symbolic of when Yahshua will live and reign with us on a restored Earth, following the Resurrection and Judgement.

It's amazing how many professed Christians will dogmatically argue holy day observance isn't required. Below is an example of several verses that speaks to those who say holy days were only intended for those of Jewish descent:

"And other sheep I have, which are not of this fold: them also I must bring, and they shall hear my voice; and there shall be one fold, and one shepherd." John 10:16

Zechariah writes 600 years before Yahshua's birth, describing events following the Resurrection of the Dead:

"And the Lord shall be king over all the earth: in that day shall there be one Lord, and his name one." Zec 14:9

Zechariah's prophecies mention Feast of Tabernacles observance three times:

"It shall come to pass, that every one that is left of all the nations which came against Jerusalem shall even go up from year to year to worship the King, the Lord of hosts, and to keep the **feast of tabernacles**. The Lord will smite the heathen that come not up to keep the **feast of tabernacles**. This shall be the punishment of Egypt, and the punishment of all nations that come not up to keep the **feast of tabernacles**." Zec 14:16, 18–19

If we had to observe the Feast of Tabernacles in the past, and we have to observe it in the future, how can you logically say we don't have to observe it now?

Christmas

As with Easter, it's ingrained into Western culture and followed by all manner of people, regardless of religious belief. Invariably, people have pondered the relevance of trees and a fat man in a red suit, with regards to the birth of Yahshua.

Pagan Origins

Numerous Pagan customs are intertwined with Christmas—holly was adopted as a symbol of Yahshua's crown of thorns; red berries as a symbol of His blood and the evergreen tree, a metaphor for His life after death. Pagan festivities at the end of December would typically last two weeks centred around the winter solstice, leading to the 'Twelve Days of Christmas'. Christmas trees, wreaths, carols, holly, mistletoe, gift-giving it's all Pagan. Burning Yule logs symbolised the rebirth of the *sun*, not the Son. Glittering lights all over your Pagan Christmas trees are derived from candles that traditionally adorned them, representing miniature suns.

'Father Christmas', Satan, er, I mean, Santa, is a counterfeit Yahshua. Santa comes from the north.

"Ho, ho, come forth, and flee from the land of the north." Zech 2:6

Besides Santa, who else has white hair?

"And in the midst of the seven candlesticks one like unto the Son of man ... His head and his hairs were white like wool, as white as snow" Rev 1:13–14

Santa ventures down chimneys, doesn't he? What lies at the bottom of a chimney?

"And his feet like unto fine brass, as if they burned in a furnace." Rev 1:15

What colour would you associate with Santa?

"And he was clothed with a vesture dipped in blood: and his name is called The Word of God." Rev 19:13

Yahshua and Santa were carpenters. Have you seen the chair Santa sits on? 'Throne' would be a better word.

"A throne was set in heaven, and one sat on the throne." Rev 4:2

Does this sound familiar? "Santa Claus is coming to town. He's making a list, And checking it twice; Gonna find out Who's naughty and nice." Where have we heard something similar?

"And I saw the dead, small and great, stand before God; and the books were opened: and another book was opened, which is the book of life: and the dead were judged out of those things which were written in the books, according to their works." Rev 20:12

There are numerous other correlations between the two.

Three centuries following Yahshua's Resurrection, Roman Emperor Constantine wanted to blend Pagan Roman practices with Christianity. Christmas and Easter were some of the outcomes. Christians have wondered why Christmas trees aren't in the Bible. They're pleasantly surprised when I tell them they are. Confusion takes hold once I state they're in the Old, rather than the New Testament, recorded in the Book of Jeremiah, 2,000 years before the birth of Yahshua:

"Thus saith the Lord, Learn not the way of the heathen, for the customs of the people are vain: for one cutteth a tree out of the forest, the work of the hands of the workman, with the axe. They deck it with silver and with gold; they fasten it with nails and with hammers, that it move not. They are upright as the palm tree, but speak not." Jer 10:2–5

How are Christmas trees related to Yahshua's birth, when they're described 2,000 years before his birth? Why are there no directions in Scripture to observe the customs of the people. In particular, Christmas and Easter? On that note, why aren't we observing the holy days we're commanded to? Yahshua and His followers observed them. After Yahshua's Resurrection, His followers continued to observe them. What makes you think we shouldn't?

Do you think Yahshua, His parents, and His siblings sat around a tinsel-covered tree, decked with silver and gold, singing carols and stuffing themselves with Christmas ham? How about His apostles and disciples?

Another Serve of Knuckle Sandwiches

I almost had a punch-up with an alleged Christian during dinner with our wives at his house. They'd served us an entrée which included prawns. Awkwardly, we explained we didn't eat prawns, apologising for not having made mention of this previously. They quizzed us as to why we didn't eat prawns, though we brushed off their questions. We knew our stance would be inflammatory. The last thing we wanted was for the subject of clean and unclean meat to arise in discussion.

They were persistent, dragging it out of us. In vain we tried to change the subject. They were unwilling to drop the issue, insisting we weren't required to observe those laws. Finally, I'd had enough. I went on the offensive hitting him right where it hurt—Christmas. I told him to fetch his Bible, then showed him Christmas trees in the Old Testament.

In icy silence, he stared at the text. "They're not talking about Christmas trees."

"Mate, 'blind Freddy' could see they're describing a Christmas tree."

Enraged and aggressive in his demeanour and tone of voice, he attempted to intimidate me. Although he was bigger, I stood my ground. While waiting for him to flip the dining table, which would've been my call to action, I remember thinking, *This is ridiculous, we're going to have a punch-up over this?* It didn't eventuate. I don't recall the reason. It's possible his wife calmed him down.

Another Christian insinuated I was an awful father. He stated with a contemptuous tone he "liked giving his children gifts at Christmas," implying I was uncaring towards my children. I pointed out that during the seven days of the Feast of Tabernacles; our children were given a gift every day. It was an underhanded comment on his behalf, and I wanted to do nothing less, than to smash my fist into his face.

Nowhere in the Bible is there anything telling us to observe and commemorate Yahshua's birth. There's no mention of Him or any of His followers celebrating anyone's birthday. Early Christians never celebrated His birth. Besides, He wasn't born in late December. This date is tied to the Pagans' belief in the birth of the sun, not the Son. Attributing the date of 25th December to the birth of Yahshua was a compromise with Paganism, a dance with the Devil. Since they were unable to stamp out Christianity, they decided to blend it with Pagan practices and customs, thereby rendering it null and void.

There are two strong arguments advocating as to why 25th December is unlikely as Yahshua's birthday. Luke records there were shepherds in the field at night, watching over their flock:

"And she brought forth her firstborn son, and wrapped him in swaddling clothes, and laid him in a manger; because there was no room for them in the inn. And there were in the same country shepherds abiding in the field, keeping watch over their flock by night." Luke 2:7-8

Late December in Israel is cold and wet. Temperatures often drop below freezing. As such, the flock would be undercover, not left to the elements.

Secondly, Yahshua's parents had travelled to Bethlehem for the sole purpose of attending a Roman Census:

"And it came to pass in those days, that there went out a decree from Caesar Augustus that all the world should be taxed. (And this taxing was first made when Cyrenius was governor of Syria.) And all went to be taxed, every one into his own city. And Joseph also went up from Galilee, out of the city of Nazareth, into Judaea, unto the city of David, which is called Bethlehem; (because he was of the house and lineage of David:) To be taxed with Mary his espoused wife, being great with child." Luke 2:1-5

Considering the weather conditions, there's no way they would've scheduled the Census for when inhabitants had to travel all over the country, in the middle of winter. While some will dispute whether there was a Census, the Bible is never wrong. Further, besides being a medical doctor, Luke was also a historian.

Counterfeit Christianity

"SATAN is not fighting churches; he is joining them. He does more harm by sowing tares than by pulling up wheat. He accomplishes more by imitation than by outright opposition." (Vance Havner)

Modern churches are rah-rah, happy-clappy, feel-good motivational centres, filled with lily-livered, cowardly little Christians. Songs sung at these services aren't the beautiful hymns of yester-year, derived from Scripture. Often, they're just monotonous, repetitive dribble.

Rarely will you hear repentance of sin, wages of sin—hellfire, and subsequent soul death preached. If anything, you'll likely be told you'll be thrown into the 'lake of puppies and pikelets'. Their prosperity gospel offers you everything Satan offered Yahshua. The vast majority of Christian churches erroneously believe we aren't required to observe the Ten Commandments. As for holy days commanded by our Creator? You can forget those, though they do observe Pagan worship days.

What's a Christian?

A friend mentioned how he'd met a new acquaintance, then proceeded to tell me this person was a Christian. I suppose, in his eyes that was meant to tell me something about that person. It didn't. 'Christian' is the vaguest term I know. If he'd told me this person was a Muslim, I would know he likely worshipped on a Friday and didn't eat pork or drink alcohol.

If someone claims to be a Christian, do they attend church? If they do, is it on the Sabbath, or Sunday? Or, do they 'pick a day', as they often tell me to do? Are they pro-abortion, or anti-abortion? Do they steal from their employer? Do they engage in fornication, or don't they?

When I ask Christians to define a Christian, I often hear, "Someone who believes in Jesus and God." This causes Yahshua's words to spring to mind:

"Thou believest that there is one God; thou doest well: the devils also believe, and tremble." James 2:19

On a Sunday about six years ago, my teenage son wanted to attend church. Having attended this particular church previously, I was curious to see if it'd changed. The church is called 'Inspire'. Could you imagine the apostles attending a church named that? Modern churches are nonsense. There's no real preaching, just motivational garbage to tickle ears.

Stepping through the door, we were handed a church 'show bag', the sort you obtain from a side-show alley. Contents included a chocolate bar and a coffee voucher for their café, following the service. Yes, this 'church' had a café. This was a weak, motivational, theatrical, lukewarm, feel-good presentation, with some stupid songs lacking any substance thrown in. I don't recall the point of the sermon. All I remember is how they had a 'prop' on stage. It was wooden framework supporting a door. The pastor would continually go through the door while trying to make a point, much to the delight of the audience. Sighing, I began reading the Bible. I'd always benefited more from doing that, than sitting there watching an infantile church exhibition.

Another time, the sermon amounted to the pastor admonishing his congregation for having unwashed cars, saying it would reflect poorly on Christianity when their colleagues would see their dirty cars. Members of the church murmured, nodding their heads. This whole concept of 'church' is a mockery.

Richard Dawkins says a lot of nonsensical things. Though at times, clarity breaks through his veil of delusion, succinctly summing up typical 'Christians', "Don't ask God to cure cancer and world poverty. He's too busy finding you a parking space and fixing the weather for your barbecue." Yes, and if He's not doing that, He's curing your headache or providing you with the numbers for next week's Lotto draw.

Fair Dinkum Christian

Fair-weather Christians are those living comfortable lives who do believe in God—up until calamity strikes, causing them to abandon their faith. Suffering separates the men from the boys. You must become a fair dinkum Christian. Job the Prophet is an illustration of the faith this entails. You've probably heard the expression, 'The patience of Job'. It's derived from his immense suffering as recorded in the Book of Job.

Yahshua illustrates some people upon hearing the gospel, in His 'Parable of the Sower':

"Hearken; Behold, there went out a sower to sow: And it came to pass, as he sowed, some fell by the way side, and the fowls of the air came and devoured it up." Mark 4:3–4

Fair-weather Christians are described:

"And some fell on stony ground, where it had not much earth; and immediately it sprang up, because it had no depth of earth: But when the sun was up, it was scorched; and because it had no root, it withered away." Mark 4:5–6

Beware of with whom you associate. Birds of a feather, flock together:

"And some fell among thorns, and the thorns grew up, and choked it, and it yielded no fruit." Mark 4:7

Now, for fair dinkum Christians:

"And other fell on good ground, and did yield fruit that sprang up and increased; and brought forth, some thirty, and some sixty, and some an hundred." Mark 4:8

Slain In the Spirit

Have you heard of this nonsense before? Alleged pastors would have us believe they can send the power of the Holy Spirit, causing us to fall backwards, writhing on the floor. All the while, uttering or screaming incomprehensible babble. Pentecostal churches are notorious for this garbage. The whole exhibition is demonic. These charlatans refer to this sick sideshow as being, 'slain in the spirit'. The term itself invokes satanic undertones.

Twenty years ago, one of these fraudsters, Benny Hinn, was coming to Australia. The newspaper had published an article about this event, along with a photo of him performing his act. I still have the article; I'm looking at it now. There's a man standing, head tilted back. He knows the direction he'll fall. Standing in front of him is Benny, the pathetic showman, arm raised in the air, ready to perform his antics. Standing behind the victim/willing participant is another man, supposedly ready to catch the participant as he falls backwards. You'd expect this bloke to have his hands out, possibly near shoulder height. Instead, all you see is his hand grasping the belted top of the man's trousers. It's pretty clear at the appointed time, he'll yank this man backwards.

Speaking In Tongues

Many of these 'churches' adhere to alleged 'speaking in tongues'. I've seen and heard many examples of this firsthand. It is *not* Biblical. It's diabolical. You'll sense this yourself when subjected to it. If you don't, you're part of the problem, so pay attention. This is *not* what the Bible refers to as speaking in tongues!

Biblically, speaking in tongues is proclaiming the gospel by speaking in a foreign language, so that their countrymen will understand. This ability is gifted to you via the Holy Spirit.

"When the day of Pentecost was fully come, they were all with one accord in one place. And suddenly there came a sound from heaven as of a rushing mighty wind, and it filled all the house where they were sitting. And there appeared unto them cloven tongues like as of fire, and it sat upon each of them. And they were all filled with the Holy Ghost, and began to speak with other tongues, as the Spirit gave them utterance. And there were dwelling at Jerusalem Jews, devout men, out of every nation under heaven. Now when this was noised abroad, the multitude came together, and were confounded, because that every man heard them speak in his own language. And they were all amazed and marvelled, saying one to another, Behold, are not all these which speak Galilaeans? And how hear we every man in our own tongue, wherein we were born? Parthians, and Medes, and Elamites, and the dwellers in Mesopotamia, and in Judaea, and Cappadocia, in Pontus, and Asia, Phrygia, and Pamphylia, in Egypt, and in the parts of Libya about Cyrene, and strangers of Rome, Jews and proselytes, Cretes and Arabians, we do hear them speak in our tongues the wonderful works of God. And they were all amazed, and were in doubt, saying one to another, What meaneth this?" Acts 2:1–12

Doug Batchelor recounts a story where he was driving in the US and picked up a hitchhiker who only spoke Spanish. Doug wanted to share the Good News, so racked his brain for vestiges of Spanish learnt during his first year of high school.

After dropping his passenger off hours later, the realisation hit him, he'd been conversing in fluent Spanish the whole time. This, is what the gift of tongues entails. It's not strange babblings.

Under Grace
Within modern churches, they love to rabbit on with the feel-good nonsense of being 'under grace'. They claim your sins have been

forgiven and stay that way. I heard a pastor tell his congregation to, "Go out and sin more, as you'll receive more grace."

If we're no longer 'under the Law', as they claim, then we cannot break the Law. So, if you haven't broken God's Law, you don't need grace. Grace has no bearing on the matter. If you're driving without wearing a seatbelt, you've broken man's law. A Policeman/woman may issue you a fine, or they may extend grace to you, in that, they withhold the punishment, the fine.

Imagine wearing a seatbelt wasn't a law and a policeman or woman pulled you over, saying you were under grace so they wouldn't extend a punishment for not wearing it. You'd politely tell them they're being ridiculous, for without a law, there cannot be a concept of grace. Do you get it? If not, keep re-reading until you do. Put it down, go away, do something else, then read it again, and keep reading it, until you do.

In the meantime, stop going to your rah-rah, happy-clappy, so-called 'church'. It's watered-down nonsense. They fall over themselves not to offend anyone, the opposite of Biblical teachings. Read Matthew 10.

Boiled down, their mantra is reduced to this, 'Once saved, always saved'. Another catchphrase they love parroting is, 'It was nailed to the cross'. They spout this regarding commandment observance. Well, the only thing that was nailed to a cross was Yahshua Himself. Consider the verse below:

"And the Word was made flesh, and dwelt among us." John 1:14

Keeping this in mind, do you remember algebra? Are you one of those people asking, "What was the relevance of learning algebra in high school?" If so, you're about to find out. Yahshua was nailed to the cross. The Bible says the 'word' (Scripture), became Yahshua Himself. In other words, according to you, the 'Word/Scripture' was 'nailed to the cross'. So, by your own logic, Scripture was 'done away with; no longer needed; made obsolete'.

Gandhi

Gandhi was asked how problems between India and Britain may be resolved. He responded, "When your country and mine shall get together on the teachings laid down by Christ in the Sermon on the Mount, we shall have solved the problems not only of our countries but those of the whole world." (Siahyonkron Nyanseor, 2002, 'Ignorance of History is No Excuse!' *The Perspective*, website)

Martin Luther King Jr

Martin Luther King Jr, in turn, adapted the methods of Gandhi, in his quest for civil rights, "It was in this Gandhian emphasis on love and nonviolence that I discovered the method for social reform that I had been seeking. I came to feel that this was the only morally and practically sound method open to oppressed people in their struggle for freedom." (Martin Luther King Jr, 1960, 'Pilgrimage to Nonviolence', Stanford: The Martin Luther King Jr Research and Education Institute, website)

Sermon On the Mount

"Blessed are the poor in spirit: for theirs is the kingdom of heaven. Blessed are they that mourn: for they shall be comforted. Blessed are the meek: for they shall inherit the earth. Blessed are they which do hunger and thirst after righteousness: for they shall be filled. Blessed are the merciful: for they shall obtain mercy. Blessed are the pure in heart: for they shall see God. Blessed are the peacemakers: for they shall be called the children of God. Blessed are they which are persecuted for righteousness' sake: for theirs is the kingdom of heaven. Blessed are ye, when men shall revile you, and persecute you, and shall say all manner of evil against you falsely, for my sake. Rejoice, and be exceeding glad: for great is your reward in heaven: for so persecuted they the prophets which were before you. Let your light so shine before men, that they may see your good works, and glorify your Father which is in heaven."

"Think not that I am come to destroy the law, or the prophets: I am not come to destroy, but to fulfil. Till heaven and earth pass, one jot or one tittle shall in no wise pass from the law, till all be fulfilled. Whosoever therefore shall break one of these least commandments, and shall teach men so, he shall be called the least in the kingdom of heaven: but whosoever shall do and teach them, the same shall be called great in the kingdom of heaven."

"Ye have heard that it was said by them of old time, Thou shalt not commit adultery: But I say unto you, That whosoever looketh on a woman to lust after her hath committed adultery with her already in his heart. It hath been said, Whosoever shall put away his wife, let him give her a writing of divorcement: But I say unto you, That whosoever shall put away his wife, saving for the cause of fornication, causeth her to commit adultery: and whosoever shall marry her that is divorced committeth adultery."

"Ye have heard that it hath been said, Thou shalt love thy neighbour, and hate thine enemy. But I say unto you, Love your enemies, bless them that curse you, do good to them that hate you, and pray for them which despitefully use you, and persecute you."

"When ye pray, use not vain repetitions, as the heathen do: for they think that they shall be heard for their much speaking. Be not ye therefore like unto them: for your Father knoweth what things ye have need of, before ye ask him."

'Our Father'

"After this manner therefore pray ye: Our Father which art in heaven, Hallowed be thy name. Thy kingdom come, Thy will be done in earth, as it is in heaven. Give us this day our daily bread. And forgive us our debts, as we forgive our debtors. And lead us not into temptation, but deliver us from evil: For thine is the kingdom, and the power, and the glory, for ever. Amen."

"For if ye forgive men their trespasses, your heavenly Father will also forgive you: But if ye forgive not men their trespasses, neither will your Father forgive your trespasses."

"Lay not up for yourselves treasures upon earth, But lay up for yourselves treasures in heaven. For where your treasure is, there will your heart be also. Therefore take no thought, saying, What shall we eat? or, What shall we drink? or, Wherewithal shall we be clothed? (For after all these things do the Gentiles seek) for your heavenly Father knoweth that ye have need of all these things. But seek ye first the kingdom of God, and his righteousness; and all these things shall be added unto you."

"Judge not, that ye be not judged. For with what judgment ye judge, ye shall be judged: and with what measure ye mete, it shall be measured to you again. And why beholdest thou the mote that is in thy brother's eye, but considerest not the beam that is in thine own eye? Or how wilt thou say to thy brother, Let me pull out the mote out of thine eye; and, behold, a beam is in thine own eye? Thou hypocrite, first cast out the beam out of thine own eye; and then shalt thou see clearly to cast out the mote out of thy brother's eye."

"Give not that which is holy unto the dogs, neither cast ye your pearls before swine, lest they trample them under their feet, and turn again and rend you. Ask, and it shall be given you; seek, and ye shall find; knock, and it shall be opened unto you: For every one that asketh receiveth; and he that seeketh findeth; and to him that knocketh it shall be opened. Therefore all things whatsoever ye would that men should do to you, do ye even so to them: for this is the law and the prophets."

"Enter ye in at the strait gate: for wide is the gate, and broad is the way, that leadeth to destruction, and many there be which go in thereat: Because strait is the gate, and narrow is the way, which leadeth unto life, and few there be that find it."

"Beware of false prophets, which come to you in sheep's clothing, but inwardly they are ravening wolves. Ye shall know them by their fruits. A good tree cannot bring forth evil fruit, neither can a corrupt tree bring forth good fruit. Every tree that bringeth not forth good fruit is hewn down, and cast into the fire. Wherefore by their fruits ye shall know them."

"Not every one that saith unto me, Lord, Lord, shall enter into the kingdom of heaven; but he that doeth the will of my Father which is in heaven. Many will say to me in that day, Lord, Lord, have we not prophesied in thy name? and in thy name have cast out devils? and in thy name done many wonderful works? And then will I profess unto them, I never knew you: depart from me, ye that work iniquity. Therefore whosoever heareth these sayings of mine, and doeth them, I will liken him unto a wise man, which built his house upon a rock: And the rain descended, and the floods came, and the winds blew, and beat upon that house; and it fell not: for it was founded upon a rock. And every one that heareth these sayings of mine, and doeth them not, shall be likened unto a foolish man, which built his house upon the sand: And the rain descended, and the floods came, and the winds blew, and beat upon that house; and it fell." Matt 5–7

That sermon was filled with 'works' instructions, including several references to the Ten Commandments, expounding them by adding detail. Notice the many instructions related to 'works', further in the chapter of Matthew:

"Then shall the King say unto them on his right hand, Come, ye blessed of my Father, inherit the kingdom prepared for you from the foundation of the world: For I was an hungred, and ye gave me meat: I was thirsty, and ye gave me drink: I was a stranger, and ye took me in: Naked, and ye clothed me: I was sick, and ye visited me: I was in prison, and ye came unto me."

"Then shall the righteous answer him, saying, Lord, when saw we thee an hungred, and fed thee? or thirsty, and gave thee drink? When saw we thee a stranger, and took thee in? or naked, and clothed thee? Or when saw we thee sick, or in prison, and came unto thee? And the King shall answer and say unto them, Verily I say unto you, Inasmuch as ye have done it unto one of the least of these my brethren, ye have done it unto me."

"Then shall he say also unto them on the left hand, Depart from me, ye cursed, into everlasting fire, prepared for the devil and his angels: For I was an hungred, and ye gave me no meat: I was thirsty, and ye gave me no drink: I was a stranger, and ye took me not in: naked, and ye clothed me not: sick, and in prison, and ye visited me not. Then shall they also answer him, saying, Lord, when saw we thee an hungred, or athirst, or a stranger, or naked, or sick, or in prison, and did not minister unto thee?"

"Then shall he answer them, saying, Verily I say unto you, Inasmuch as ye did it not to one of the least of these, ye did it not to me. And these shall go away into everlasting punishment: but the righteous into life eternal." Matt 25:34-46

How do we show our belief, our faith? By our works, attempting to follow the Law, asking for forgiveness when we fail and endeavouring to do better. If there's no Law to break, there's no need to ask forgiveness. Paul said Christians should not only stop sinning, they should do the opposite:

"Let him that stole steal no more: but rather let him labour, working with his hands the thing which is good, that he may have to give to him that needeth." Eph 4:28

Love, is a verb, not a noun. It's an action, or 'doing' word. In other words, 'love', is 'works'. You demonstrate love by your actions.

"And, behold, a certain lawyer stood up, and tempted him, saying, Master, what shall I do to inherit eternal life? He said unto him, What is written in the law? how readest thou? And he answering said, Thou shalt love the Lord thy God with all thy heart, and with all thy soul, and with all thy strength, and with all thy mind; and thy neighbour as thyself. And he said unto him, Thou hast answered right: this do, and thou shalt live." Luke 10:25:8

"Let your light so shine before men, that they may see your good works, and glorify your Father which is in heaven." Matt 5:16

One important purpose of the Law is to demonstrate we cannot attain eternal life, based on our own merits. The concept of works, adhering to the Law, is always discussed when mentioning the concept of, 'being under grace'. Those using these terms don't understand the connection, the relationship these two concepts share.

It's as if they think everyone who believes we have to keep the Ten Commandments, thinks the only way to go to Heaven is by your actions. I suppose many Jews hold this belief. Christians know the way to salvation is through the Saviour, Yahshua. By His sacrifice upon the cross, He took the punishment for sin, death. By accepting this truth, His death becomes a payment, an atonement, of our sins. That doesn't mean we can go and do as we please. We must continue to abide by the rules. Only by doing so, shows our repentance is genuine.

Good Samaritan

"Therefore all things whatsoever ye would that men should do to you, do ye even so to them: for this is the law and the prophets." Matt 7:12

The Parable of the Good Samaritan is an illustration of this directive. Another way of saying it is, "Treat others the way you want to be treated." This directive falls into the category of 'works'. Samaritans were despised by Jews. The feeling was mutual.

"And, behold, a certain lawyer stood up, and tempted him, saying, Master, what shall I do to inherit eternal life? He said unto him, What is written in the law? how readest thou? And he answering said, Thou shalt love the Lord thy God with all thy heart, and with all thy soul, and with all thy strength, and with all thy mind; and thy neighbour as thyself. And he said unto him, Thou hast answered right: this do, and thou shalt live. But he, willing to justify himself, said unto Jesus, And who is my neighbour? And Jesus answering said, A certain man went down from Jerusalem to Jericho, and fell among thieves, which stripped him of his raiment, and wounded him, and departed, leaving him half dead. And by chance there came down a certain priest that way: and when he saw him, he passed by on the other side. And likewise a Levite, when he was at the place, came and looked on him, and passed by on the other side. But a certain Samaritan, as he journeyed, came where he was: and when he saw him, he had compassion on him, And went to him, and bound up his wounds, pouring in oil and wine, and set him on his own beast, and brought him to an inn, and took care of him. And on the morrow when he departed, he took out two pence, and gave them to the host, and said unto him, Take care of him; and whatsoever thou spendest more, when I come again, I will repay thee. Which now of these three, thinkest thou, was neighbour unto him that fell among the thieves? And he said, He that shewed mercy on him. Then said Jesus unto him, Go, and do thou likewise." Luke 10:25-37

Cairns High School Bus Crash

The other day, I travelled down the Gillies Highway, south of Cairns, one of the most dangerous stretches of road in Australia. It has 263 turns in only nineteen kilometres of road, over an elevation change of 800 metres.

It was the scene of a harrowing tragedy on the 4th of February, 1987. A school bus from Cairns State High School containing forty-three year twelve students and two teachers careered over the side, plunging twenty metres, killing eight students:

Mark Fisher *Judith Frericus* *Amanda Garrone*
Monique Perresi *Erica Strooper* *Elizabeth Zelmer*
Jody Keen *Lee-Anne Willis*

The bus rolled several times on the way down, crushing its roof, coming to rest upside-down in a gully. Subsequent buses witnessed the carnage. An investigation proved it was due to a mechanical fault.

At the time, I was in grade nine at St Augustine's College. It's something those of us living in Cairns when this occurred, will never forget. Students were returning from a camp on the Atherton Tablelands, which many schools in the area had a pilgrimage to, including mine. My eldest sister had attended the all-girls school, St Monica's College. While in grade eleven she'd decided to do her senior year, grade twelve, at Cairns High the following, fateful year. During a church service at her current school, she found herself suddenly deciding to stay at St Monica's and if she wished, repeat year twelve at Cairns High, which is what she did, possibly circumnavigating an early demise.

Hear from my eldest sister herself, "Like all those other times/occasions when this type of thing happened, it wasn't a thought, and I also hadn't been consciously thinking about it. It seemed to have come out of nowhere. It was a 'knowing'."

This story highlights you never know the hour of your death. They were in their very last year of school. Ironically too, the accident occurred near the base of the mountain. Mountain View Hotel sits at the bottom, with a beautiful creek out the back. If you're ever fortunate enough to visit Cairns, drop in.

This particular day, a car had driven into a steep ditch outside of the pub. Both senior occupants were unharmed. I stopped to see if I could offer assistance. A 19-year-old, Samuel, had already done the same, over an hour earlier. While we realised there wasn't a lot we could do, we were aware our presence helped put these elderly visitors to the area at ease.

Sometime later another bloke, Solomon, stopped. We were there for a few hours. It turned out all three of us were Bible believers. Quite a few people offered to help. We thanked them, letting them know a tow truck was on its way. It wasn't lost on us, the only people who stopped, and stayed, were Bible believers. I suppose we were aware of Yahshua's admission to, 'Do unto others, as you would have them do unto you', 'Love your neighbour' and the 'Parable of the Good Samaritan'.

The Tragic Tale of Judith Frericus

Judy was one of the eight who'd lost her life. In a cruel twist of fate, she'd confided in her twin sister, Ruth Mcleod, she'd felt she wouldn't be returning. Ruth wasn't on the ill-fated trip. The sisters had completed their senior year of high school the previous year. Judy had her heart set on becoming a criminal lawyer and had to return that fateful year to complete a few subjects before being permitted into university.

Once Saved, Always Saved?

No, of course not. Many modern churches tout this nonsense. People can fall away again. Just because we were once repentant and asked for forgiveness, it doesn't mean we're in the clear. It's not a get-out-of-jail-free card. There are obligations. This verse shall suffice to put an end to the, "Once saved, always saved," doctrine:

"For if we sin wilfully after that we have received the knowledge of the truth, there remaineth no more sacrifice for sins." Heb 10:26

We must follow the law. There are exceptions to the rule, of course. An obvious example being the thief on the cross. Like us, he was a sinner and as a result, deserving of death. Gospels show initially, both thieves crucified alongside Yahshua mocked him. As time passed, it appears one had a change of heart, chastising his companion before asking Yahshua for forgiveness. Although he wasn't in a position to prove his faith, by works, as such, he was told he'd be in the kingdom with Yahshua.

Below, John is talking about the 'pearly gates' to the Kingdom of Heaven:

"Blessed are they that do his commandments, that they may have right to the tree of life, and may enter in through the gates into the city." Rev 22:14

Heaven and Hell

"Marvel not at this: for the hour is coming, in the which all that are in the graves shall hear his voice, And shall come forth; they that have done good, unto the resurrection of life; and they that have done evil, unto the resurrection of damnation." John 5:28–29

THIS was an interesting one. Learning the truth regarding this topic took quite a bit of time. Going back to Catholic school teachings, we were taught hellfire was eternal. The vision of an evil man in a red suit, black goatee, tail and pitchfork was paramount. Even so, I couldn't reconcile how an alleged loving God could subject someone to being burnt alive, for eternity. I didn't believe anyone could be capable of that. Interestingly, it's a major obstacle for many people to believe in the concept of the Judeo-Christian God.

Heaven was a strange concept too. Would we have wings, be dressed in white, sit on clouds, and not do anything, other than play the harp for eternity?

I was taught to believe that when you die you either go to Heaven or Hell—smoking, or non-smoking. Almost everyone who believes in Heaven thinks they are going there. What does the Bible have to say?

"Enter ye in at the strait gate: for wide is the gate, and broad is the way, that leadeth to destruction, and many there be which go in thereat: because strait is the gate, and narrow is the way, which leadeth unto life, and few there be that find it." Matt 7:13–14

Many people believe there's no Hell, while others erroneously believe Hell is a concept of the life they're living now.

What happens after death?

You go to sleep, to await the Resurrection and Judgement.

"But I would not have you to be ignorant, brethren, concerning them which are asleep, that ye sorrow not, even as others which have no hope. For if we believe that Jesus died and rose again, even so them also which sleep in Jesus will God bring with him." 1 Thess 4:13–14

"And many of them that sleep in the dust of the earth shall awake, some to everlasting life, and some to shame and everlasting contempt." Dan 12:2

For this reason, headstones would often be inscribed with 'RIP', 'rest in peace'. You could also add, 'until the resurrection'.

"For the living know that they shall die: but the dead know not any thing." Ecc 9:5

"Whatsoever thy hand findeth to do, do it with thy might; for there is no work, nor device, nor knowledge, nor wisdom, in the grave, whither thou goest." Ecc 9:10

"And no man hath ascended up to heaven, but he that came down from heaven, even the Son of man which is in heaven." John 3:13

"Men and brethren, let me freely speak unto you of the patriarch David, that he is both dead and buried, and his sepulchre is with us unto this day." Acts 2:29

And,

"For David is not ascended into the heavens." Acts 2:34

This Biblical doctrine was one of the hardest I dealt with. Due to experiences during séances, I didn't see how it could be true. There too, was the perceived problem of reincarnation. I'd seen documentaries and read books and articles on the topic. The only possible explanation for people's uncanny memories I had at the time, was the concept of reincarnation. However, since I'd decided I'd change my beliefs to be congruent with Scripture, I discarded my previous beliefs on the afterlife and accepted the Bible at its word, trusting the truth would be revealed.

Further study showed spirits we thought we'd been communicating with weren't those of the deceased, but rather, demonic beings impersonating the deceased. This deception extends back to the very beginning, back to Genesis. Our ancestors were told not to eat from the Tree of the Knowledge of Good and Evil, otherwise, they'd die:

"And the Lord God commanded the man, saying, Of every tree of the garden thou mayest freely eat: But of the tree of the knowledge of good and evil, thou shalt not eat of it: for in the day that thou eatest thereof thou shalt surely die." Gen 2:16–17

A Lie From the Beginning

Do you recall the serpent's reply? It was incredibly sly, aimed to plant a seed of doubt:

"Now the serpent was more subtil than any beast of the field which the Lord God had made. And he said unto the woman, Yea, hath God said, Ye shall not eat of every tree of the garden?" Gen 3:1

Whenever I present Biblical truth and someone questions that, which I know to be true, I've trained myself to hear, slyly spoken, "Yea, hath God really said …?" The serpent didn't tempt Adam and Eve to sin, only to question God's word.

Eve responded,

"We may eat of the fruit of the trees of the garden: But of the fruit of the tree which is in the midst of the garden, God hath said, Ye shall not eat of it, neither shall ye touch it, lest ye die." Gen 3:3-3

The serpent countered,

"Ye shall not surely die." Gen 3:4

There it is, the original lie—'You shall not die'. Whereas, our Creator says emphatically, sinners *shall* die:

"The soul that sinneth, it shall die." Ezek 18:20

"And fear not them which kill the body, but are not able to kill the soul: but rather fear him which is able to destroy both soul and body in hell." Matt 10:28

The deceiver is perpetuating the myth from the beginning, utilising ghost sightings, revelations, encounters and séances. Throughout the Bible it repeatedly states **the soul that sins shall die** – NOT live forever.

Talking Snake

While on the topic, let's bring up the validity of a talking snake. Many scoff at this in their perceived wisdom, ridiculing the possibility of a serpent communicating with a human. Clearly, these same people are unable to think outside the box. After all, everyone's familiar with communication between humans and animals on some level. Who's to say this ability was not further developed in humans at the time of Creation?

Every human generation since Creation has been a copy, of a copy. What tends to happen to the subsequent quality, following copying? That's right, it diminishes. It's been said that every single human generation has an associated 100 mutations, however minute.

That aside, these dullards believe in talking monkeys and fish, which emerged from an explosion/expansion of 'nothing'.

Regardless, demonic possession itself can account for a talking serpent.

Inherited Memories

These explain phenomena attributed to reincarnation. Memories are encoded into DNA, then passed on to offspring. This offers a scientific explanation for strange experiences following organ transplants. Donor recipients of various organs have been known to take on the quirks, beliefs, fears, phobias, memories and tastes of their donor.

Inherited memories also explain how someone can appear to be talented. In that, they may pick up a musical instrument for the first time and play as if they'd been doing so for years.

Heaven Is a Place on Earth

As a child, my parents made me recite prayers nightly. Namely, 'Our Father'.

"After this manner therefore pray ye: Our Father which art in heaven, Hallowed be thy name. Thy kingdom come, Thy will be done in earth, as it is in heaven. Give us this day our daily bread. And forgive us our debts, as we forgive our debtors. And lead us not into temptation, but deliver us from evil: For thine is the kingdom, and the power, and the glory, for ever. Amen." Matt 6:9–13

I used to say, ignorantly, "Our Father which *aren't* in heaven." This did my head in. After all, *if He wasn't there, where was He?* I was astounded to learn this prayer was in the Bible. Especially the last line. I'd never heard that before.

Christians say we go to Heaven or Hell at death. Yet, it dawned on me many years later, the truth of the matter is contained within 'Our Father':

"Thy kingdom come, Thy will be done in earth, as it is in heaven." Matt 6:10

Heaven Will Be on a Restored Earth

"And I saw a new heaven and a new earth: for the first heaven and the first earth were passed away; and there was no more sea. And I John saw the holy city, new Jerusalem, coming down from God out of heaven, prepared as a bride adorned for her husband. And I heard a great voice out of heaven saying, Behold, the tabernacle of God is with men, and he will dwell with them, and they shall be his people, and God himself shall be with them, and be their God. And God shall wipe away all tears from their eyes; and there shall be no more death, neither sorrow, nor crying, neither shall there be any more pain: for the former things are passed away. And he that sat upon the throne said, Behold, I make all things new." Rev 21:1–5

Continuing:

"And he shewed me a pure river of water of life, clear as crystal, proceeding out of the throne of God and of the Lamb. In the midst of the street of it, and on either side of the river, was there the tree of life, which bare twelve manner of fruits, and yielded her fruit every month: and the leaves of the tree were for the healing of the nations." Rev 22:1–2

Did the Tree of Life ring a bell? It was planted in the Garden of Eden, at Creation:

"And out of the ground made the Lord God to grow every tree that is pleasant to the sight, and good for food; the tree of life also in the midst of the garden, and the tree of knowledge of good and evil." Gen 2:9

The Book of Revelation states the Tree of Life is currently in Heaven, which will be here on Earth. This will follow the Resurrection of the Dead and sentencing at the Great White Throne Judgement.

"And he carried me away in the spirit to a great and high mountain, and shewed me that great city, the holy Jerusalem, descending out of heaven from God." Rev 21:3–10

The Day of the Lord

"Behold, the day of the Lord cometh, and thy spoil shall be divided in the midst of thee. For I will gather all nations against Jerusalem to battle; and the city shall be taken." Zec 14:1–2

The 'day of the Lord' is a Biblical reference for Yahshua's return.

"And his feet shall stand in that day upon the Mount of Olives, which is before Jerusalem on the east, and the mount of Olives shall cleave in the midst thereof toward the east and toward the west, and there shall be a very great valley; and half of the mountain shall remove toward the north, and half of it toward the south." Zec 14:4

The Judgement

When priests use a Bible during a sermon, they don't read much, usually just a few verses, then make a huge story around those verses. Sitting in St Francis Xavier's church as a child, Father Lennon approached the pulpit and commenced preaching:

"For the Lord himself shall descend from heaven with a shout, with the voice of the archangel, and with the trump of God: and the dead in Christ shall rise first." 1 Thess 4:16

This confused me, as Catholics teach that you're assigned Heaven, Hell, or purgatory, three days after you die. I don't recall whether Father Lennon also stated the verse below, though it highlights the doctrinal error, if you hold the Bible as truth:

"And I saw a great white throne, and him that sat on it, from whose face the earth and the heaven fled away; and there was found no place for them. And I saw the dead, small and great, stand before God; and the books were opened: and another book was opened, which is the book of life: and the dead were judged out of those things which were written in the books, according to their works. And the sea gave up the dead which were in it; and death and hell delivered up the dead which were in them: and they were judged every man according to their works. And death and hell were cast into the lake of fire. This is the second death. And whosoever was not found written in the book of life was cast into the lake of fire." Rev 20:11–15

I'm sure you appreciate the problem. Anyone with a sprinkling of logic could. You can either believe you go to Heaven or Hell at death, or you can believe the Bible. You can't do both.

Mary is dead. She's not in Heaven. She's 'resting in peace', awaiting the Resurrection and Judgement:

"And as it is appointed unto men once to die, but after this the judgement." Heb 9:27

There are no Scriptures that state she's risen from the dead. So, who are Catholics praying to? Unlike 'Our Father', there's no 'Hail Mary' in the Bible.

Thief on the Cross

People will disagree with the Biblical concept of soul death, presenting various, obscure verses. Remember, I once thought as you. I probably have more reasons to believe in life after death than you. Any Scripture or arguments put forward; I've seen it all before. It's always the same old, tired arguments. This isn't to say they're weak arguments, only that over the years, I keep hearing the same ones, over, and over again. For instance:

"And Jesus said unto him, Verily I say unto thee, Today shalt thou be with me in paradise." Luke 23:43

It seems to suggest upon death, that very day, Yahshua and the thief would be in Heaven. Keep in mind, Yahshua proceeded to be entombed for three days and nights. After appearing to Mary Magdalene following His resurrection, He tells her He hasn't been to Heaven:

"Jesus saith unto her, Touch me not; for I am not yet ascended to my Father." John 20:17

This appears to be contradictory to what Yahshua had told the thief. One thing I've learnt is, any supposed or alleged contradictions are not so, upon further learning and study. While I agree there *are* supposed contradictions, I'm as yet unable to give an explanation for, it does not mean there *isn't* a satisfactory explanation. In all fairness, it also doesn't mean there *is* a satisfactory explanation. Regardless, based on past experiences, I've chosen to believe there *is* an explanation, if one searches for it.

Scripture was written without punctuation. Below, I will present Luke 23:43 twice. The only difference between verses shall be the placement of the comma:

"And Jesus said unto him, Verily I say unto thee, *Today shalt thou be with me in paradise.*" Luke 23:43

Contrast with:

"And Jesus said unto him, *Verily I say unto thee today*, shalt thou be with me in paradise." Luke 23:43

Here's a common thought, often tossed around concerning death. Most would like to think if they, a friend or family member was to die, it'd be a quick, painless, death. The problem is, that person may not have repented of their sins, and now the opportunity has passed. So, while the possibility of a prolonged death is shunned, it does have its benefits. Remember this when dealing with the untimely death of someone you love.

Thief Contradiction?

This is another example of what appears to be a contradiction, isn't. Mark and Matthew allude to both thieves mocking Yahshua. Conversely, Luke writes a thief chastises the other thief for mocking Yahshua.

"Let Christ the King of Israel descend now from the cross, that we may see and believe. And *they that were crucified with him reviled him.*" Mark 15:32

And:

"Likewise also the chief priests mocking him, with the scribes and elders, said, He saved others; himself he cannot save. If he be the King of Israel, let him now come down from the cross, and we will believe him. He trusted in God; let him deliver him now, if he will have him: for he said, I am the Son of God. *The thieves also, which were crucified with him, cast the same in his teeth.*" Matt 27:41-44

Whereas Luke's account appears contradictory:

"And one of the malefactors which were hanged railed on him, saying, If thou be Christ, save thyself and us. But *the other answering rebuked him,* saying, Dost not thou fear God, seeing thou art in the same condemnation? And we indeed justly; for we receive the due reward of our deeds: but this man hath done nothing amiss. And he said unto Jesus, Lord, remember me when thou comest into thy kingdom." Luke 23:39-42

The condemned men were on the cross for hours. It's likely both were initially mocking Yahshua. Though, as time drifted by, one had a change of heart. Did he see or hear something the other didn't? Remember, the thieves were crucified either side of Yahshua:

"Then were there two thieves crucified with him, one on the right hand, and another on the left." Matt 27:38

There's no reason both accounts can't be true. So, you see, given time for reflection, dying slowly, as opposed to dying quickly, allowed the thief to have sins forgiven. Here's another alleged contradiction. It references the inscriptions all four Gospels recorded for the sign on the cross:

"This is Jesus, the King of the Jews." Matt 27:37

"The king of the Jews." Mark 15:26

"THIS IS THE KING OF THE JEWS." Luke 23:38

"Jesus Of Nazareth The King Of The Jews." John 19:19

Blind Freddy himself can see all four inscriptions contain, 'King of the Jews'. Only a simpleton would conclude they weren't reading the same sign. This demonstrates the authenticity of the historical recordings. It's clear the four writers hadn't gathered together and collaborated.

Easter Fairy Tale

EASTER was approaching. We were reading from the Book of Matthew in grade seven, with Father Grundy:

"Then certain of the scribes and of the Pharisees answered, saying, Master, we would see a sign from thee. But he answered and said unto them, An evil and adulterous generation seeketh after a sign; and there shall no sign be given to it, but the sign of the prophet Jonas: For as Jonas was three days and three nights in the whale's belly; so shall the Son of man be three days and three nights in the heart of the earth." Matt 12:38–40

Where's the Proof?

This was puzzling. They were asking for proof Yahshua was God's Son. He in turn said the only proof He'd give, is that He'd be entombed for three days and three nights. Sunset Good Friday, until dawn Easter Sunday, *isn't* three days and three nights. At best, it's two nights and one and a half days. That being the case, He *couldn't* be the Son of God—by his own admission.

I pointed this out to the priest. He claimed when Yahshua died, the sky went dark, making it the first night. Even as a child, I couldn't believe such nonsense. It bothered me for many years. Intuitively I knew the Bible was true, so there had to be an explanation. There was.

After the passing of fifteen years, I discovered the truth. Yahshua was executed on a Wednesday, not on a Friday. He didn't rise on Sunday. He rose on Saturday, the weekly Sabbath at sunset, exactly three days and three nights later, just as He said He would.

Debating online one night, I stated nowhere in the Bible did it say Yahshua rose from the dead on a Sunday. A bloke challenged me so I asked for proof, knowing full well the Scripture he would, and did, present:

"And very early in the morning the first day of the week, they came unto the sepulchre at the rising of the sun. And they said among themselves, Who shall roll us away the stone from the door of the sepulchre? And when they looked, they saw that the stone was rolled away: for it was very great. And entering into the sepulchre, they saw a young man sitting on the right side, clothed in a long white garment; and they were affrighted. And he saith unto them, Be not affrighted: Ye seek Jesus of Nazareth, which was crucified: he is risen; he is not here: behold the place where they laid him."
Mark 16:2–6

I pointed out it didn't say when He rose, only when the empty tomb was discovered. If they'd gone to the tomb during the night, they'd have discovered it empty then.

The key is that there were two Sabbaths that week. The weekly Sabbath day (Saturday), and one of the seven annual High-day Sabbaths, the first day of the Feast of Unleavened Bread (Thursday that year).

Jewish Passover

Passover is a seven-day period. At the time, Jews had two names for the same festival; it was called the 'Feast of the Passover', or the 'Feast of Unleavened Bread'. The first month in the Jewish calendar is Nisan (March /April). The Passover meal is observed on the 14th of Nisan every year.

"In the fourteenth day of the first month at even is the Lord's Passover." Lev 23:5

This particular meal that night, came to be known as 'The Last Supper'.

Jewish Calendar and Definition of 'Day'

The Jewish calendar is modelled after the circling of the moon, while the Roman calendar we use follows the solar cycle. Jewish days are calculated from sunset to sunset, commencing and ending at six p.m. (sunset). Daylight hours are counted from six a.m. In the Gospels, you'll see reference to the 'third hour', 'sixth hour' and 'ninth hour'. While this may seem weird to us, our method of calculating days would appear weird to them. With our Roman calendar, a day commences and ends at midnight.

First hour – Dawn to 8 a.m.
Second hour – 8 to 9 a.m.
Third hour – 9 to 10 a.m.
Fourth hour – 10 to 11 a.m.
Fifth hour – 11 to noon.
Sixth hour – Noon to 1 p.m.
Seventh hour – 1 to 2 p.m.
Eighth hour – 2 to 3 p.m.
Ninth hour – 3 to 4 p.m.
Tenth hour – 4 to 5 p.m.
Eleventh hour – 5 to 6 p.m.

The Last Supper and Crucifixion occurred the same day. At this point, you're probably wondering how this is possible, as Yahshua ate the Last Supper (Passover) at night, yet was crucified during the day. Their Wednesday commences at sunset on Tuesday. So, even though they partook of the Last Supper on what we would call Tuesday night, it was a Jewish Wednesday.

The High-day Sabbath on Thursday, commenced at sunset on Wednesday, hence the urgency to retrieve Yahshua from the cross before sunset, which would herald the beginning of Thursday, and therefore the High-day Sabbath, the First Day of Unleavened Bread:

"The Jews therefore, because it was the preparation, that the bodies should not remain upon the cross on the sabbath day, (for that sabbath day was an high day,) besought Pilate that their legs might be broken, and that they might be taken away." John 19:31

"After two days was the feast of the passover, and of unleavened bread: and the chief priests and the scribes sought how they might take him by craft, and put him to death. But they said, Not on the feast day, lest there be an uproar of the people." Mark 14:1–2

Tuesday 13th of Nisan

"Now the feast of unleavened bread drew nigh, which is called the Passover." Luke 22:1

Yahshua and His twelve apostles arrive in Jerusalem after travelling from Bethany, to partake of the Passover meal. They send John and Peter ahead to locate the place of the meal and to prepare for it:

"Now the first day of the feast of unleavened bread the disciples came to Jesus, saying unto him, Where wilt thou that we prepare for thee to eat the passover? And he said, Go into the city to such a man, and say unto him, The Master saith, My time is at hand; I will keep the passover at thy house with my disciples. And the disciples did as Jesus had appointed them; and they made ready the passover. Now when the even was come, he sat down with the twelve." Matt 26:17–20

Wednesday 14th of Nisan

Yahshua and His disciples ate the Passover meal on a Tuesday evening. 'Wednesday' started at sunset on Tuesday.

Following the Last Supper, they walked across the Valley of the Shadow of Death, to the Mount of Olives. Yahshua was betrayed by Judas at an olive grove in Gethsemane at the foot of this mountain. He was arrested, then brought before the high priest, Caiaphas. The trial ended at dawn, Wednesday.

This is the preparation day for one of the annual Sabbaths, the First day of Unleavened Bread, which fell on a Thursday that year. It wasn't the preparation day for the weekly Saturday Sabbath.

Wednesday morning Yahshua was brought before Pilate the Governor:

"When the morning was come, all the chief priests and elders of the people took counsel against Jesus to put him to death: And when they had bound him, they led him away, and delivered him to Pontius Pilate the governor." Matt 27:1–2

"And it was the preparation of the passover, and about the sixth hour [6 a.m. Throughout his gospel, John uses Roman timekeeping] and he saith unto the Jews, Behold your King!" John 19:14

"And it was the third hour [9 a.m.], and they crucified him." Mark 15:25

"And when the sixth hour [midday], was come, there was darkness over the whole land until the ninth hour [3 p.m.]." Mark 15:33

Due to the approaching High-day Sabbath, this occurred:

"The Jews therefore, because it was the preparation, that the bodies should not remain upon the cross on the sabbath day, for that sabbath day was an high day, besought Pilate that their legs might be broken, and that they might be taken away." John 19:31

With crucifixion, victims could use their feet to push up, taking pressure off of their lungs. Matthew 12:40 also stipulates a High-day Sabbath. It was the verse that had vexed me in grade seven, causing me to question my teacher as to what a High-day Sabbath was. She was oblivious, declaring, "It wasn't important." This was crucial, it's the key to discovering the truth regarding the true days related to the Crucifixion and Resurrection.

Yahshua, Sacrificial Lamb

All sacrificial lambs were slaughtered on the 14th Nisan (preparation day), at the **ninth hour (3 p.m.).**

"And at the **ninth hour** Jesus cried with a loud voice, saying, Eloi, Eloi, lama sabachthani? which is, being interpreted, My God, my God, why hast thou forsaken me?" Mark 15:34

Yahshua's body was placed in the tomb at twilight, Wednesday. He was buried before sunset due to the approaching High-day Sabbath, (the First Day of the Feast of Unleavened Bread). The tomb was sealed with a stone and a guard posted.

"The animal was **slain** on the eve of the Passover, on the afternoon of the 14th of Nisan, after the Tamid sacrifice had been killed, i.e., at **three o'clock**, or, in case the eve of the Passover fell **on Friday, at two**." (Executive Committee of the Editorial Board., Jacob Zallel Lauterbach, 'Passover Sacrifice (Hebrew, "zebaḥ Pesaḥ"; lit. "sacrifice of exemption")', *Jewish Encyclopedia* website)

Did the significance of what you just read smack you in the face, or did it go over your head? A sacrificial death would've occurred at the **eighth hour (2 p.m.)**—*if* it was a Friday crucifixion.

Thursday 15th of Nisan

This day commenced at sunset on Wednesday, just after Yahshua's body was sealed inside the tomb. It was the first day of the Feast of Unleavened Bread. It was also known as a High Sabbath, as it was one of seven annual Sabbaths, besides the weekly seventh-day Sabbath. Lasting twenty-four hours, this annual Sabbath finished at sunset on Thursday.

Now the next day [Wednesday sunset is the start of Thursday, so this event occurred after Yahshua had been placed in the tomb and the sun had set], that followed the day of the preparation, the chief priests and Pharisees came together unto Pilate, Saying, Sir, we remember that that deceiver said, while he was yet alive, After three days I will rise again. Command therefore that the sepulchre be made sure until the third day, lest his disciples come by night, and steal him away, and say unto the people, He is risen from the dead: so the last error shall be worse than the first. Pilate said unto them, Ye have a watch: go your way, make it as sure as ye can. So they went, and made the sepulchre sure, sealing the stone, and setting a watch." Matt 27:62–66

Friday 16th of Nisan

With the annual High-day Sabbath now over, the women bought and prepared spices and ointments for anointing Yahshua's body:

"And when the sabbath was past, Mary Magdalene, and Mary the mother of James, and Salome, had bought sweet spices, that they might come and anoint him." Mark 16:1

Once they'd bought spices from the market, they went home to prepare them:

"And they returned, and prepared spices and ointments; and rested the sabbath day according to the commandment." Luke 23:56

The weekly Sabbath begins at sunset.

Saturday 17th of Nisan

This was the weekly Sabbath. The women rested on this weekly Sabbath, as they always did.

Yahshua rose around sunset, exactly three days and three nights after burial, to fulfil the sign of Jonah, authenticating Yahshua's claim that He was, Son of the living God, Yahweh.

The weekly Sabbath ends at sunset. It's also when Sunday begins, by Jewish reckoning.

Sunday 18th of Nisan

Mary Magdalene is confronted by an open, empty tomb when she arrives at dawn to anoint the body:

"The first day of the week cometh Mary Magdalene early, when it was yet dark, unto the sepulchre, and seeth the stone taken away from the sepulchre." John 20:1–2

"And very early in the morning the first day of the week, they came unto the sepulchre at the rising of the sun." Mark 16:2

Two Sabbaths That Week

The Bible is like a jigsaw. Finding a piece will often present clues to finding other pieces. It's also finely interwoven. The key to understanding the chronology surrounding Yahshua's Crucifixion and Resurrection is, there were two Sabbaths that week, Thursday (annual Sabbath day), and Saturday (regular weekly Sabbath). In between was Friday, the weekly day of preparation.

Wednesday, the Crucifixion day, was also the day of preparation for Thursday, which was the High-day Sabbath, the First Day of Unleavened Bread.

Before, and Yet, *After*, the Sabbath?

John records that the day following Yahshua's Crucifixion was a High-day Sabbath, as opposed to the weekly seventh-day Sabbath:

"The Jews therefore, because it was the preparation, that the bodies should not remain upon the cross on the sabbath day, for **that sabbath day was an high day**, besought Pilate that their legs might be broken, and that they might be taken away." John 19:31

Compare Mark 15:43–47 with Luke 23:56

"Joseph of Arimathaea, an honourable counsellor, which also waited for the kingdom of God, came, and went in boldly unto Pilate, and craved the body of Jesus. And Pilate marvelled if he were already dead: and calling unto him the centurion, he asked him whether he had been any while dead. And when he knew it of the centurion, he gave the body to Joseph. And he bought fine linen, and took him down, and wrapped him in the linen, and laid him in a sepulchre which was hewn out of a rock, and rolled a stone unto the door of the sepulchre. And Mary Magdalene and Mary the mother of Joses beheld where he was laid. And **when the sabbath was past**, Mary Magdalene, and Mary the mother of James, and Salome, had **bought sweet spices**, that they might come and anoint him." Mark15:43-47

Now, for Luke's account:

"This man went unto Pilate, and begged the body of Jesus. And he took it down, and wrapped it in linen, and laid it in a sepulchre that was hewn in stone, wherein never man before was laid. And that day was the preparation, and the sabbath drew on. And the women also, which came with him from Galilee, followed after, and beheld the sepulchre, and how his body was laid. And they returned, and **prepared spices and ointments; and rested the sabbath day according to the commandment**." Luke 23:52-56

It was almost dark when Yahshua was laid in the tomb, heralding the Sabbath day, the annual, High-day Sabbath, beginning Wednesday at sunset. It's forbidden to buy, work or sell on a Sabbath, so the day before is called a preparation day, as they have to prepare for the coming day of rest.

This being the case, they couldn't have done this if the crucifixion was on a Friday. By sunset on Friday, the weekly Sabbath would've commenced. They wouldn't have been able to purchase spices and ointments on Saturday, let alone, prepare them on Saturday. Once the spices and ointments were purchased and prepared, (on Friday), they rested on the weekly Sabbath (Saturday), as per the Fourth Commandment. Then early Sunday morning they went to anoint the body, thereby discovering the empty tomb.

Mark's account, buying and preparing spices after the High-day Sabbath:

"And when the sabbath was past, Mary Magdalene, and Mary the mother of James, and Salome, had bought sweet spices, that they might come and anoint him. And very early in the morning the first day of the week, they came unto the sepulchre at the rising of the sun." Mark 16:1-2

Luke's account, buying and preparing spices on Friday, then resting on the weekly Sabbath day, ready to anoint the body early Sunday morning:

"Prepared spices and ointments; and rested the sabbath day **according to the commandment**." Luke 23.56

According to both accounts, they bought spices and prepared them after the Sabbath, and yet before the Sabbath. Logically, there have to be two Sabbaths involved, with the day of preparation between them.

Owing to the vast majority not knowing the truth of two Sabbaths that week, the ignorant have falsely proclaimed the preceding two verses as a contradiction. Granted, to the ignorant, it would certainly seem that way. After all, Mark claims spices were purchased and prepared after the Sabbath, whereas Luke states this occurred before the Sabbath.

They were both correct. Without the extra insight, it would appear a glaring contradiction. Keep this in mind when any other implied contradictions are raised. Ignoramuses use this conundrum as evidence against the Bible, insisting it's a contradiction. This is how they present their apparent contradiction:

Q. When did the women buy the spices? Before the Sabbath, or after?

"And when the sabbath was past, Mary Magdalene, and Mary the mother of James, and Salome, had bought sweet spices, that they might come and anoint him." Mark 16:1

Or:

"And the women also, which came with him from Galilee, followed after, and beheld the sepulchre, and how his body was laid. And they returned, and prepared spices and ointments; and rested the sabbath day according to the commandment." Luke 23:55-56

While there may appear to be contradictions within the Bible, further study destroys them. Clearing up this alleged contradiction led to the solving of another alleged contradiction, that of the three days and three nights. Not only that, the solving of the apparent contradiction destroyed the contradiction of Matthew 12:40 which seemed to show Yahshua wasn't Yahweh's son.

Matthew 12:40 Prophecy Fulfilled

Yahshua died on Wednesday, just before sunset.

Wednesday sunset, to Thursday sunset—1 day (first night and day in the heart of the earth).

Thursday sunset, to Friday sunset—1 day (second night and day in the heart of the earth).

Friday sunset, to Saturday sunset—1 day (third night and day in the heart of the earth).

Exactly three days and three nights, just as He said He would. Mary discovered the empty tomb at dawn on Sunday.

To be clear, nowhere in the Bible does it say Yahshua rose on a Sunday. It says the tomb was discovered on Sunday, while it was still dark. If they'd gone there the night before, they would've discovered the empty tomb then.

Yahshua's prophesy was fulfilled, exactly as He prophesied. He'd declared that, like the Prophet Jonah, He'd be entombed three days and three nights, before rising from the dead on the third day.

"For as Jonas was three days and three nights in the whale's belly; so shall the Son of man be three days and three nights in the heart of the earth." Matt 12:40

"And shall deliver him to the Gentiles to mock, and to scourge, and to crucify him: and the third day he shall rise again." Matt 20:19

"And while they abode in Galilee, Jesus said unto them, The Son of man shall be betrayed into the hands of men: And they shall kill him, and the third day he shall be raised again." Matt 17:22–23

Disclaimer

While I've laboured extensively on this point, it's necessary. It took me a long time to get my head around it. Each time I discussed this with someone, their objections sent me back to the Bible, where I'd go through the same process, again and again, to ensure what I was saying, was true. It is.

Cognitive Dissonance

If you disagree, that's natural, but do you want to believe man, or the Bible? Try to refute it with Scripture. You can't. Cognitive dissonance is the mental conflict that occurs when someone's behaviours and beliefs don't align. It also occurs when a person holds two contradictory beliefs.

It happened to me many times. It also happened to the Seventh-day Adventist Bible study facilitator. I'd mentioned the whole debacle of the three days and nights to him. Naturally, he'd expressed opposition to what I was saying so I gave him some information to take home.

Visiting a week later, he was sombre, quiet, conflicted. Eventually, the time came for him to leave. Slowly, he walked down the path as I watched from the landing at my front door. Pausing before the gate, he turned with downcast eyes, "I looked at the information you gave me."

"What did you think?" I enquired.

Speaking softly, his words conveyed the heaviness of his heart, "I've been with the church for twenty years. Sometimes, you just have to believe what they believe." With that, he turned, walking heavily to his car. I never brought it up again. Neither did he.

April Fool

According to one theory, 1st of April is the day Yahshua was sent from Pontius Pilate to Herod and back again, a journey which has also been associated with the old expression of sending someone on a 'fool's errand'. It also applies to Roman soldiers mocking Him while He was blindfolded, by striking Him, then demanding He identify who'd struck Him.

It's not a coincidence April Fools often coincides with Passover.

Eggs and Rabbits

Nowhere in the Bible is there mention of a chicken, let alone a rabbit who delivers decorated chocolate eggs on Easter Sunday. Yet, the Easter bunny has emerged as a prominent symbol of Christianity's most sacred holiday. Eggs are ancient Pagan symbols of fertility. Rabbits are renowned as prolific procreators. Why else do you think the rabbit is the symbol for Playboy magazine?

Roman Guard

There's great opposition to the teachings of Yahshua today, just as there was when He walked the earth. Religious leaders were so incensed by it, they killed Him. Jews were aware of Yahshua's claim He'd rise from the dead. While they didn't believe He would, they did believe His disciples would endeavour to steal the body and hide it, as evidence He'd risen from the dead. They implored the Romans to place a guard over the tomb to prevent this from occurring.

According to those who killed Him and numerous people today, Yahshua wasn't God on Earth. Therefore, He couldn't rise from the dead. With the guard in place, there's no way the disciples could fake Yahshua's Resurrection. The natural outcome would be His new movement would die with Him. It did. The apostles were hiding, cowering, fearful of the same fate. Then, with Yahshua's Resurrection, this new movement subsequently resurrected and flourished. If you want another proof the Bible is true, there it is. One-third of Earth's population is Christian. You know why, deep down, don't you?—The empty tomb.

Calvary Conspiracies

OPPONENTS propose a number of absurd conspiracy theories in a feeble, pathetic attempt to explain away the empty tomb. The most common story is, 'Yahshua's body was stolen'.

Stolen Body

Conspiracy theorists claim the guards fell asleep and disciples stole His body.

Really? Is that the best explanation they have to explain away the empty tomb? If so, we're still stuck with the problem of trying to explain away how the risen Messiah appeared to hundreds of eyewitnesses. Many appearances were to groups of people at once. Perhaps this conspiracy is the most common one, as that's the excuse given at the time:

"Now when they were going, behold, some of the watch came into the city, and shewed unto the chief priests all the things that were done. And when they were assembled with the elders, and had taken counsel, they gave large money unto the soldiers, Saying, Say ye, His disciples came by night, and stole him away while we slept. And if this come to the governor's ears, we will persuade him, and secure you. So they took the money, and did as they were taught: and this saying is commonly reported among the Jews until this day." Matt 28:11–15

It's claimed the disciples came during the night, stealing the body. Instead, His followers were panicked, hiding, cowering. They'd just seen their Leader publicly humiliated, flogged, tortured and executed and were expecting a similar fate:

"Then the same day at evening, being the first day of the week, when the doors were shut where the disciples were assembled for fear of the Jews, came Jesus and stood in the midst, and saith unto them, Peace be unto you." John 20:19

They'd also bolted when Yahshua was arrested:

"And they all forsook him, and fled." Mark 14:50

So much for trying to take their Leader's body from under the nose of an armed guard.

Another obstacle for those opposed to the reality of the empty tomb is the fact ten apostles were martyred for their belief. At any point they could've renounced their claim Yahshua had risen, sparing their lives. Peter was martyred, crucified upside-down. Three times he'd denied even knowing Him. Who willingly dies for something they know is a lie?

Death and Resurrection of Christianity

Christianity died with Yahshua. Jews were intent on ensuring Yahshua stayed dead, posting an armed guard. His apostles and disciples were terrified. Even if they weren't and managed to overpower an armed guard and take a body; where, and how, would they've disposed of it?

If a body had been produced, either within or outside the tomb, Christianity would've been stopped dead in its tracks. Instead, it flourished. The fact it flourished is, in itself, overwhelming proof of the empty tomb. All they had to do, was open the tomb three days and nights later, revealing the body. It's what they wanted—to end His following. They didn't. You know why they didn't, don't you? They couldn't. You also know why they couldn't, don't you? That's right, the tomb was empty.

As the death and burial of Yahshua was simultaneous with the death and burial of Christianity, so too was the resurrection and revival of Yahshua simultaneous with the resurrection and revival of Christianity.

Keep in mind, **Jews never disputed the validity of the empty tomb.** Every one of their fanciful excuses was aimed at explaining away the empty tomb. Several cold-case investigators have sifted the evidence. Their conclusion—the tomb was empty.

Christian-killer's Conversion

Paul wrote a great portion of the New Testament. Before his conversion, he was known as Saul of Tarsus and crusaded against Christians, seeking their death and administering their persecution:

"And Saul, yet breathing out threatenings and slaughter against the disciples of the Lord, went unto the high priest, And desired of him letters to Damascus to the synagogues, that if he found any of this way, whether they were men or women, he might bring them bound unto Jerusalem." Acts 9:1–2

Things were about to change:

"And as he journeyed, he came near Damascus: and suddenly there shined round about him a light from heaven: And he fell to the earth, and heard a voice saying unto him, Saul, Saul, why persecutest thou me? And he said, Who art thou, Lord? And the Lord said, I am Jesus whom thou persecutest: it is hard for thee to kick against the pricks. And he trembling and astonished said, Lord, what wilt thou have me to do? And the Lord said unto him, Arise, and go into the city, and it shall be told thee what thou must do. And the men which journeyed with him stood speechless, hearing a voice, but seeing no man." Acts 9:3–7

God appeared in a vision to a certain disciple at Damascus, named Ananias and told him to minister to Paul. However, Paul's reputation for hatred had preceded him:

"Then Ananias answered, Lord, I have heard by many of this man, how much evil he hath done to thy saints at Jerusalem: And here he hath authority from the chief priests to bind all that call on thy name." Acts 9:13–14

God was quick to allay his concerns:

"But the Lord said unto him, Go thy way: for he is a chosen vessel unto me, to bear my name before the Gentiles, and kings, and the children of Israel: For I will shew him how great things he must suffer for my name's sake." Acts 9:15–16

Anasis did as he was asked, restoring Paul's sight which God had taken, three days earlier:

"And Ananias went his way, and entered into the house; and putting his hands on him said, Brother Saul, the Lord, even Jesus, that appeared unto thee in the way as thou camest, hath sent me, that thou mightest receive thy sight, and be filled with the Holy Ghost. And immediately there fell from his eyes as it had been scales: and he received sight forthwith, and arose, and was baptized." Acts 9:17–18

Paul began his public testimony that Yahshua was indeed, God on Earth. His abrupt, opposing change in belief confounded religious leaders, who then sought to kill him:

"Then was Saul certain days with the disciples which were at Damascus. And straightway he preached Christ in the synagogues, that he is the Son of God. But all that heard him were amazed, and said; Is not this he that destroyed them which called on this name in Jerusalem, and came hither for that intent, that he might bring them bound unto the chief priests? But Saul increased the more in strength, and confounded the Jews which dwelt at Damascus, proving that this is very Christ. And after that many days were fulfilled, the Jews took counsel to kill him: But their laying await was known of Saul. And they watched the gates day and night to kill him. Then the disciples took him by night, and let him down by the wall in a basket. And when Saul was come to Jerusalem, he assayed to join himself to the disciples: but they were all afraid of him, and believed not that he was a disciple. But Barnabas took him, and brought him to the apostles, and declared unto them how he had seen the Lord in the way, and that he had spoken to him, and how he had preached boldly at Damascus in the name of Jesus. And he was with them coming in and going out at Jerusalem. And he spake boldly in the name of the Lord Jesus, and disputed against the Grecians: but they went about to slay him." Acts 9:19–29

Explain all of that, logically and coherently, without an empty tomb and an un-Resurrected Son of God.

Swoon Theory

This pathetic claim is, Yahshua didn't die on the cross, He merely fainted, and was, 'later revived in the cool air of the tomb'. Even if this was the case, you'd still have to explain the empty tomb, which was under a heavy guard, and the radical change in Yahshua's cowering, fearful apostles.

Yahshua had been beaten and whipped. A crown of long thorns had been hammered onto his head. Forced to carry a heavy cross, He fell three times before having his hands and feet nailed to it.

Speared For Good Measure

He was crucified with two thieves. All three could use their feet to push on the cross, enabling them to breathe easier. Since their executioners wanted to speed up their deaths, to have the bodies taken down before sunset, they set out to break their legs:

"But when they came to Jesus, and saw that he was dead already, they brake not his legs." John 19:33

He was dead. Do you think Roman executioners were mistaken? The fact that His legs weren't broken was a fulfilment of another two prophecies:

"In one house shall it be eaten; thou shalt not carry forth ought of the flesh abroad out of the house; neither shall ye break a bone thereof." Ex 12:46

And:

"They shall leave none of it unto the morning, nor break any bone of it: according to all the ordinances of the passover they shall keep it." Num 9:12

Both of these were written 1,500 years before Yahshua's birth.

Although they saw He was dead, as an extra measure, they speared Him. Which was a fulfilment of another ancient prophecy:

"But one of the soldiers with a spear pierced his side, and forthwith came there out blood and water. And he that saw it bare record, and his record is true: and he knoweth that he saith true, that ye might believe. For these things were done, that the scripture should be fulfilled, A bone of him shall not be broken. And again another scripture saith, They shall look on him whom they pierced." John 19:34–37

Here's the prophecy written 500 years before the fact, referencing the future spearing of Yahshua, upon the cross:

"And I will pour on the house of David and on the inhabitants of Jerusalem the Spirit of grace and supplication; then they will look on Me whom they pierced." Zech 12:10

It's pretty clear He was dead. So too, is the nonsensical swoon theory.

"And he stooping down, and looking in, saw the linen clothes lying; yet went he not in. Then cometh Simon Peter following him, and went into the sepulchre, and seeth the linen clothes lie, And the napkin, that was about his head, not lying with the linen clothes, but wrapped together in a place by itself." John 20:5–7

If anyone had stolen the body, they wouldn't have gone to the trouble of undressing it in the tomb. That's ridiculous. So too, is the assumption tied to the Swoon Conspiracy—a man beaten to the point of death manages to break free from his wrappings, open a sealed tomb from the inside, and escape—under the nose of an armed guard.

Mass Hallucinations

Another denial of the obvious, logical, and historical facts is the claim the disciples and hundreds of others who witnessed the risen Messiah on several occasions were hallucinating. Mass hallucinations do not exist. For the sake of the argument, let's say they did. We'd still have the problem of the empty tomb.

Atheists Admit Resurrection Is Scientifically Possible

This concept hasn't occurred to those who believe in Evolutionism. They believe an explosion/expansion of 'nothing', produced 'everything', including 'life', itself. The law of biogenesis and the scientific method say otherwise. It states life can only arise from life, not non-life.

Darwinian Evolution invokes 'abiogenesis', also known as 'spontaneous generation', meaning, life arising from non-living matter. This is scientifically impossible. For this to occur, it would be deemed miraculous—outside the bounds of scientific law. The problem is, believers of Evolutionism deny the possibility of miracles. Thereby, they deny their religious doctrine of abiogenesis. On the other hand, if they want to twist science to fit their religious doctrines, as they do (saying life can arise from non-living matter), they then have to admit the Resurrection is scientifically possible.

Since Evolutionism believers profess to believe in abiogenesis, falsely believing this to be scientific, they cannot deny the

Resurrection. It's far more probable than their claims. After all, Yahshua was only dead for three days. There was a body ready to go. You'd just have to kick-start it, by adding life, and possibly do a bit of maintenance. With Evolutionism's creation story, they have to start from an explosion/expansion of 'nothing'.

It's amusing when an Evolutionism believer scoffs at the possibility of the Resurrection. Then after you point out the truth above, they're reluctantly forced to admit, according to Evolutionism dogma, the Resurrection is scientifically possible. When they attempt to rubbish the scientific possibility of the Resurrection, they're ridiculing their own religious beliefs.

The conversation would proceed like this:

Intelligent Designer: "How do you get life from an explosion/expansion of nothing?"

Evolutionism Believer: "Well, once upon a time, there was 'nothing', then it exploded. Er, I mean, it expanded, producing rocks. It rained on the rocks for '♪ millions of years ♪', producing a pond scum. One day, this pond scum was zapped by lightning, and here we are. I rest my case."

Intelligent Designer: "So, life was produced from non-living, inorganic matter?"

Evolutionism Believer: "Yes!"

Intelligent Designer: "Wouldn't that then make the Resurrection scientifically possible?"

Evolutionism Believer: *speechless*

If Evolutionism believers want to say the Resurrection isn't scientifically possible, by default, they have to admit their fanciful creation story isn't either.

No Greater Love

"Greater love hath no man than this, that a man lay down his life for his friends." John 15:13

Yahshua also laid down His life for His enemies ...

Despite all they did to Him, He had this to say:

"Father, forgive them; for they know not what they do." Luke 32:34

"Before Abraham Was, I Am"

DURING grade seven, opening statements of John's Gospel were perplexing.

"In the beginning was the Word, and the Word was with God, and the Word was God. The same was in the beginning with God. All things were made by him; and without him was not any thing made that was made." John 1:1–3

Who was in the beginning with God? Who was, The Word? I kept reading.

"He was in the world, and the world was made by him, and the world knew him not. He came unto his own, and his own received him not." John 1:10–11

It appears to say Yahshua was the Creator, not Yahweh the Father. How could this be? He wasn't born yet. I was utterly confused. It was in stark contrast to what I'd believed my entire life. *What else does it say?* A few more verses and any shadow of a doubt would be removed:

"And the Word was made flesh, and dwelt among us." John 1:14

Let's go to the very first book of the Bible, Genesis. Notice the words 'us' and 'our'. To whom do you think He may be referring?

"And God said, Let us make man in our image, after our likeness." Gen 1:26

This passage seems to suggest Yahshua Himself, is eternal:

"But thou, Bethlehem Ephratah, though thou be little among the thousands of Judah, yet out of thee shall he come forth unto me that is to be ruler in Israel; whose goings forth have been from of old, from everlasting." Micah 5:2

It makes sense, seeing as Scripture says He was the Creator and the first thing created was time, itself:

"In the beginning." Gen 1:1

Moses wrote the first five books of the Bible, including Exodus, which Paul refers to, below:

"Moreover, brethren, I would not that ye should be ignorant, how that all our fathers were under the cloud, and all passed through the sea; And were all baptized unto Moses in the cloud and in the sea; And did all eat the same spiritual meat; And did all drink the same spiritual drink: for they drank of that spiritual Rock that followed them: and that Rock was Christ." 1 Cor 10:1–4

Yahshua, Himself:

"For had ye believed Moses, ye would have believed me: for he wrote of me. But if ye believe not his writings, how shall ye believe my words?" John 5:46–47

Alleged Contradiction

"No man hath seen God at any time." John 1:18 and John 4:12

Without knowing it was Yahshua, not Yahweh, interacting with Moses, there appears to be a significant contradiction. Applying study to alleged contradictions leads to greater knowledge. Contextually, it's obvious he is referring to God the Father. Yahshua Himself, makes the distinction:

"And the Father himself, which hath sent me, hath borne witness of me. Ye have neither heard his voice at any time, nor seen his shape." John 5:37

Here, too:

"Not that any man hath seen the Father, save he which is of God, he hath seen the Father." John 6:46

Without knowing it was Yahshua interacting with people in the Old Testament, these and numerous other Scriptures would appear contradictory. We're told many people did see God. These include Abraham, Isaac, Aaron, Jacob, Moses, Joshua, Gideon, and let's not forget, Adam and Eve.

So, whom did these individuals see, when they saw God? Yahshua was the great 'I AM' who spoke to Moses and others as God, during the Old Testament events. John describes a heated debate between Yahshua and religious leaders.

They'd asked Yahshua, "Art thou greater than our father Abraham, which is dead?" John 8:53

Yahshua responded, "Your father Abraham rejoiced to see my day, and he saw it, and was glad." John 8:56

The Jewish religious leaders were shocked by His implication, "Thou art not yet fifty years old, and hast thou seen Abraham?" John 8:57

Here it is, the verse that would ultimately lead to His Crucifixion and Resurrection, filling numerous, ancient, detailed prophecies in the process, "Verily, verily, I say unto you, Before Abraham was, I am." John 8:58

Incensed religious leaders grabbed rocks intending to stone Him to death for claiming to be God. Yahshua had claimed to be the burning bush, which hadn't been consumed. A voice from this bush had given a message to Moses, saying He'd deliver the Israelites from their enslavement in Egypt. When Moses had asked whom he should say the message was from, this was the answer:

"I Am That I Am. Thus shalt thou say unto the children of Israel, I Am hath sent me unto you." Ex 3:14

Yahshua had given Moses the stone tablets with the Ten Commandments, written with His own finger. Whose commandments did Yahshua say they were:

"If ye love me, keep my commandments." John 14:15

Yahshua Was the Creator

"For by him were all things created, that are in heaven, and that are in earth, visible and invisible, whether they be thrones, or dominions, or principalities, or powers: all things were created by him, and for him." Col 1:16

"And, Thou, Lord, in the beginning hast laid the foundation of the earth; and the heavens are the works of thine hands:" Heb 1.10

"Who hath delivered us from the power of darkness, and hath translated us into the kingdom of his dear Son: In whom we have redemption through his blood, even the forgiveness of sins: Who is the image of the invisible God, the firstborn of every creature: For by him were all things created, that are in heaven, and that are in earth, visible and invisible, whether they be thrones, or dominions, or principalities, or powers: all things were created by him, and for him: And he is before all things, and by him all things consist. And he is the head of the body, the church: who is the beginning, the firstborn from the dead; that in all things he might have the preeminence." Col 1:13–18

Bible Perversions Hide Our Creator

If you're open-minded and willing to leave your bias aside, you'd logically conclude Yahshua pre-existed. Perverted Bible versions have purposefully hidden the truth from you. In the King James Bible, the Scripture is clear:

"All things were made by him; and without him was not any thing made that was made." John 1:3 KJB

Look at the subtle word change the New King James Version uses:

"All things were made through Him, and without Him nothing was made that was made." John 1:3 NKJV

They change 'by', to 'through'.

It's subtle, as subtle as the serpent, "Yea, hath God said?" It's a slippery slope. In time, 'updated' versions will erode Scriptural truth further.

Bible Versions

WHILE living in Brisbane I encountered Christadelphians. They'd dropped literature in our letterbox, offering a free Bible study course. One of the six subject matters they taught was—Bible translations. This seemed like a complete waste, *Why have something so trivial as one of only six subjects? They all say the same thing anyway,* or so I thought.

Undertaking homework from the Christadelphians, I noticed several leading questions and statements seemed to be levelled against the King James Bible. This intense bias piqued my curiosity. I hated the KJB—all the thees and thous of Early Modern English. I possessed most English Bible versions, my preference being the New King James Version. It became evident this alleged study was purely an attack on the KJB. As I delved deeper, I discovered the KJB was superior to all modern English Bible versions. After all, that's what they are, versions. They're not God's word. They're counterfeits. Keep in mind, at the time, I loathed the KJB, despised it.

Peter's Vision

Every week we'd meet back as a class. There was a woman there who, like me, was seeking truth. Referencing an element of the homework, she asked a question regarding clean and unclean meat. The homework had been misleading, presenting a case which on the surface, implied we were no longer required to adhere to dietary rules.

The pastor told her food laws were 'done away with', citing Scripture describing a sheet, filled with unclean meat. This event had occurred in Old Jaffa, about a half-hour walk from Tel Aviv. I've visited Simon the Tanner's house where this occurred.

"Peter went up upon the housetop to pray about the sixth hour: And he became very hungry, and would have eaten: but while they made ready, he fell into a trance, And saw heaven opened, and a certain vessel descending upon him, as it had been a great sheet knit at the four corners, and let down to the earth: Wherein were all manner of fourfooted beasts of the earth, and wild beasts, and creeping things, and fowls of the air. And there came a voice to him, Rise, Peter; kill, and eat. But Peter said, Not so, Lord; for I have never eaten any thing that is common or unclean. And the voice spake unto him again the second time, What God hath cleansed, that call not thou common. This was done thrice: and the vessel was received up again into heaven." Acts 10:9–16

On the surface, it did seem to suggest dietary regulations were obsolete. Though I'm sure you realise if that was the case, the subject matter appears out of context. I knew this was a misunderstanding. It was an analogy regarding preaching the gospel to Gentiles.

"Now while Peter doubted in himself what this vision which he had seen should mean, behold, the men which were sent from Cornelius had made enquiry for Simon's house, and stood before the gate, And called, and asked whether Simon, which was surnamed Peter, were lodged there. While Peter thought on the vision, the Spirit said unto him, Behold, three men seek thee. Arise therefore, and get thee down, and go with them, doubting nothing: for I have sent them." Acts 17:20

Peter knew Yahshua wasn't implying dietary laws were to be discarded:

"For I am the Lord, I change not." Mal 3:6

Peter realised the vision was a metaphor, so he was trying to establish what the vision meant. He was about to find out.

The three men were Gentiles, (non-Jewish). They had been sent by Cornelius the Centurion, who'd become the first Gentile to convert to Christianity. Before his baptism, only Jews had converted to Christianity.

"Then Peter went down to the men which were sent unto him from Cornelius; and said, Behold, I am he whom ye seek: what is the cause wherefore ye are come? And they said, Cornelius the centurion, a just man, and one that feareth God, and of good report among all the nation of the Jews, was warned from God by an holy angel to send for thee into his house, and to hear words of thee. Then called he them in, and lodged them. And on the morrow Peter went away with them, and certain brethren from Joppa accompanied him. And the morrow after they entered into Caesarea. And Cornelius waited for them, and he had called together his kinsmen and near friends. And as Peter was coming in, Cornelius met him, and fell down at his feet, and worshipped him. But Peter took him up, saying, Stand up; I myself also am a man. And as he talked with him, he went in, and found many that were come together." Acts 10:21–27

Here it comes, Peter's realisation of what the vision which had perplexed him truly meant:

"And he said unto them, Ye know how that it is an unlawful thing for a man that is a Jew to keep company, or come unto one of another nation; but God hath shewed me that I should not call any man common or unclean." Acts 10:28

There you have it! The vision had nothing to do with the overruling of our Creator's laws, but everything to do with telling Peter to begin preaching the gospel to all, not just the Jews.

As the pastor attempted to sell the woman on the idea it was now acceptable to eat unclean meat, I interrupted, "That's not true." I didn't think the pastor was aware he was misleading her.

I innocently assumed he didn't know, so I started explaining the true meaning. The pastor became uncomfortable, nervous eyes darting to the other pastor, who attempted to silence me.

I was incensed, dumbstruck. I couldn't believe it. I glared at them, "You knew!" They attempted to pacify me, to silence me. It had the opposite effect, "No, you knew! Here's this woman, just looking for the truth, and you are blatantly lying to her!"

How ironic, from a denomination that believes there's no Devil, no Satan, no Father of Lies.

"Ye are of your father the devil, and the lusts of your father ye will do. He was a murderer from the beginning, and abode not in the truth, because there is no truth in him. When he speaketh a lie, he speaketh of his own: for he is a liar, and the father of it." John 8:44

"Yea, Hath God Said?"

You could say, the premise of every English version of the Bible since the publication of the KJB could be summed up from Genesis,

"Yea, hath God said ...?" Gen 3:1

The Byzantine Text is the name given to 6,000 copies of the New Testament, in Greek. It's also known as the Majority Text, due to the vast number of copies. When the printing press was invented in the West, the Bible was the first book printed. Five of the Byzantine manuscripts were utilised for the New Testament. The Codex Bezae was used also. Written in ancient Greek and Latin, it was one of the oldest manuscripts of the New Testament. The finished product was called the Textus Receptus, the Received Text. It was the standard Greek text for centuries, the bedrock of the King James Bible.

Unlike foundational Scripture used for modern versions, the Textus Receptus is untainted with Egyptian philosophy and heresies. It hasn't been corrupted by deletions, additions or amendments.

During the mid 1800s, the world's oldest New Testament manuscript, the Codex Sinaiticus was discovered at Mount Sinai in Egypt. It was poorly written, with missing words, horrific grammar and shocking spelling. While it's natural to assume oldest manuscripts are the best, that's not always the case. Remember, it's the 'oldest surviving'. Manuscripts being copied, read and passed around will wear out.

Most corrupted texts appeared early in the first century. These had been compiled and influenced by the Gnostics, originating from Alexandria in Egypt. They'd discard verses they didn't like.

Another old text, the Vaticanus, which had also originated from Alexandria, was discovered inside the Vatican library. This too, was peppered with appalling spelling mistakes, horrific grammar, and copious omissions.

While the 6,000 Byzantine texts are consistent with each other, the Alexandrian manuscripts argue with each other. Not only do both the Codex Sinaiticus and Vaticanus differ significantly from the Majority text, they also disagree with themselves over 3,000 times, in the four Gospels alone.

"For many bare false witness against him, but their witness agreed not together." Mark 14:56

A lot is missing from these Egyptian texts, including Yahshua forgiving the woman for committing adultery. Yet, modern versions decided to include it. Regardless, Gnostic scribes had chosen to omit it when they copied the manuscripts. So, which is the right foundation to use for a translation into the English language? The Byzantine, Majority Texts; or the corrupted, minority, Egyptian Alexandrian texts?

As early as 55 AD, Alexandrian Gnostics were wresting Scripture. Peter has a letter showcasing this, warning the church had been infiltrated by wolves in sheep's clothing, infiltrators with insatiable and destructive intentions:

"But there were false prophets also among the people, even as there shall be false teachers among you, who privily shall bring in damnable heresies, even denying the Lord that bought them, and bring upon themselves swift destruction. And many shall follow their pernicious ways; by reason of whom the way of truth shall be evil spoken of." 2 Peter 2:1–2

Alexandrians are recorded arguing with first-century disciples:

"Then there arose certain of the synagogue, which is called the synagogue of the Libertines, and Cyrenians, and Alexandrians, and of them of Cilicia and of Asia, disputing with Stephen." Acts 6:9

Despite Egyptian scribes and editors of both manuscripts being some of the most hostile 'translators' of God's words, their translation was the foundation for many modern English versions' New Testament. Because of this, Alexandrian texts continue to dispute the teachings of the disciples, as recorded in the Majority Text, which is the foundation of the King James' New Testament.

Westcott and Hort

This hostile 'translation' occurred in the 1800s under two men, Brook Foss Westcott and Fenton John Anthony Hort. The Septuagint is a corrupted translation of the Hebrew Bible into Greek. They used the Septuagint, Codex Sinaiticus and Vaticanus, despite knowing they had errors. Neither man believed in Yahshua's deity.

Hort didn't believe the Bible was infallible and revered the writings of Charles Darwin, "The book which has most engaged me is Darwin. Whatever may be thought of it, it is a book that one is proud to be contemporary with. My feeling is strong that the theory is unanswerable." (*Life and letters of Fenton John Anthony Hort*, Vol. I, p. 416)

Hort didn't believe Yahshua's death was atonement for our sins, "The popular doctrine of substitution is an immoral and counterfeit. Nothing can be more unscriptural than the limiting of Christ's bearing our sins and sufferings to His death, but indeed that is only one aspect of an almost universal heresy." (Hort to Westcott, *Life and Letters of Fenton John Anthony Hort*, Vol. I, p. 430)

Westcott didn't believe the first three chapters of Genesis, or that Heaven existed, "I reject the infallibility of Holy Scriptures overwhelmingly." (Westcott, *The Life and Letters of Brook Foss Westcott*, Vol. I, p. 207)

Westcott's words below, remind me of the Catholic priest during my religion lesson in grade seven, "No one now, I suppose, holds that the first three chapters of Genesis, for example, give a literal history. I could never understand how anyone reading them with open eyes could think they did."—Westcott had written this in a letter to a clergyman in 1890 (*Life and Letters of Fenton John Anthony Hort*, Vol. II, p, 69). Westcott didn't believe in Heaven or Hell either, "Hell is not the place of punishment of the guilty, it is the common abode of departed spirits." (Westcott, *Historic Faith*, pp. 77–78)

Critics claim traditional Bible manuscripts add material. The absurdity of this claim is proven by the following Scripture:

"For this, Thou shalt not commit adultery, Thou shalt not kill, Thou shalt not steal, Thou shalt not bear false witness, Thou shalt not covet; and if there be any other commandment, it is briefly comprehended in this saying, namely, Thou shalt love thy neighbour as thyself." Rom 13:9 KJB

The phrase 'Thou shalt not bear false witness' is missing from the Alexandrian texts, and thereby, most modern versions. Now, ask yourself, "What's more likely, someone removed a self-incriminating commandment, or added one?" KJB preserves the Ninth Commandment, whereas most modern versions have removed it. Surely common sense would cause you to see those who corrupt God's word remove the very phrase that incriminates them? What do you think Yahshua would have to say on the matter?

"For verily I say unto you, Till heaven and earth pass, one jot or one tittle shall in no wise pass from the law, till all be fulfilled." Matt 5:18

It's no surprise the corrupt NIV, New International Version, removed the Ninth Commandment. A more appropriate title would be, 'The No Idea Version' or 'Never Inspired Version'. Unfortunately, it's currently the best-selling version. Many alleged scholars claim the NASB, New American Standard Bible is the most accurate English Bible translation. However, they also removed the Ninth Commandment. Logic and common sense should suffice for you to realise it cannot be the most accurate translation.

Check your Bible. If they've abolished the Ninth Commandment, throw it in the bin. Better still, burn it and obtain a KJB.

King James Bible Tells Us To Study

"Study to shew thyself approved unto God, a workman that needeth not to be ashamed, rightly dividing the word of truth."
2 Tim 2:15 KJB

Modern versions, including the alleged, 'New' King James Version, omit the instruction to study.

"Be diligent to present yourself approved to God, a worker who does not need to be ashamed, rightly dividing the word of truth."
2 Tim 2:15 NKJV

Archaic

It's often said the KJB uses words no longer in use, so should be discarded. That being the case, to be true to their argument, they should discard the Scriptures. After all, the original Scriptures used words that were archaic at the time. For example, the archaic word 'seer' had already been replaced with 'prophet':

"And the servant answered Saul again, and said, Behold, I have here at hand the fourth part of a shekel of silver: that will I give to the man of God, to tell us our way. (Beforetime in Israel, when a man went to enquire of God, thus he spake, Come, and let us go to the seer: for he that is now called a Prophet was beforetime called a Seer.) Then said Saul to his servant, Well said; come, let us go. So they went unto the city where the man of God was. And as they went up the hill to the city, they found young maidens going out to draw water, and said unto them, Is the seer here?" 1 Sam 9:8-11

Thees and Thous

My biggest problem with the KJB was the use of words such as 'thee' and 'thou'. In my ignorance, I believed it was the desire for those uttering such words to appear pious or learned. Instead, the use of 'ye', 'thee' and 'thou' would become one of many reasons I became King James Bible only, or 'KJBO'.

In modern English, 'you' refers to both one person, or several—it's ambiguous. King James Bible wasn't written in the everyday language of common people in 1611. It's written to let us know whether Scripture is directed at one person, or several. 'Thee' or 'thou' means one person is being addressed, 'ye' or 'you', means several. This distinction aids translation and interpretation, rendering King James Bible the clearest translation of the Bible into English.

Thee, Thou, Thy, Thine = Singular, referring to one person (They all start with the letter T). 'Thy' and 'thine' correspond to 'your' and 'yours'.

You, Ye, Your, Yours = Plural, referring to more than one person (They all start with the letter Y).

There's a misconception that the use of thee or thou are a reference to a Deity. Their use serves purely to clarify the translation into English. When the KJB was first penned, so to speak, these words were archaic. They were utilised to make the translation clear.

"Marvel not that I said unto THEE [Nicodemus], YE [everyone] must be born again." John 3:7

For comparison, the NIV: "You should not be surprised at my saying, 'You must be born again'."

See the difference? The NIV infers it's only Nicodemus, who has to be born again. There are countless examples of similar ambiguities in modern Bible versions.

"And the eye cannot say unto the hand, I have no need of thee: nor again the head to the feet, I have no need of you." 1 Cor 12:21

'Hand' is singular, meaning one hand, as opposed to 'hands' meaning two, or more. Therefore, it's referred to as 'thee'. On the other hand, pun intended, 'feet' is plural, meaning more than one, (as opposed to saying foot, meaning one). Accordingly, it's referred to as 'you.'

"And the Lord said, Simon, Simon, behold, Satan hath desired to have *you* [all apostles], that he may sift *you* [all apostles], as wheat: But I have prayed for *thee* [Simon], that thy faith fail not: and when thou art converted, strengthen thy brethren." Luke 22:31–32

Author of Confusion

Besides the destruction of pure doctrine, scriptural accuracy, prophetic links and fulfilments, there are other problems with the deluge of false Scriptures. What happens today when a preacher reads Scripture? You follow along in your head, until you can't. The words in your mind are different from the preacher's. Confusion reigns. The Father of Confusion is also the Father of Lies. The two go hand-in-hand. The church is not on the same page. It flies in the face of this:

"Fulfil ye my joy, that ye be likeminded, having the same love, being of one accord, of one mind." Phil 2:2

The church is not of one accord. While undertaking my study, differing versions caused incredible frustration. A denomination would make a claim, alongside a Scripture reference which wouldn't agree with their reasoning. While a large part is likely due to wishful thinking or bias on their behalf, it could be due to conflicting Bible versions.

'But If Not'

Early in World War Two, close to half of the British army was stranded on the shores of France at Dunkirk, separated from their island home by the English Channel. Facing annihilation from the German army and air force, they gazed forlornly across the waves to where their parents, wives, siblings and children lived.

"'Nothing but a miracle can save the BEF (British Expeditionary Force) now, and the end cannot be very far off.' General Alan Brooke, Commander of II Corps." (Stavros Atlamazoglou, 'Dunkirk: The German Half of the Story', 2021, SOFREP website)

Cabled home to London were just three words, 'But if not'. Upon receipt of the cryptic message, their countrymen instantly understood the severity of their predicament, and that they'd refuse to surrender. King George VI immediately called for a national day of prayer. Places of worship were filled. *The Four Miracles of Dunkirk*, written by Evan Miller and available at guideposts.org is essential reading.

As with the three men about to be thrown into a fiery furnace over 2,500 years previously, the situation across the English Channel was dire:

"If it be so, our God whom we serve is able to deliver us from the burning fiery furnace, and he will deliver us out of thine hand, O king. **But if not**, be it known unto thee, O king, that we will not serve thy gods, nor worship the golden image which thou hast set up." Dan 3:17–18

The besieged British understood Yahweh expects us to respect His sovereignty as to whether or not He'll deliver us from a predicament. There's power in the King James Bible. It's incredible how three simple words, instantly recognised by so many, could convey so much.

Poetic

King James Bible, 'KJB', has been heralded as, "The noblest monument of English prose, the highest point of achievement of English composition" (Cheryl Lowe, *The Noblest Monument of English Prose*, 2011, memoriapress.com). I implore all of you to read this article in its entirety.

"The plays of Shakespeare and the English Bible [the KJV] are, and will ever be, the twin monuments not merely of their own period, but of the perfection of English, the complete expressions of the literary capacities of the language." (George Saintsbury, English literary historian)

The KJB has poetic form, metre and beat. Even non-Christians are affected by it in ways they may not realise. Its language has influenced generations of artists, writers and songwriters. Numerous KJB phrases permeate our language. The famous opening line, 'Four score and seven years ago' from President Abraham Lincoln's Gettysburg Address was inspired by the KJB. His entire speech imitated its wording, structure and rhythm, incorporating a Shakespearean style.

Richard Dawkins speaks highly of the King James Bible, "You can't not appreciate English literature, unless you are, to some extent at least, steeped in the King James Bible ... Proverbial phrases, phrases that make echoes in people's minds, they haunt our minds ... And not to know the King James Bible, is to be, in some small way, a barbarian." (Professor Richard Dawkins, King James Bible Trust, London, England)

He's also said it this way, "A native speaker of English who has never read a word of the King James Bible is verging on the barbarian." Yet, in his book, *The Greatest Show on Earth*, he says the Bible was written by "Bronze Age desert tribesmen," and insinuates it's only worthy for readers of the same ilk.

During the aforementioned interview, Dawkins reads from a two-page list of words and phrases he believed people didn't realise originated from the KJB, "A coat of many colours; Amid the alien corn; New wine in old bottles; Shake off the dust of your feet; Seeds falling on stony ground; A stranger in a strange land; Beat their swords into ploughshares; Weeping and gnashing of teeth."

"In celebration of the four hundredth anniversary of the King James Bible in 2011, the famed unbeliever Christopher Hitchens paid it gushing homage in Vanity Fair magazine, where he argued that the dignity of its prose, the beauty of its expression, and the appropriateness of its linguistic form to its exalted subject matter make it one of the greatest works of the English language—a 'repository and edifice of language which towers above its successors'." (Martin Cothran, 'Archaic On Purpose: A Defence Of The King James Bible,' 2021, Memoria Press website)

Common King James Bible Sayings

Here is an extremely small sample of everyday sayings gleaned from the King James Bible:

"The writing is on the wall; The apple of my eye; A law unto himself; A man after his own heart; Fight the good fight; Sign of the times; Rise and shine; Root of the mater; A stumbling block; Like a thief in the night; At your wits end; Salt of the earth; Bottomless pit; An eye for an eye; Fallen from grace; Fell by the wayside; Fell flat on his face; God forbid; Holier than thou; Out of the mouths of babes; Putting words in my mouth; Cast the first stone; Ashes to ashes, dust to dust; Scapegoat; Blind leading the blind; Broken heart; Can a leopard change its spots?; The powers that be; Forbidden fruit; The love of money is the root of all evil; Reap what you sow; See eye to eye; How are the mighty fallen; To give is better than to receive; Turn the other cheek; Two edged sword; Go the extra mile; A wolf in sheep's clothing; Skin of my teeth; The truth shall make you free; Pride comes before a fall; Good Samaritan; As white as snow; and Eat, drink and be merry."

It Has a Beat

The King James Bible has a rhythm, a beat. It can be easily set to music. Hence, the beautiful, powerful hymns of yesteryear. Do you recall the song 'Turn', performed by the band The Byrds? It was taken straight from the KJB:

"To every thing there is a season, and a time to every purpose under the heaven: A time to be born, and a time to die; a time to plant, and a time to pluck up that which is planted; A time to kill, and a time to heal; a time to break down, and a time to build up; A time to weep, and a time to laugh; a time to mourn, and a time to dance; A time to cast away stones, and a time to gather stones together; a time to embrace, and a time to refrain from embracing; A time to get, and a time to lose; a time to keep, and a time to cast away, A time to rend, and a time to sew; a time to keep silence, and a time to speak; A time to love, and a time to hate; a time of war, and a time of peace." Ecc 3:1–8

King James Bible uses powerful and colourful imagery, painting pictures in your mind while beautifully espousing truths.

"Though your sins be as scarlet, they shall be as white as snow; though they be red like crimson, they shall be as wool." Isa 1:18

"He maketh me to lie down in green pastures: he leadeth me beside the still waters. He restoreth my soul." Ps 23:2–3

Many examples listed earlier as common sayings today, which originated with the KJB, could also be listed here, such as:

"Beware of false prophets, which come to you in sheep's clothing, but inwardly they are ravening wolves." Matt 7:15

Other than the NKJV, all modern versions are 65,000 words shorter than the KJB. Though, peculiarly, their sentence structure is wordier. King James Bible has the least number of words per sentence and the least number of syllables per word.

Most popular 'Bibles' have 'updated' versions, rendering previously memorised verses obsolete. Don't buy into the nonsense that we have better clarification on how to translate words. It's just a cover for, "Yea, hath God said?" KJB translators were superior for the task of translating ancient texts into English, as you shall see.

Memorisation

Scripture memorisation is a lost art, coinciding with the arrival of Bible versions. Whole congregations memorised passages of Scripture when the King James Bible was read aloud during services. Due to its rhythm, beat and powerful imagery coupled with its small vocabulary of many one or two-syllable words, it's easily memorised.

"Thy word have I hid in mine heart, That I might not sin." Ps 119:11

There'll come a time when having Bibles in Western countries will be illegal, eventually punishable by death. Those who know, know— 'The writing is on the wall'. The only place we'll be safely able to access it, will be within the confines of our memories.

Ask people to quote John 3:16, the Beatitudes, the 23rd Psalm, or say the 'Our Father.' Almost all will do so with KJB Scripture, even though they read other versions. They're quoting the last version they memorised. Memorisation ceased when people began reading Bible versions. Pastors constantly quote from different versions, even during one sermon.

KJB Translators

I spent a lot of time researching this. The outcome was the accuracy and knowledge of these translators were superior to those of other versions. Several times I've been sitting in church hearing some idiot pastor reading Scripture before singling out a word, saying it was translated incorrectly. They'll often do this with the KJB. These pastors, who've done a few years of Greek language study, if they're lucky, then proceed to enlighten us with what the Bible should've translated a particular word as. All I hear is, "Yea, hath God said?" echoing in my mind.

Forty-seven scholars and clergymen translated the KJB over seven years. They used superior manuscripts, Hebrew and Greek, for the Old and New Testaments. They used a superior technique with their translation method. Unlike Bible versions, they didn't paraphrase. It was pure, a literal word-for-word translation.

Of the translators, forty-one were university professors, thirty-nine held Masters's degrees, thirty held PhDs, and thirteen were masters of the Hebrew language. Ten had mastered Greek, five were deans and four were college presidents.

Unlike Westcott and Hort, the fathers of all modern English Bible versions, every man involved in the King James Bible translation believed in the inspiration of Scripture and the deity of Yahshua. As such, they referred to the Bible as, "God's Word, God's Truth, God's testimony, and The Word of salvation." Many were not only master linguists and Biblical scholars, but also preachers. (Bill Bradley, 'The Translators of the King James Bible Brief Summary,' 2023, *Safeguard Your Soul* website)

A Few of the KJB Translators

Below are short biographies of a handful of the noble, scholarly men who translated the King James Bible. While the information is scant, you may read to your heart's content where it was taken from (kingjamesbibletranslators.org and Bill Bradley's article, listed above).

Dr Lancelot Andrews was a superior translator. He'd mastered fifteen languages and spent five hours a day in prayer. While studying at Cambridge during his youth, he learned a new language each year during Easter holidays. After several years, he'd mastered most European languages. He spoke Latin, Greek, Hebrew, Arabic and seventeen other languages.

Dr William Bedwell was famed in Arabic learning, writing an Arabic dictionary in three volumes and had begun a Persian dictionary. He translated Scriptures into Hebrew, Arabic and two other languages. A master of Semitic languages, he provided great insight into Hebrew words and phrases, which had found their way into the Greek language of the New Testament.

Dr Miles Smith 'a walking library', was an expert in Hebrew, Syriac, Chaldee and Arabic. These languages were as familiar to him as English. He'd studied writings of Latin and Greek church fathers, and was final editor on the KJB, writing its preface.

Sir Henry Saville was proficient in mathematics and Greek, tutoring these subjects to Queen Elizabeth I.

John Bois was an expert in Hebrew and Greek. By the age of five, he'd read the entire Bible in Hebrew. By age six, he could write Hebrew in a precise, elegant style. He was often seen studying Greek for fifteen hours a day and had memorised the New Testament. While at University, he'd tutored several fellow students in Greek, with many of his Greek professors attending.

John Spencer was elected as Greek lecturer at Oxford University at age nineteen.

John Reynolds became a Greek lecturer at Corpus Christi College at age twenty-three. He studied the Scriptures in their original languages. He'd read all the Greek and Latin fathers and all records of the ancient church. He was known as a 'third university', (Oxford, Cambridge, and John Reynolds).

These translators had mastered English, Hebrew, Aramaic and Greek. They knew related languages which shed light on ancient Scriptures, such as Aramaic, Arabic, Persian, Coptic and Syriac.

'Translators' of modern versions were perplexed when they encountered a word they didn't understand. Conversely, the vast pool of knowledge of KJB translators enabled them to easily translate difficult words.

Wrested Scripture

Would you read a Bible that ~~does this~~ to Scripture? Below is an extremely small sample of entire verses or parts of verses 'removed' from the Holy Bible, by modern Bible versions.

"~~For the Son of man is not come to destroy men's lives, but to save them~~. And they went to another village." Luke 9:56

"~~For the Son of man is come to save that which was lost.~~" Matt 18:11

"~~And the scripture was fulfilled, which saith, And he was numbered with the transgressors.~~" Mark 15:28

"~~Two men shall be in the field; the one shall be taken, and the other left.~~" Luke 17:36

"And whosoever shall not receive you, nor hear you, when ye depart thence, shake off the dust under your feet for a testimony against them. ~~Verily I say unto you, It shall be more tolerable for Sodom and Gomorrha in the day of judgment, than for that city.~~" Mark 6:11

Do you know what the Alexandrian manuscripts do to the words, 'should not perish', from the Scripture below? They erase them:

"That whosoever believeth in him should not perish, but have eternal life." John 3:15 KJB

This is how NIV renders the Scripture, "That everyone who believes may have eternal life in him."

Most modern versions don't fare much better. They've removed, 'whosoever believeth in him' and also, 'should not perish', attempting to eradicate 'soul death'. In other words, they're endeavouring to perpetrate the lie from the beginning, "Ye shall not surely die." Gen 3:4

Here's another wresting of Scripture where they destroy God's sovereignty:

"Verily, verily, I say unto you, He that believeth on me hath everlasting life." John 6:47 KJB

This is how the NIV wrests it, "Very truly I tell you, the one who believes has eternal life." Believes what? Fish can swim? It's removed the crucial words, "on me". Other modern versions remove these words too.

"Go ye up unto this feast: I go not up yet unto this feast." John 7:8 KJB

How does the NIV render it? "You go to the festival. I am not going up to this festival."

Other versions are similar. They remove, "yet". By the way, it wasn't a festival, it was the Feast of Tabernacles. True to His word in the KJB, Yahshua would later attend the Feast. If you hold fast to most of the modern versions, then, by default, you're claiming Yahshua is a liar. This is another example where ignoramuses will point to the alleged discrepancy and declare it's a contradiction, that Yahshua is a liar, or both. Due to counterfeit Bibles, who could blame them? That said, from my experience, many who would know the truth in this instance, would choose to overlook it, and continue to use an argument they know is fraudulent.

"Lo, I see four men loose, walking in the midst of the fire, and they have no hurt; and the form of the fourth is like the Son of God." Dan 3:25 KJB

Compare it with the NIV: "He said, 'Look! I see four men walking around in the fire, unbound and unharmed, and the fourth looks like a son of the gods'."—'Like a son of the gods', need I say more?

It gets worse. Compare the two following NIV passages:

"I, Jesus, have sent my angel to give you this testimony for the churches. I am the Root and the Offspring of David, and the bright **Morning Star**." Rev 22.16 NIV

Now for the second passage:

"How you have fallen from heaven, **morning star**, son of the dawn! You have been cast down to the earth, you who once laid low the nations! You said in your heart, "I will ascend to the heavens; I will raise my throne above the stars of God; I will sit enthroned on the mount of assembly, on the utmost heights of Mount Zaphon. I will ascend above the tops of the clouds; I will make myself like the Most High." Isa 14:12–14. NIV

Did you spot the similarity? The NIV is calling Yahshua, 'Satan'.

Here's how Scripture records the above verse:

"How art thou fallen from heaven, **O Lucifer**, son of the morning! how art thou cut down to the ground, which didst weaken the nations!" Isa 14:12 KJB

Another Scriptural Assault

"But I say unto you, Love your enemies, bless them that curse you, do good to them that hate you, and pray for them which despitefully use you, and persecute you." Matt 5:44 KJB

How it's rendered in the NIV, "But I tell you, love your enemies and pray for those who persecute you."

Below is another example of, "Hath God said?" The NIV adds the words, "with passion." That's taken out of context. The KJB is clearly addressing the sin of fornication, and subsequent punishment, soul death in the Lake of Fire:

"I say therefore to the unmarried and widows, it is good for them if they abide even as I. But if they cannot contain, let them marry: for it is better to marry than to burn." 1 Cor 7:8–9 KJB

This is how the NIV butchers it, "Now to the unmarried and the widows I say: It is good for them to stay unmarried, as I do. But if they cannot control themselves, they should marry, for it is better to marry than to burn with passion."

The 2011 NIV replaces references of just men, to both men *and* women. In the 1984 NIV Mark 4:25 says, "Whoever has will be given more; whoever does not have, even what he has will be taken from him." The 2011 version replaces the 'he' and 'him' with 'they' and 'them'. Below, counterfeits take God's word and flip it on its head:

"Judah yet ruleth with God, and is faithful with the saints." Hosea 11:12 KJB

"Judah is unruly against God, even against the faithful Holy One." NIV

"Judah is still unruly against God, Even against the Holy One who is faithful." NASB

Pure

Our Creator tells us He's preserved His word:

"The words of the Lord are pure words: as silver tried in a furnace of earth, purified seven times. Thou shalt keep them, O Lord, thou shalt preserve them from this generation for ever." Ps 12:6–7 KJB

The NIV's bastardisation of His promise to preserve His word to us:

"And the words of the Lord are flawless, like silver purified in a crucible, like gold refined seven times. You, Lord, will keep the needy safe and will protect us forever from the wicked." Ps 12:6–7 NIV

"Heaven and earth shall pass away, but my words shall not pass away." Matt 24:35

Bible Versions

Only the KJB claims to be the preserved word of God in English. Its supporters claim it's pure, free from error. This is in stark contrast to all English Bible versions.

NIV removes 65,000 words, such as sodomite, fornication, effeminate, slothful, vanity, damnation, devils and Lucifer. Here is one of several examples, from the NIV, where modern versions have also omitted words:

"And Jesus answered him, saying, It is written, That man shall not live by bread alone, but by every word of God." Luke 4:4 KJB

Compare God's inspired word, above, with the Never Inspired Version below:

"Jesus answered, "It is written: 'Man shall not live on bread alone." Luke 4:4 NIV

These are not trivial changes, by any stretch of the imagination. Here's another:

"Unto you first God, having raised up his Son Jesus, sent him to bless you, in turning away every one of you from his iniquities." Acts 3:26 KJB

All other versions choose to omit the words, 'Son Jesus', replacing it with the solitary word, 'servant'.

King James Bible translators were committed to an accurate, unadulterated Bible translation. Occasionally words were added to aid translation. Every time this occurred, KJB translators used the added word in italics, so we'd know the word wasn't original. Using italics proves the sincerity of KJB translators to bring you God's word.

With the KJB Scriptures in this book, I haven't included the italics. This is because when I'm making a point, I've italicised words, to help make my point clearer. Besides, you're meant to obtain your own Bible, so you can test all you read.

Doctrinal Destructions

Modern versions also destroy yet another fulfilment of prophecy. Old Testament prophet Isaiah had prophesied that the Messiah would be born of a virgin:

"Behold, a virgin shall conceive, and bear a son, and shall call his name Immanuel." Isa 7:14 KJB

See if you notice how modern versions destroy the 'virgin birth' doctrine courtesy of the Revised Standard Version, RSV: "Therefore the Lord himself will give you a sign. Behold a young woman shall conceive and bear a son, and shall call his name Immanuel."

Along with the Scripture regarding the virgin birth, there is this problem as well:

"And Joseph and his mother marvelled at those things which were spoken of him." Luke 2:33 KJB

This is the NIV's deplorable wresting of the above Scripture: "The child's father and mother marvelled at what was said about him." Father? What nonsense! Our Creator was the father, Joseph was the male parent.

Here's another crucifying of Scripture:

"And as they went on their way, they came unto a certain water: and the eunuch said, See, here is water; what doth hinder me to be baptized? And Philip said, If thou believest with all thine heart, thou mayest. And he answered and said, I believe that Jesus Christ is the Son of God. And he commanded the chariot to stand still: and they went down both into the water, both Philip and the eunuch; and he baptized him." Acts 8:36–38 KJB

It reads as if there was a prerequisite to becoming baptised, namely, the declaration that, "Jesus Christ is the Son of God."

The NIV not only leaves out "Jesus Christ is the Son of God," but the entire verse, verse 37: "As they traveled along the road, they came to some water and the eunuch said, 'Look, here is water. What can stand in the way of my being baptized?' And he gave orders to stop the chariot. Then both Philip and the eunuch went down into the water and Philip baptized him." NIV

They'd come across a body of water, causing the subject of baptism to be brought up. They then proceeded 'down into the water' to be baptised. This demonstrates full immersion is required for baptism, symbolic of being washed clean, not just sprinkled with water, or fired upon, by a water pistol filled with 'holy water'. Not only that, the subject had to be fully aware of what was taking place. Catholics, how can babies possibly fulfil this requirement?

Christians are largely unaware Bible versions aren't translated from the same texts used by King James translators. The KJB utilises superior manuscripts and translators. They used a superior translation technique. Their translation method was pure. They didn't alter grammar. They didn't take a noun and twist it into a verb. They converted Hebrew words directly into English, using the same process with Greek words.

I hate throwing anything out, especially books, preferring instead to take items to second-hand shops. However, following my investigation of Bible versions, anything within my possession other than a King James was thrown in the bin. Do you have a Bible, or a Bible version?

The Bible Was Written by Man?

WE'VE all heard this ridiculous argument before. Some of you've probably said it. Technically, it was penned by man, but man was the scribe—the middle man. You could argue our Creator literally wrote a portion of the Bible Himself:

"And the Lord delivered unto me two tables of stone written with the finger of God; and on them was written according to all the words, which the Lord spake with you in the mount out of the midst of the fire in the day of the assembly." Deut 9:10

When someone states the Bible was written by man, a normal response would be, "Yeah, so?" Who cares what the writing instrument was? Whether the writing instrument was a tool, or a combination of a man holding a tool, the recorded message still came from the same source. If you were to write a book with a typewriter, would you say you wrote it, or the typewriter wrote it? Or, how about if you dictated information and others recorded it? Would you say you were the author, or those recording it were?

To those insinuating Scripture isn't inspired, I say, "How would you know?" Those who claim the Bible was written by man insist there's no such thing as absolute truth. To those who believe there's no absolute truth, I ask, "How could your claim, 'God didn't write the Bible,' possibly be true?"

If they respond, "How do you know the Bible's true?" I counter with, "How do you know it's not true?" If you're ever in a similar conversation, whatever they say, I recommend asking them if their words are true. If they say yes, remind them they previously declared there isn't absolute truth.

"I have a fundamental belief in the Bible as the Word of God, written by those who were inspired. I study the Bible daily." (Sir Isaac Newton, mathematician, physicist, astronomer)

Archaeology

Archaeologists use the Bible to determine where to dig. Over 25,000 archaeological digs have been conducted, directly related to the Bible. Every single one confirms the Bible's authenticity.

Agnostic archaeologist Nelson Gluek declares, "It may be stated categorically that no archaeological discovery has ever controverted a Biblical reference," and "Scores of archaeological findings have been made which confirm in clear outline or exact detail historical statements in the Bible." (John Stonestreet and Kasey Leander, 'Archeology Continues to Confirm Biblical Record,' 2023, *Breakpoint* website)

Although the Smithsonian Institution is hostile toward the Bible, most of it is directed at the first few chapters of Genesis. Despite their bias, they're willing to concede this, "Much of the Bible, in particular the historical books of the Old Testament are as accurate historical documents as any that we have from antiquity and are in fact more accurate than many of the Egyptian, Mesopotamian, or Greek histories." ('Smithsonian Letter,' The Bible as History, National Museum of Natural History, Smithsonian Institution, Washington DC 20560)

Hittite Empire

The Bible was mocked as being false due to it mentioning a huge Hittite Empire, one of the most powerful empires at the time.

However, there was no archaeological evidence to support this Biblical claim; until recent times, when Hattusa, the capital city of the empire was unearthed. Relics, tablets, and documents from this time were also discovered. We see this scenario play out, time, and time again.

Pilate Stone

Almost everyone is familiar with Pontius Pilate's role in the events concerning Yahshua's Crucifixion. Outside of the New Testament, there's hardly any evidence he'd existed at all. That changed in 1961 with the discovery of the 'Pilate Stone', a piece of carved limestone inscribed, "Pontius Pilate, prefect of Judea." Before this, his very existence had been questioned.

King Sargon

"In the year that Tartan came unto Ashdod, (when Sargon the king of Assyria sent him,) and fought against Ashdod, and took it." Isa 20:1

Sceptics asserted there was never a king named Sargon, as this name was unknown in any other record. Others contended Isaiah confused this name with another. Then, archaeological diggings found King Sargon's palace in Iraq. They uncovered proof that under the rule of Sargon, the Assyrian army invaded Ashdod during the time of Isaiah. What's more, it showed that Sargon didn't accompany the invasion. Instead, it was led by Tartan, and the city was conquered, just as the Bible had declared. Some of this information was recorded on palace walls.

I could provide example after example where the Bible's authenticity has been proven. The cows could come home and I still wouldn't be anywhere near finished. Incredibly, there are still dullards who spout nonsense such as, "The Bible was written by 'illiterate' goat-herders."

Exodus

El Arish Stone was discovered in the late 1800s lying on an Egyptian farm. Weighing two tonnes, it's comprised of engraved hieroglyphics on black granite. Moses is referred to as 'Prince of the Desert', and Israelites are named, 'evil ones'. It tells the story from Pharaoh's view, corroborating the Biblical plagues of Egypt, Pharaoh's daughter (who raised Moses), fleeing with the Israelites and the Red Sea parting, allowing the Israelites to escape Egypt.

"It mentions a specific location next to where the sea parted. The place is called 'Pekharti'. Remarkably, this exact place is mentioned in Exodus 14:2,9 as the location where the Israelites camped just prior to the parting of the sea. In the Book of Exodus, it is called 'Pi-hahiroth'. (Simcha Jacobovici, 'Proof of the Exodus!' 2013, *SimchaJacoboviciTV* website)

"Speak unto the children of Israel, that they turn and encamp before Pihahiroth, between Migdol and the sea, over against Baalzephon: before it shall ye encamp by the sea." Ex 14:2

King David

Do you recall the story of David slaying Goliath with a projectile hurled from a slingshot? He went on to become a musician, Israel's greatest king, the writer of the Book of Psalms and a direct ancestor of Yahshua. Despite this, critics denied he'd ever existed. Archaeology has unearthed undeniable proof of his existence, most notably, the Tel Dan Stele. Uncovered from the ancient city of Dan was a rock inscribed in Aramaic, 'House of David', which translates as, 'Dynasty of David'. Other portions were discovered that recorded the details of a battle from the same period, corroborating Scripture from 2 Kings 9.

Uncovered in Jordan was the Moabite Stone, or, Mesha Stele, which has references to events recorded in 2 Kings 3, and also contains the phrase, 'House of David'.

There are Egyptian hieroglyphs, 'The Karnak Inscription', which references conquering land in Israel from the 'Heights of David'.

Numerous other proofs have been uncovered corroborating the Biblical account of David, including the remains of his palace.

Harmonious

There were approximately forty writers of the Bible, from three different continents, three languages, written over 1,500 years. Occupations of the writers were diverse, including Prince, Shepard, Army Commander, Tent Maker, King, Prophet, Fisherman, Tax Collector and Medical Doctor. None were authors or writers, except maybe Ezra, who was a scribe. What's more, the majority of them had never met each other.

Even so, the Bible is harmonious throughout its writings, comprising a total of sixty-six different books, yet it appears to be authored by the same person. Placed together, these books fit seamlessly, effortlessly becoming one.

Do you recall the expression, "Too many cooks spoil the broth"? Well, not in this case. This observation alone shows inspiration arises from one source.

"All scripture is given by inspiration of God, and is profitable for doctrine, for reproof, for correction, for instruction in righteousness." 2 Tim 3:16

Dead Sea Scrolls

For those adamant the Bible wasn't inspired by the Creator, I have three words for you—Dead Sea Scrolls.

Accidently discovered in a cave near the shore of the Dead Sea by teenage shepherds in 1947, were the first seven Dead Sea Scrolls. Most were written in Hebrew, with a smaller number in Aramaic or Greek. More were found up until 1956. There's speculation as to how these documents came to be in the caves. More than likely, it was during a time of the Jews endeavouring to escape Roman persecution.

All the books of the Hebrew Bible are referenced except for Nehemiah and Esther. In some cases, several copies of the same book were found. For example, thirty copies of Deuteronomy. A new set of Dead Sea Scrolls has been found in an Israeli desert.

'Chinese Whispers'

Often, an argument is put forward stating the Bible cannot be trusted, due to 'Chinese Whispers'. How each passing on of a message, changes the message. It's imperative to compare apples with apples. With this method, the message, each time it's repeated, isn't repeated by the original person who instigated the message. The message is filtered down, through any number of people. Contrast this with Bible translations. Every time, the writer of the new translation returns to the original manuscripts. The 'relayed message' is always firsthand.

'Chinese Whispers' is an accidental change of the original message, whereas the modern Bible versions are actively seeking to destroy the original message. Or, at the very least, dilute it. Unlike the King James Bible, the other modern English versions now translate from corrupted ancient texts. The truth will always be attacked by the 'Father of Lies'.

The Dead Sea Scrolls have proved the accurate recording of Old Testament Scripture over the past several thousand years. New Testament writings are superior to other works of antiquity, such as Homer, Aristotle, Tacitus, Plato, and Caesar. New Testament Scriptures have greater numerical and earlier documentation than any other ancient book. Most of the aforementioned works only have a few manuscripts attesting to their existence.

Scholars use the Bibliographic Test against all ancient literature, since original documents of ancient literature don't exist. They have to determine whether existing copies are reliable. The greater the quantity of copies, and the earlier their dating, the easier it is to reconstruct a text closer to the original. It also serves to identify discrepancies or errors in subsequent copies. This test confirmed the New Testament has been accurately transmitted over time.

Not only do we have thousands of ancient manuscripts of the New Testament, we also have numerous early citations taken from them, "The textual critic has available the numerous scriptural quotations included in the commentaries, sermons, and other treatises written by early Church fathers. Indeed, so extensive are these citations that if all other sources for our knowledge of the text of the New Testament were destroyed, they would be sufficient alone for the reconstruction of practically the entire New Testament." (Bruce M. Metzger and Bart D. Ehrman, 2005, *The text of the New Testament: Its transmission, corruption, and restoration*, 4th ed, Oxford: Oxford University Press)

Existence of the Jews and Israel

King Louis XIV of France asked Blaise Pascal, the great Christian philosopher more than 300 years ago, to give him proof of the existence of God. Pascal answered, "Why the Jews, Your Majesty, the Jews!" ('The Torah: Divinely-Inspired or Man-Made?' *The Rational Believer: An Intellectual Journey Through Belief in Judaism and Torah Theology*, jewishbelief.com)

When people leave their homeland, they lose their national identity within five generations, or disappear completely. Jews have maintained their identity for over 4,000 years. They're the only nation to return, after surviving an exile. They did it twice—Babylonian and Roman exiles. For thousands of years, Jews have been subjected to battles, conquests, and rioting to massacre or displace them. There were several crusades, the Inquisition, and let's not forget the Holocaust of World War Two. Surrounded by enemies, they live under the constant threat of sudden war.

Other empires and cultures have vanished completely, or were assimilated. At the time of the Hebrews, there were Hittites,

Jebusites, Canaanites, Moabites, Edomites, Ammonites, Chaldeans, Amalekites and Philistines. They constantly waged war with Israel and have disappeared from the face of the earth. Powerful Roman, Babylonian, Egyptian and Assyrian Empires have collapsed. Yet, Jews remain. How? Why?

God commanded Abraham 4,000 years ago, to leave Egypt and to obey Him faithfully. If not, others would fight them, banish them and they'd suffer persecution everywhere they went:

"And among these nations shalt thou find no ease, neither shall the sole of thy foot have rest: but the Lord shall give thee there a trembling heart, and failing of eyes, and sorrow of mind: And thy life shall hang in doubt before thee; and thou shalt fear day and night, and shalt have none assurance of thy life." Deut 28:65–66

Jews have been banished from almost every country they've settled in. Hatred of the Jews is so widespread they're the only group in the world with a unique term for their persecution. Anti-Semitism is rife, always has been. There've been countless attempts to eradicate them. Proportionally, there aren't many more Jews today, than there were before the Roman expulsion, 2,000 years ago.

"And the LORD shall scatter you among the nations, and ye shall be left few in number among the heathen, whither the LORD shall lead you." Deut 4:27

If you want to eradicate a people and its customs, scatter them. Every trace of them should've disappeared, due to their scattering across the earth. Especially their ancient language, Hebrew, and their customs and traditions. Despite being exiled to numerous countries across the Earth, Jews have remained as 'one people'.

Detailed Prophecies
Recorded in the Bible are 300 prophecies concerning the birth, life, death and Resurrection of Yahshua. All have been fulfilled. The probability of one man fulfilling just eight of those prophecies

is 1 in 100,000,000,000,000,000. ('The Mathematical Probability that Jesus is the Christ,' Empower International, empower.global)

For those who wish to believe the Bible isn't true, added to your many woes is this indisputable evidence; the Old Testament brims with detailed, specific prophecies. Verifiable historical records document the accurate fulfilment of prophecies by Yahshua during His time on Earth. These historical facts have caused many hostile to truth, to insist Old Testament books such as Daniel, must've been written after the fact, as the fulfilment of prophecies was too precise.

Thousands of years later, copies of Old Testament books, the Dead Sea Scrolls, confirmed the authenticity of the foretelling of prophecies, centuries and even thousands of years before their accurate fulfilment. The prediction and fulfilment of these prophecies qualifies it as being authenticated by God:

"For the prophecy came not in old time by the will of man: but holy men of God spake as they were moved by the Holy Ghost."
2 Peter 1:21

The Bible is a collection of sixty-six verified historical documents, harmonious in theme, despite it having forty different writers, from over three continents and three languages. The documents span thousands of years. Writers are of diverse occupations, including kings, fishermen, tax collector, military commander, prince, tentmaker and medical doctor. Yet it reads as if there was only one Author—there was. These documents were recorded by eyewitnesses, during the lifetime of other eyewitnesses. They record supernatural events, which accurately fulfil specific prophecies. They insist their writings are not their own, but are of Divine origin. This statement was formulated from a similar commentary, penned by Voddie Baucham, American pastor, author, and educator.

Ancient Historian

Besides being a Gospel writer, Luke was also a medical doctor and historian. Below he's making a declaration of what the apostles believe. He too, now believes, after his careful investigation. Referencing the Scriptures, Luke notes they were recorded by eyewitnesses. He felt it was his duty to investigate and write these historical events in chronological order. This way, others may be certain the words he wrote are true:

"Forasmuch as many have taken in hand to set forth in order a declaration of those things which are most surely believed among us, even as they delivered them unto us, which from the beginning were eyewitnesses, and ministers of the word. It seemed good to me also, having had perfect understanding of all things from the very first, to write unto thee in order, most excellent Theophilus, that thou mightest know the certainty of those things, wherein thou hast been instructed." Luke 1:1-4

Archaeologist and Oxford University professor Sir William Ramsay set out to destroy the authenticity of the Biblical Book of Acts, written by Luke. Upon the culmination of his thirty-year study, this was his conclusion, "Luke is a historian of the first rank; not merely are his statements of fact trustworthy. ...[He] should be placed along with the very greatest of historians." (Sir William Mitchell Ramsay, 1915, *The Bearing of Recent Discovery on the Trustworthiness of the New Testament*, p. 222)

"Sir Ramsay found no historical or geographical mistakes in the Book of Acts. This is amazing when we realize that in the book of Acts, Luke mentions 32 countries, 54 cities, nine Mediterranean islands and 95 people and he did not get one wrong. Compare that with the Encyclopedia Britannica. The first year the Encyclopedia Britannica was published it contained so many mistakes regarding places in the United States that it had to be recalled." (Russ Whitten, 'Have You Wondered: Is the Bible historically accurate?' 2017, *The Destin Log* website)

"Why Hast Thou Forsaken Me?"

Psalm 22 was written at least 500 years before the Crucifixion, yet describes this event in detail. Incredibly, the writer had never witnessed nor heard of a crucifixion before. Do you know why? It was written at least 200 years before crucifixion was invented. To read it, you'd think he'd witnessed Yahshua's crucifixion firsthand.

Rather than do a side-by-side comparison of the prophecies and their fulfilment, I've elected to highlight in bold the various prophecies that were fulfilled. Read all about it in Matthew 27, Mark 15, Luke 23 and John 19.

"My God, my God, why hast thou forsaken me? why art thou so far from helping me, and from the words of my roaring? But I am a worm, and no man; **a reproach of men**, and **despised of the people**. All **they that see me laugh** me to scorn: they **shoot out the lip**, they **shake the head, saying, he trusted on the Lord that he would deliver him: let him deliver him**, seeing he delighted in him. But thou art he that took me out of the womb: thou didst make me hope when I was upon my mother's breasts. I was cast upon thee from the womb: thou art my God from my mother's belly. Be not far from me; for trouble is near; for there is none to help. **Many bulls have compassed me**: strong bulls of Bashan have beset me round. **They gaped upon me with their mouths**, as a ravening and a roaring lion. I am **poured out like water**, and **all my bones are out of joint**: my heart is like wax; it is melted in the midst of my bowels. My strength is dried up like a potsherd; and **my tongue cleaveth to my jaws**; and thou hast brought me into the dust of death. For **dogs have compassed me**: the assembly of **the wicked have inclosed me**: they **pierced my hands and my feet**. I may **tell all my bones**: they **look and stare upon me**. They **part my garments among them**, and **cast lots upon my vesture**."

Ps 22:1–18

Did you catch all the prophecies? You'd be forgiven for thinking it was written after the fact, not 500 years earlier. Yahshua knew what was happening—the fulfilment of ancient prophecy. He was drawing attention to it. That's why he recited the very first line of the ancient Psalm. Matthew and Mark recorded this fact:

"And about the ninth hour Jesus cried with a loud voice, saying, Eli, Eli, lama sabachthani? that is to say, My God, my God, why hast thou forsaken me?" Matt 27:46

Ignoramuses love to ask with a silly smirk on their mugs, "If Yahshua was all-knowing, why did he say 'My God, my God, why have you forsaken me?' It sounds to me like He didn't know what was going to happen to him after all. Why did God abandon him?"

Ignorant Christians will erroneously answer, "It's because God had to turn His back on Him, as at that very point, Yahshua took on the sins of the world.

They're both wrong.

At the time, Scriptures weren't broken into numbered chapters and verses. Instead, Scripture was referenced by saying the first few words. Yahshua was drawing attention to the prophecies of Psalm 22, which had just unfolded right before their very eyes.

Forbidden Chapter

You're about to read the remarkable, detailed, fulfilled prophecies (in bold), of Isaiah 53, 'The Forbidden Chapter'. Jews will not read this in their synagogues. Read it, and find out why:

"For he shall grow up before him as a tender plant, and as a root out of a dry ground: **he hath no form nor comeliness**; and when we shall see him, there is **no beauty** that we should desire him. He is **despised and rejected** of men; a man of sorrows, and **acquainted with grief**: and we hid as it were our faces from him; he was **despised**, and we esteemed him not. Surely **he hath borne our griefs**, and **carried our sorrows**: yet we did esteem him **stricken**, smitten of God, and afflicted. But **he was wounded for our transgressions**, he was **bruised for** our iniquities**: the chastisement of our peace was upon him; and **with his stripes we are healed.** All **we like sheep have gone astray**; we **have turned everyone to his own way**; and **the Lord hath laid on him the iniquity of us all**. He was **oppressed, and he was afflicted, yet he opened not his mouth**: he is **brought as a lamb to the slaughter**, and **as a sheep before her shearers is dumb, so he openeth not his mouth**. He was **taken from prison and from judgment**: and who shall declare his generation? for he was cut off out of the land of the living: **for the transgression of my people was he stricken**. And he **made his grave with the wicked**, and **with the rich in his death**; because **he had done no violence, neither was any deceit in his mouth**. Yet it pleased the Lord to bruise him; he hath put him to grief: when thou shalt make **his soul an offering for sin**, he shall see his seed, he shall prolong his days, and the pleasure of the Lord shall prosper in his hand. He shall see of the travail of his soul, and shall be satisfied: by his knowledge shall my righteous servant justify many; **for he shall bear their iniquities**. Therefore will I divide him a portion with the great, and he shall divide the spoil with the strong; because he hath poured out his soul unto death: and **he was numbered with the transgressors**; and he **bare the sin of many**, and **made intercession for the transgressors**." Isa 53:2–12

These Scriptures are peppered with prophecies, intricate in detail. Psalm 22 was written by King David 500 years before Yahshua's birth. The Forbidden Chapter was written 700 years before His birth. They were written 200 years apart. Do you still choose to believe these writings were written by man? How is that possible?

Virgin Birth

Isaiah wrote of a virgin birth. How's that for a prophecy? How's that prediction possible?

"Therefore the Lord himself shall give you a sign; Behold, a virgin shall conceive, and bear a son." Isa 7:14

Predicted Birthplace

Micha named the place Yahshua would be born:

"But thou, Bethlehem Ephratah, though thou be little among the thousands of Judah, yet out of thee shall he come forth unto me that is to be ruler in Israel; whose goings forth have been from of old, from everlasting." Micah 5:2

What are the chances of that? Micah predicted the birth of the Ruler of Israel, as being born in Bethlehem and it wasn't even the town His parents lived in. Take note of how the prophet alludes to this Ruler being at the Beginning, as well as the End. In short, he's establishing Yahshua's declaration, that He was God on Earth.

Bible Prophecy Fulfilled During the 21st Century

"Who hath heard such a thing? who hath seen such things? Shall the earth be made to bring forth in one day? or shall a nation be born at once?" Isa 66:8

On 14th May 1948, the nation of Israel was created in one day, fulfilling a 2,500-year prophecy. Never had a persecuted, scattered ancient people managed to preserve their identity over twenty centuries, to then re-establish themselves in their original homeland.

This miraculous outcome was instigated due to another miraculous event. The liberation of Israel during World War One, leading to the signing of the Balfour Declaration. Light Horsemen from Australia and New Zealand overcame incredible odds to take Beersheba in a daring cavalry charge, which opened the way to Jerusalem's liberation. The youngest nation, Australia, liberated the oldest nation, Israel. Poetic.

The Creator says He'll bring His people home:

"For thus saith the Lord God; Behold, I, even I, will both search my sheep, and seek them out. As a shepherd seeketh out his flock in the day that he is among his sheep that are scattered; so will I seek out my sheep, and will deliver them out of all places where they have been scattered in the cloudy and dark day. And I will bring them out from the people, and gather them from the countries, and will bring them to their own land, and feed them upon the mountains of Israel by the rivers, and in all the inhabited places of the country." Ez 34:11–13

Jews scattered around the world are returning to their ancestral home in droves. This has to occur, to allow for the final fulfilment of Biblical prophecies, those of the Last Days.

The Law of Return

An Israeli law, The Law of Return, passed in 1950, gives Jews, or people with one or more Jewish grandparents, and their spouses, the right to relocate to Israel and obtain Israeli citizenship. While touring Israel, I encountered several people who were there on a Birthright program. It's a mission to allow every young Jewish adult the opportunity to explore Israel at least once in their lifetime. The program is funded through the generous donations of philanthropists and the State of Israel. Their whole journey is free, including the airfare.

Israel has exhibited divine, unexplained intervention when it comes to defending itself from aggressors. Former Israeli Prime Minister, David Ben-Gurion once stated, "In Israel, in order to be a realist, you must believe in miracles."

Six Day War

In 1967 a six-day war ensued with Egypt. Israel's Arab neighbours vowed to turn the Mediterranean Sea red with the blood of Jews. Israel was outgunned and outmanned on three fronts—Egypt, Jordan and Syria. The aggressors had double the number of soldiers, triple the number of tanks and quadruple the number of planes. Catastrophe was imminent. Instead, Israel destroyed her enemies. In the process, she tripled her land. What's more, she did it all in six days.

Surely you can see the hand of God in that? It was a miracle. There's no other explanation for it. The following day, the secular commander of the Israeli army wrote an inscription on a piece of paper, placing it within a Western Wall crevice:

"This is the Lord's doing; it is marvellous in our eyes." Ps 118:23

Parallels with the Biblical story of Gideon, winning a decisive victory over an army, despite a vast numerical disadvantage, didn't go unnoticed.

"We Do Aim Them, but Their God Changes Their Path in Mid-air."

Israel possesses an extraordinary defence system. 'Iron Dome' intercepts and destroys incoming missiles. Despite its incredible ability, it isn't infallible. In 2014, Israel was once again under attack. Disaster was imminent. Three intercepting rockets from Iron Dome failed to destroy an incoming rocket. Miraculously, with four seconds to spare, a sudden gale blew the rocket harmlessly into the ocean.

Those managing Iron Dome witnessing the events unfold are adamant it was God's doing. Even those who perpetrated the attacks had this to say, "We do aim them, but their God changes their path in mid-air."

Catholics

NUMEROUS people discredit the Bible, based on actions and beliefs of Catholics. Or, unsubstantiated allegations against Catholics. Although the Catholic Church is satanic, based on how it's continually at odds with Scripture, this doesn't extend to all the congregation.

Many of my relatives are Catholic. I used to be one. Several close friends are Catholic. This isn't an attack on members of the Catholic congregation. It's an attack on the institution of the Roman Catholic Church.

Paedophiles

While mockers are quick to play the paedophile card when attempting to bash the Bible or Catholics, here are some points to consider. An extreme minority of Catholic priests are paedophiles. However, the vast majority of paedophile priests are homosexual.

Did you catch that? Read it again, slowly. Absorb it. Don't read further until you've grasped this truth. What does the Bible say about sodomy? Is it for, or against?

"Thou shalt not lie with mankind, as with womankind: it is abomination." Lev 18:22

"And likewise also the men, leaving the natural use of the woman, burned in their lust one toward another." Rom 1:27

I rest my case. How could you possibly, logically and honestly, declare people acting in direct violation of Scripture, are ambassadors for Scripture? Their actions prove they aren't followers of God.

What's another name for someone who isn't a believer, let alone, a follower of God? 'Atheist' fits the bill, doesn't it? Priests don't become paedophiles, paedophiles become priests. If you were a paedophile, which occupation would give you access to boys? Which occupation would offer an umbrella of trust? Further, which occupation would make your non-attraction to women inconspicuous?

Just because someone 'claims' to be a Catholic or a Christian, it doesn't mean they are. Someone could claim to be a World War Two veteran. They may even have old photos, medals and a uniform. It doesn't prove anything.

Vain Repetitions

"But when ye pray, use not vain repetitions, as the heathen do: for they think that they shall be heard for their much speaking." Matt 6:7

Catholics will sit with rosary beads for hours, muttering vain repetitions. They trust priests without question, instead of searching the Scriptures for themselves.

"Come out from among them, and be ye separate." 2 Cor 6:17

Mary Worship

"For there is one God, and one mediator between God and men, the man Christ Jesus." 1 Tim 2:5

Catholics have invented their own prayer, 'Hail Mary'. As established earlier, Mary is dead. So, who, or what, are they praying to, pray tell? At school, I was taught to pray to Mary, as Yahshua would listen to her. If you visit a priest for 'confession', rest assured, you'll be prescribed a liberal dose of 'Hail Marys' to recite.

Virgin Mary

"Then Joseph being raised from sleep did as the angel of the Lord had bidden him, and took unto him his wife: And *knew her not till she had brought forth her firstborn son*: and he called his name Jesus." Matt 1:24–25

Catholics believe Mary was a perpetual virgin, and that Joseph and Mary had a celibate marriage. She wasn't, and they didn't.

Yahshua Is an Only Child

Yahshua had four brothers and at least two sisters. Step-brothers and sisters, as it was Joseph who fathered His siblings. All four brothers are named in Scripture, and 'sisters' is plural, so He had at least two.

"Is not this the carpenter, the son of Mary, the brother of James, and Joses, and of Juda, and Simon? and are not his sisters here with us?" Mark 6:3

Catholics maintain they were cousins, not half-siblings. Paul is clear:

"But other of the apostles saw I none, save James the Lord's brother." Gal 1:19

This half-brother wrote the Book of James.

Immaculate Conception

Catholics claim Mary was sinless. She was human. There's only one sinless person who walked the earth—her Firstborn.

Idol Worship

Catholics violate the Second Commandment:

"Thou shalt not make unto thee any graven image, or any likeness of any thing that is in heaven above, or that is in the earth beneath, or that is in the water under the earth. Thou shalt not bow down thyself to them, nor serve them." Ex 20:4-5

Their churches are full of statues. Their altars contain relics of alleged saints, such as strands of hair, bone fragments, teeth or clothing. Father Grundy told us this in primary school. Even then, it didn't sit well with me. He showed us where remnants of Saint Therese had been concealed in the altar of our school's church. We're commanded not to make statues to worship. Let alone, bow down or serve them. Catholic churches are filled with graven images. Upon entering, you must kneel towards a graven image of a man on a cross.

During one of three Easter services I had to attend yearly as a child, a huge crucifix was taken off the wall. One after the other, we had to kneel and kiss the feet of the graven image.

"It was not until Christianity began to be Paganized that the cross came to be thought of as a Christian symbol. It was in 431 A.D. that crosses in churches and chambers were introduced, while the use of crosses on steeples did not come until about 586 A.D." (Ralph Woodrow, *Babylonian Mystery Religion*, p. 50)

The crucifix/cross is an idol. Worse, its symbolism is of Pagan origin, worshipping a Babylonian sun god. The 'ankh', a cross with a loop atop, is one of Egypt's oldest symbols. When Constantine's Christians adopted the Pagan cross, the Coptic Christians of Egypt adopted the ankh. Anything related to a cross is idolatry. Catholics and Christians will attempt to justify with pious garbage such as, "No, no. This cross represents my Lord and Saviour dying on the cross, for my sins."

No, it doesn't. That's your justification. Good luck trying to sell Yahshua on that when you stand before Him on Judgement Day.

Changing Commandments

The Second Commandment didn't sit well with Catholics, so they got rid of it.

"And he shall speak great words against the most High, and shall wear out the saints of the most High, and think to change times and laws." Dan 7:25

After destroying the Second Commandment, they turned their attention towards the Fourth Commandment. They changed the Sabbath day from the seventh day of the week, to the first day of the week.

Changing Days and Times

"Remember the sabbath day, to keep it holy. Six days shalt thou labour, and do all thy work: But the seventh day is the sabbath of the Lord thy God." Ex 20:8–10

Catholics changed it to Sunday, the first day of the week, to commemorate the sun. They allege after the death of Yahshua, disciples started holding their services on a Sunday. They didn't. Yet, they ignore observing the holy days commanded by God.

"And he shall speak great words against the most High, and shall wear out the saints of the most High, and think to change times and laws." Dan 7:25

Observing Pagan Customs

Rather than observing God's holy days, Catholics instead observe man's holidays. Namely, Christmas and Easter with all of their associated customs and traditions.

Pope

Catholics say Peter was the first Pope. Nothing in Scripture or other historical documents supports this. Priests take a vow of celibacy. They're forbidden to marry. Peter was married:

"And when Jesus was come into Peter's house, he saw his wife's mother laid, and sick of a fever." Matt 8:14

Many Christs

"For there is one God, and one mediator between God and men, the man Christ Jesus." 1 Tim 2:5

In the verse above, Catholics have changed one mediator into many:

"Catholic priests serve primarily as mediators between God and man ... Ultimately, the priest is 'another Christ', God's chosen instrument of salvation." ('The Priest: Mediator Between God and Man,' SSPX, Society of Saint Pius X, sspx.org)

Catholics also teach their congregation to use Mary as an intercessor.

Fish Worship

'Dagon' is a Philistine and Babylonian 'fish god'. Dagon's priests wear a religious hat, called a 'mitre'. From the side, it appears as the open mouth of a fish. The Pope occasionally wears the same hat, as do bishops. There are two lengths on the back, similar to the cloth attached to the back of Dagon's mitre, marked to represent scales. Catholics will vehemently insist their headdress isn't symbolic of the 'fish god'. Your eyes and common sense shall tell you otherwise.

"For religious reasons, most of the Syrian peoples had special days for eating fish, a practice that one is naturally inclined to connect with the worship of a fish god." (*The Catholic Encyclopedia*, 1913, Encyclopedia Press, Inc.)

There are two fertility goddesses in ancient European mythology—Frigg and Freya. It's likely both are one and the same. Friday is derived from 'Freya's Day'. If you feel there is something familiar about the word 'Frigg', you wouldn't be mistaken. 'Frigging' is an old English word meaning 'sexual intercourse'. The same word is occasionally today used in lieu of another word. The symbol for these two goddesses was the fish.

Since Pagan fish symbolism, including the rite of eating fish on Friday, was rife throughout the Roman Empire, it was therefore adopted into Catholicism. Christians don't fare much better. Are you familiar with the 'Jesus Fish'? It's a symbol they say represents Christianity. They have several just-so stories to explain away the association. The truth is, they too, have adopted the Pagan symbolism.

Blasphemy

Catholics refer to their priests as 'Father'.

"And call no man your father upon the earth: for one is your Father, which is in heaven." Matt 23:9

Whore of Babylon

'Woman' in Bible prophesy represents, 'church'.

"I saw a woman sit upon a scarlet coloured beast, full of names of blasphemy, having seven heads and ten horns. And the woman was arrayed in purple and scarlet colour, and decked with gold and precious stones and pearls, having a golden cup in her hand full of abominations and filthiness of her fornication: And upon her forehead was a name written, Mystery, Babylon The Great, The Mother Of Harlots And Abominations Of The Earth." Rev 17:3–5

Picture a church, featuring purple and scarlet colours, gold, jewels and a golden chalice. I'm not saying the Roman Catholic Church is the Whore of Babylon, though it certainly looks that way. They also have an early history of murdering Protestants:

"And I saw the woman drunken with the blood of the saints, and with the blood of the martyrs of Jesus." Rev 17:8

Rome has always been known as, the 'City of Seven Hills'. "It is within the city of Rome, called the city of seven hills, that the entire area of Vatican State proper is now confined." (Thomas Nelson, 1976, *The Catholic Encyclopedia*, under the heading, 'Rome')

"The seven heads are seven mountains, on which the woman sitteth." Rev 17:9

"And the woman which thou sawest is that great city, which reigneth over the kings of the earth." Rev 17:18

Satanic Symbolism

A satanic inverted cross was visible on the backrest of the Pope's throne during a 2,000 service in Israel. While Catholics say it's representative of Peter who was crucified upside-down, surely you hear alarm bells ringing? If that wasn't bad enough, the Pope often holds a bent cross which has a distorted body attached to it. It reeks of satanism.

The cross itself is Pagan, stemming from worship of Tammuz. The cross represents a 'T'.

Sun Worship

Besides fertility gods, Catholics worship sun gods:

"Thou shalt see greater abominations that they do. Then he brought me to the door of the gate of the LORD'S house which was toward the north; and, behold, there sat women weeping for Tammuz. Then said he unto me, Hast thou seen this, O son of man? turn thee yet again, and thou shalt see greater abominations than these. And he brought me into the inner court of the LORD'S house, and, behold, at the door of the temple of the LORD, between the porch and the altar, were about five and twenty men, with their backs toward the temple of the LORD, and their faces toward the east; and they worshipped the sun toward the east." Ez 8:13–16

That's why we had to attend Midnight Mass on Easter Sunday. During the service we had to walk outside and turn east, to face the direction of the rising sun.

Cannibals

During my primary school years, the ritual of Catholic 'communion' unnerved me. A priest held up some wafers, claimed it was now the body of Yahshua, and told us to eat it.

Then, he held up a chalice of wine, declaring it was Yahshua's blood, and told us to drink it. We did all he asked. Even as a child, I understood there was something abhorrently wrong with this ritual. It appears Catholics have misunderstood what took place at the Last Supper. The bread and wine didn't become the body and blood of Yahshua, as Catholics claim. It was a symbolic representation:

"And he took bread, and gave thanks, and brake it, and gave unto them, saying, This is my body which is given for you: this do in remembrance of me. Likewise also the cup after supper, saying, This cup is the new testament in my blood, which is shed for you."
Luke 22:19–20

We are to remember Yahshua's sacrifice for our sins, with the act of breaking bread and consumption of wine, at Passover. Catholics claim they're following Yahshua's example at their services. They're not. Yahshua was celebrating Passover and the Feast of Unleavened Bread. Catholics are celebrating the Pagan festival of Easter. Yahshua said the bread and wine were symbolic of His body and blood. Catholics insist the bread and wine have *become* His body and blood. Passover occurs once a year. Catholics practise their cannibalistic ritual weekly, on the wrong day, in a building filled with graven images.

Non-Practising Messianic Jew

FOR those who insist on placing a label on others, this shall suffice for me. Messianic is an extension of Judaism. It's what Yahshua and His disciples were—a harmonious blend of Judaism with Christianity. They were, and remained, Jewish. They didn't start a new religion, theirs expanded. Gentiles, once converted, worshipped in the synagogues on the seventh day of the week, the Sabbath day. They kept the holy days as commanded by our Creator and adhered to food laws.

Although the Forbidden Chapter, Isaiah 53, was written 700 years before Christ, the accuracy of its numerous prophecies has caused many Jews to turn to Christianity.

Back when I was observing the holy days and the food laws, I told people I was a Messianic Jew. Events happened in my life, people change and I fell away. All things aside, I kept the dietary laws. During my falling away years, when asked what religion I was, I'd say, "Non-practising Messianic Jew."

Messianic Jew

This changed when I caught a taxi at four a.m. to take me to the airport to commence my journey to Egypt and Israel. You wouldn't believe it—the driver was Messianic. What are the chances? Messianic are as rare as hens' teeth. Not only that, this was Wagga Wagga, a regional town in New South Wales. I cannot remember the last time I'd encountered a Messianic. It must've been at least twenty years ago at a Messianic church in Brisbane.

When I told the taxi driver, I was an un-practising Messianic Jew, she asked if I was Jewish. Her question made me think. As far as I knew, I didn't have a Jewish background, although anything is possible. Her words made me realise; *I probably shouldn't be including the 'Jew' tag at the end*. After all, 'Messianic' is an extension of Judaism—Followers of Yahshua, the Jewish Messiah, Son of Yahweh.

The early church was Messianic. At the time, some had referred to it as 'Christian.' The Greek word is derived from the Hebrew word, 'Messiah'. Modern Christianity is NOT what the early church practiced. The Catholic church corrupted the Messianic early church by mixing it with Pagan customs and traditions. Modern Christianity would later break away from this apostasy, yet retain many vestiges of it.

Arab/Israeli Debate

Staying in Nazareth for three nights and four days, it wasn't what I'd expected. During Yahshua's time growing up there, the population would've been a few hundred. When I was there, 2022, it was approximately 80,000. Nazareth is known as the Arab capital of Israel. Of these, seventy per cent are Muslim. Christians make up the remaining thirty per cent.

I encountered an Arab there who took an instant dislike to me. I believe it was due to the Star of David around my neck. At twenty-three, he was one year older than my eldest son. He was sly, taking cheap shots at people, but did so in a way that was clandestine, borderline. The Arab/Israeli debate wasn't one I wanted to engage in. He had his beliefs, I had mine. His were shaped by his upbringing, what he saw or heard, or chose to see, or hear. No doubt, the lens he viewed the world through was coloured by those around him. By the same token, I was also coming from a biased position. The difference was, I knew it, whereas, I don't feel he did.

Despite our differences, we were similar in some ways. This could've been a problem. He tried taking me to task for wearing the Star of David, "You're not Jewish, so you shouldn't wear it. People will assume you're Jewish."

By this time, my logic meter had well and truly exploded. His mild rant was peppered with numerous assumptions. *How the hell would you know anyway? You're not family,* "We both don't know if I have Jewish ancestry, or not. Just because I'm unaware of any, doesn't mean I don't have any."

As for, "Other people may think you're Jewish."

"… Yeah … so …?" He had no answer. "If people want to think I'm Jewish, so be it. We make assumptions about others all the time, so what's the difference?"

He wasn't backward in coming forward with his opinions, "You should wear a cross."

I countered with, "Why should I?" Slumped shoulders and averted eyes signalled his defeat.

During our interaction, he'd reluctantly conceded a point. Present was a young German couple, along with this bloke's French girlfriend. She'd made the assertion she wasn't religious, thereby securing my full attention, "Yes, you are. Everyone is religious."

She began to protest. I told her she either had to believe there was a Supreme Intelligent Being that created everything; or, there was an explosion/expansion of 'nothing', caused by 'nothing', for 'no reason', which produced 'everything'. Continuing, I told her both positions were based on faith, thereby making them religious.

As her mouth began to open in protest, my adversary reluctantly cautioned her, "No, he's right." His words hit her like a freight train. Interestingly, when she'd disputed the idea of everything arising from nothing, fervently claiming everything came from atoms, the agnostic German girl, (studying to be a Lawyer), who'd been listening intently and learning fast, laughed, "Where did the atoms come from?"

Exiting the discussion and walking away, the Arab attempted to drag me back into the conversation. Before long, I declined to answer any more questions, telling him it was pointless, as we were going in circles. Afterwards, it seemed the tension was broken and there was somewhat of a mutual understanding between us.

Every Cloud Has a Silver Lining

Strangely, there was something poignant I discovered from this exchange, which gave me a greater understanding of passages of Scripture, and the way modern Jews conducted themselves. During our encounter, he mentioned there were various sects of Jews. Following our interaction, I researched the validity of his claims, and also that of mine.

He'd been right about various sects of Jews. In hindsight, it makes a lot of sense. It also led to a light-bulb moment—Orthodox Jews of today are descended from Pharisees of Yahshua's day. This revelation cleared up a lot of hypocrisy I'd learnt about Jews while living in Melbourne. Some would say you couldn't swat a mosquito on the Sabbath day as that action constitutes 'work'. Yes, it's ridiculous. It reminded me of Yahshua's encounter with religious leaders of His time:

"Jesus went on the sabbath day through the corn; and his disciples were an hungred, and began to pluck the ears of corn and to eat. But when the Pharisees saw it, they said unto him, Behold, thy disciples do that which is not lawful to do upon the sabbath day."
Matt 12:1–2

After Yahshua rebuked the religious leaders, this occurred:

"When he was departed thence, he went into their synagogue: And, behold, there was a man which had his hand withered. And they asked him, saying, Is it lawful to heal on the sabbath days? that they might accuse him. And he said unto them, What man shall there be among you, that shall have one sheep, and if it fall into a pit on the sabbath day, will he not lay hold on it, and lift it out? How much then is a man better than a sheep? Wherefore it is lawful to do well on the sabbath days. Then saith he to the man, Stretch forth thine hand. And he stretched it forth; and it was restored whole, like as the other. Then the Pharisees went out, and held a council against him, how they might destroy him." Mark 2:9–14

The same nonsense religious leaders presented Yahshua with, is the same nonsense I see today with Orthodox Jews. I also experienced it, and its associated hypocrisy, in my travel to Israel in 2022. I'd joined a program to experience a Sabbath (Shabbat), dinner with a Jewish family. The information stated a few other compatible travellers would join us. I'd expected a Jewish family, complete with children, and maybe two, or even three other participants. In reality, it was two Jewish people, with about twelve travellers. A few were heard to say it wasn't what they'd expected either. Most were American, at least one of them was a Jewish American, as he was wearing the small-cap Jews wore on their heads. There may have been more, as others appeared to know the Hebrew songs.

Walking into the house as a group, we were presented with a table decked with all manner of food and wine—a feast. I asked everyone to gather behind it for a photo. However, our Jewish host put a stop to it, explaining, "It wasn't lawful to use a camera for that purpose on the Sabbath day." I don't know if he was referring to the use of modern technology, or if it was related to 'works' in some capacity. So be it, although it did seem strange.

Imagine my surprise when he later described how electric lights wouldn't be turned on for Sabbath dinners. Candles were to be utilised instead. Yet, here we were, sitting under bright, electric lights. Apparently, it's acceptable to turn lights on before sunset and leave them on. I could tear holes in that argument. That aside, this bloke was working, making a fortune. The dinner cost eighty-five US dollars per person.

Mind you, when he was talking about candles and electric lights, he could sense my logic meter was exploding. Shame flickered in his eyes. It was clear to me, that he knew, that I knew. Respectfully biting my tongue, I sat there thinking about Jews swatting mosquitos and Yahshua's disciples eating corn in the fields, thinking to myself, *Here we go again*. Glancing around, it was obvious other participants remained blissfully unaware of the hypocrisy playing out before their very eyes.

Our host spoke of other petty rules and regulations. Asking if he was referring to the Talmud, he responded in the affirmative. I don't know a whole lot about their laws, customs and culture, which is the reason I was there in the first place. At one point he said the Talmud says on Sabbath, you cannot say no to a request, or something to that effect. He then proceeded to give the example of how his daughter had once walked across the lounge room while he lolled in an armchair. Smiling slyly, she'd asked him for 100 shekels. He dutifully handed her the money. This is absurd.

Sitting there, mulling over things, I began to see how Orthodox Judaism strongly resembled the Pharisees, the religious leaders, of Yahshua's time and why they, and He, were in constant conflict. For what it's worth, I don't know a lot about Judaism and don't pretend to. However, my interaction with the Nazarene Arab had gifted me great insight into my discontent with Orthodox Judaism.

While in Nazareth, I went on a tour of 'Old Nazareth'. It concluded with an extremely pro-Palestinian propaganda presentation. It's been said you can never really understand the Arab/Israeli conflict unless you've lived there for years. I don't know if that's true. My opinion on the matter reflects words I heard years previously. I believe you cannot deny the logic and truth of the following statement, if you're being honest with yourself:

"If the Arabs laid down their weapons today, tomorrow, there'd be peace in the Middle East. However, if Israel laid down their weapons today, tomorrow, there'd be no more Israel." (Benjamin Netanyahu)

Let's take it a step further, with my take on it. The land was promised to the Jews by our Creator, thousands of years ago. As such, there isn't much point arguing about it. It's a lost cause:

"In the same day the LORD made a covenant with Abram, saying, Unto thy seed have I given this land, from the river of Egypt unto the great river, the river Euphrates: The Kenites, and the Kenizzites, and the Kadmonites, And the Hittites, and the Perizzites, and the Rephaims, And the Amorites, and the Canaanites, and the Girgashites, and the Jebusites." Gen 15:18–21

Jews are descended from Isaac. Since Abraham's wife Sarah was barren, she gave Hagar, her Egyptian handmaiden to Abraham to conceive a child, Ishmael:

"Now Sarai Abram's wife bare him no children: and she had an handmaid, an Egyptian, whose name was Hagar. And Sarai said unto Abram, Behold now, the Lord hath restrained me from bearing: I pray thee, go in unto my maid; it may be that I may obtain children by her. And Abram hearkened to the voice of Sarai. And Sarai Abram's wife took Hagar her maid the Egyptian, after Abram had dwelt ten years in the land of Canaan, and gave her to her husband Abram to be his wife. And he went in unto Hagar, and she conceived." Gen 16:1–4

Later, Sarah goes on to have her own child, Isaac:

"And God said, Sarah thy wife shall bear thee a son indeed; and thou shalt call his name Isaac: and I will establish my covenant with him for an everlasting covenant, and with his seed after him. And as for Ishmael, I have heard thee: Behold, I have blessed him, and will make him fruitful, and will multiply him exceedingly; twelve princes shall he beget, and I will make him a great nation. But my covenant will I establish with Isaac, which Sarah shall bear unto thee at this set time in the next year." Gen 17:19-21

Isaac becomes the father of Esau and Jacob. Esau was the ancestor of the Edomites, while Jacob was the ancestor of the Israelites. All twelve tribes of Israel come from the twelve sons of Jacob. Our Creator made the covenant with the Jews, not the Arabs, 4,000 years ago.

"And I will give unto thee, and to thy seed after thee, the land wherein thou art a stranger, all the land of Canaan, for an everlasting possession; and I will be their God." Gen 17:8

It's for the above reason I was ticked off while discussing a potential tour in Jerusalem, covering the Israel/Palestine conflict. It'd been recommended to me by an acquaintance after telling him I wanted to understand the conflict. Dubious, I told him I'd ask the facilitators a question about the tour. Their answer would determine whether I'd participate or not.

When I asked, "How far back do you go? Do you only go as far back as the Balfour Declaration, (which occurred in 1917, during WWI), or do you go back to when the land was promised to Abraham by our Creator, 4,000 years ago?"

"No, we only go back as far as the Belfour Declaration."

I was incredulous, "How can you possibly expect people to understand the conflict when you only talk about the tip of the iceberg, and ignore the rest!?" They gave me a blank look. Unfortunately, anyone attending that tour is going to receive a flawed, biased presentation. For that reason, and coupled with the propaganda machine of the household idiot box, it's little wonder people are swayed to the wrong position on the matter.

Fingerprints of God

CREATION is proof of a Creator. Open your eyes and mind and you'll see His Creation is covered with His fingerprints. Slice a carrot in half. Do you see similarity with the human eye? Surely, you're aware of carrots being beneficial for eyesight? Do you think it's coincidence? Beta-carotene is a substance found in carrots which the body converts to vitamin A, an essential nutrient for the health of eyes.

Walnuts resemble a human brain. Plaques linked with Alzheimer's disease are broken down with walnut extract.

Slice a mushroom in half and it resembles the shape of a human ear. Mushroom consumption is beneficial for hearing. Packed with vitamin D, they're instrumental in maintaining the three bones of the inner ear. Nerve transmissions that convey sound to the brain are assisted by vitamin D. These similarities are not coincidences. You're looking at the signature of our Creator, while also seeing a glimpse of His sense of humour.

Chambers of a human heart resemble a sliced tomato. Lycopene, an antioxidant, fights several cancers and heart disease and is responsible for the tomato's colour, the same pigment as human hearts.

Almonds are eye-shaped and contain vitamin E, which prevents macular degeneration as well as cataracts.

Sliced onions resemble the cell. Removing waste from every human cell, they're known as, the 'bushman's orange'.

Do you believe this is a coincidence resulting from unguided causes? Isn't it more likely it's our Creator's signature? Perhaps a revelation of His sense of humour? Do you have a sense of humour? How, why, did that evolve? Our Creator claims we're made in His image.

Contemplate the shape of kidneys and aptly named kidney beans, which heal and help maintain kidney function.

How about similarities between bones, rhubarb, bok choy and celery? Celery is full of Vitamin K, crucial for building bone on a cellular level by regulating calcium levels and removing old bone, making way for new bone cells. Celery and bones are both twenty-three per cent sodium. If you don't have enough sodium, it's taken from bones, weakening them.

Root ginger, used as a remedy for travel sickness and upset stomachs, is shaped like a stomach.

Sweet potatoes resemble the pancreas and boost their function while reducing propensity to pancreatic cancer.

Avocados are known as 'fertility fruit', containing minerals essential for reproductive health. They resemble a uterus, with the seed resembling a baby in the womb.

Bananas resemble a smile and encourage serotonin production, the hormone of satisfaction. They're high in magnesium, a mood-booster. They're handy for ripening fruit, due to the gas they release. I often use them to ripen avocadoes. If you're in a hurry, place the unripened fruit in a paper bag with a banana—just grab a mushroom bag while you're shopping. We share over fifty per cent of our DNA with bananas, chickens and fruit flies. Do you think this proves humans are evolved bananas, chickens and fruit flies? If not, why not?

Grapes resemble lung alveoli. Emphysema and lung cancer are reduced by grape consumption. Asthma severity is reduced by a chemical contained in grape seeds. Blood resembles grape juice which decreases blood clot risk and maintains blood pressure and cholesterol levels.

Broccoli resembles lungs and contains a compound that boosts gene activity in lung cells, protecting them from damage caused by smoking and pollution.

Tree branches are similar in structure to lungs. Trees are the lungs of Earth. Tree roots are also similar to veins; the finer ends are similar to capillaries. The signature of our Creator's design doesn't stop there. Consider the similarity between the loops, arches and whorls on a tree stump, compared with your fingerprints. Fingerprints reek of uniqueness and design.

Similarity between food and its associated benefits to bodily organs is evidence of God's handiwork. They're covered with His fingerprints. His signature, if you will.

Brains Are Evolved Walnuts

Evolutionism believers point to similarities between apes and humans, insisting it proves 'common descent'. They insist since we appear similar to apes in some ways, it proves we evolved from them. Using their logic, one would have to conclude the human brain evolved from a walnut, kidneys evolved from kidney beans, hearts evolved from tomatoes, ears evolved from sliced mushrooms and fingerprints evolved from trees. Or even, 'potatoes have skin, we have skin, therefore we are potatoes'. That'd be the natural conclusion of their established thought processes.

Rather than 'common descent', this similarity denotes a 'common Designer', with an element of humour thrown in. This harmonises with science, logic and common sense.

Instinct

Instinctual behaviour isn't learnt or practised. How did birds learn to fly south before winter? The first bird would've frozen. So too, would subsequent birds. How does a caterpillar know it has to make a cocoon, let alone, how to make a cocoon? How did it learn to fly? These capabilities have been hard-wired into the brains of these creatures. Who was the Electrician/Engineer?

How did the mechanisms to spin spider webs evolve? How do spiders *know* to spin webs? How did they *learn* to spin webs? When they do, how do they achieve such stunning designs? Why do baby sea turtles head into the ocean, instead of inland? After all, they were born on land. Imagine if animals born on land, headed for the oceans.

Unlike all birds which use body heat for incubation, bush turkeys build incubators from leaf litter. After testing heat generation, eggs are laid and the female leaves indefinitely. The male ensures the heat remains at thirty-four degrees Celsius by adding or removing vegetation. Precision is required. How could this process have evolved?

Humans point to minuscule insects' brains, implying relative stupidity. Using the same logic, they'd have to conclude computer power in their mobile phones is inferior to computers of yesteryear.

Lifespans of monarch butterflies are so short they never complete the full migration route from Canada to Mexico and back again. However, butterflies that arrive in Mexico know to turn around and start heading north again. How did this evolve?

Chicken eggshells contain numerous holes invisible to the human eye until placed in warm water. These enable the chick to breathe and expel waste. After five days blood vessels have grown and attached to the cell membrane. Another vessel attaches to the yolk, the food source. By day nineteen a bump has grown on the end of its beak. Using this, the chick breaks into the air sack. Instinctively knowing he now only has six hours air supply; he immediately begins breaking a hole in the shell.

He emerges on the twenty-first day. The whole process unfolds like clockwork. If not, at any point along the way, he's dead. How could this process have evolved? How could the required instinct have evolved?

Biomimicry

This is a science that copies Intelligent Design in nature. Credited with the creation of the world's first motor-operated aeroplane, the Wright brothers had studied pigeons to understand the physics of staying aloft.

Helicopters were designed to mimic dragonflies, capable of flying in any direction or hovering. Dragonflies twist their wings at different angles allowing them to rapidly alter direction. This ability is also incorporated into the design of wind turbines and propellers.

Miniature spy planes have wings modelled after bats.

B-2 bombers are fashioned after the aerodynamic design of falcons.

Abalone makes ceramics five times stronger than ours, without using a kiln and only using seawater. Scientists are endeavouring to duplicate this advanced technology.

Swimming in schools, fish create spirals in the water, propelling them forward. After studying this, vertical-axis wind turbines are now installed close together, increasing power tenfold. When designing wind turbines, it was assumed smooth blades would reduce drag and increase lift. After observing bumps on humpback whale flippers, similar features were incorporated into turbine blades, improving stability and durability, while simultaneously reducing noise.

Mussels adhere to immovable objects via sticky fibres, preventing them from being swept away by currents or tidal action. They're being studied for the development of glue capable of withstanding wet conditions.

Japanese high-speed 'bullet' trains produced sonic booms exiting tunnels in the early days of their development. Turning to the wisdom of our Creator, it was discovered the design of a kingfisher's beak causes minimal sound and disturbance when diving through water. Designing the train in similar fashion, sonic boom was eliminated.

Urban planners in Japan studied slime mould growth to devise efficient and cost-effective road and rail systems.

Early LED light development was hampered by light being reflected backwards, reducing lighting efficiency. After analysing fireflies and incorporating the research back into LEDs, lighting was enhanced by over fifty per cent.

Elephant trunks comprise 40,000 muscles but no bones. These advanced mechanics are being incorporated into the design of robotic arms.

Spiders are studied to develop robotics, especially in off-road applications, due to their balancing ability on moving surfaces. Spider web is five times stronger than steel, on a weight-by-weight comparison. They're being utilised in roof construction design due to their lightness, strength, elasticity and ability for shock absorption. Bulletproof vests, surgical tape, ropes, nets, parachutes and artificial tendons are incorporating spider web technology.

Sonar was developed after studying dolphins. Submarines were inspired by whales for a host of reasons, though mainly for their functional and aesthetic attributes. During both world wars, whales were often mistaken for submarines and bombed.

Velcro was inspired by burrs sticking to a hiker's socks.

Mimicking miniature hairs on gecko feet enables robots to climb smooth, vertical surfaces. These hairs were incorporated into a super-adhesive tape design.

Termite nests are studied to improve the air conditioning inside of skyscrapers and the sea sponges' design is being utilised for improving ventilation in large buildings.

Light-refracting technology gives colourful iridescence to otherwise drab butterfly wings. Clothing manufacturers are endeavouring to replicate this technology to reduce the use of dyes, a major pollutant.

Dirt and water-repelling paint was inspired by the lotus plant. The texture of its leaves prevents dirt from sticking.

Scientists are attempting to produce a material that copies the squid's ability to absorb and reflect light at different wavelengths rendering it invisible, despite the changing environments it travels through. Military camouflage is often overlooked when thinking of biomimicry.

Olympic swimmers have clothing modelled after shark skin, reducing drag. Basking sharks don't move much, yet don't attract barnacles. They're studied for design innovations to prevent barnacles from sticking to ships' hulls.

Bird skulls inspire stronger and lighter building materials. Shock absorption capabilities of woodpeckers are studied for flight recording black box design.

Durable and light aerospace materials are inspired by impact-resistant surfaces of human teeth.

Concrete manufacture creates carbon dioxide, whereas coral makes its structure by utilising this waste product. Engineers are keen to duplicate the technology of coral, enabling us to substitute waste material as a raw building product.

Cats' eyes reflect light at night. This technology was copied and utilised in reflective light studs, colloquially called 'cat's eyes', installed on roads.

Drones copy the albatross design for fixed-winged models, enabling them to fly internationally without stopping.

Parasitic worms have inspired a new design for a microneedle to attach skin grafts. They're three times stronger than current methods and greatly reduce soft tissue damage.

Mosquitos occasionally feast on you incognito, due to the intelligent design of the proboscis. Comprising moving parts and slightly vibrating, it lessens the pain of insertion. The medical industry is developing needles that copy this superior technology. Surprisingly, only female mosquitos draw blood as it's required for them to be able to produce eggs. How do they know they're required to do that? How could this knowledge have 'evolved'?

If Evolutionism is true, why are we exhausting all of our time, money, resources, knowledge and intelligence, trying to attain a level that was allegedly achieved by purposeless, unguided, random, accidental copying mistakes?

Beauty

Only a Designer can add beauty for the sake of beauty. In contrast, Evolutionism has no random mechanism to explain how beauty could evolve, for beauty's sake. Beauty in Creation, such as flowers, sunsets and animal markings is evidence for a Creator.

Peacock feathers are brown. The dazzling colours and patterns are achieved through light refraction, known as iridescence. Atheists would have you believe the peacock feather is a 'frayed dinosaur scale'. How could the ornate display of a peacock's tail have evolved? Besides asking yourself "How?" ask yourself, "Why?" Then ask yourself, "What's more likely? The peacock tail randomly evolved over 'millions of years', or was it purposely designed and created by a Supreme Intelligent Being?"

It's little wonder Darwin said, "The sight of a feather in a peacock's tail, whenever I gaze at it, makes me sick." (Letter to Asa Gray, 3 April 1860, Darwin Correspondence Project, darwinproject.ac.uk)

"Fair Go Mate"

As with humans, animals have senses of fairness, humour, empathy, justice, guilt, shame, embarrassment and other complex emotions.

Our two cats were having a stand-off near the pool, much to the amusement of nearby kookaburras. One ran at the other, ending up in the pool. Immediately the air rang with peals of laughter. Emerging sheepishly from the pool, looking like a drowned rat, embarrassment was apparent in the cat's eyes.

An injured dingo pup was cared for by my sister and finally returned to the wild. Years later it returned with pups of its own. No doubt thanking my sister, as well as showing her pups the human who'd assisted her.

When my uncle was ten, he'd ridden a mare after inadequately fastening the saddle strap, causing the horse severe chaffing. The next day my uncle was leading the mare's stallion, which directed him slightly away from the usual route. Although my uncle thought it strange, he gave it no more thought—until he'd been brushed up against the notorious stinging tree. The pain is so unbearable, victims have been known to commit suicide. There's no doubt in my uncle's mind this was done intentionally, as a form of 'horse payback'.

Many animals including giraffes, magpies, foxes, elephants and gorillas hold funerals. Why? It wouldn't surprise me to learn that all animals do, to some degree. Whenever I was upset as a child, my dog would seek me out, move close and quietly look at me with sorrowful eyes.

Dogs are notorious for conveying guilt. You'll often realise there's a problem, before you discover the problem, due to their behaviour and expressions.

Golden Ratio

All beauty stems from mathematics. It's been said that beauty is symmetry. This is exemplified within the Golden Ratio. This ratio has been discovered within the blueprint of everything within the universe. From plants, to animals and snowflakes. It's a fingerprint of our Grand Designer.

Fingerprints help us discover the identity of the one it belongs to. Our Creator's fingerprints are visible within the beauty and symmetry of a peacock's tail, or the pattern of a sunflower's seeds. Similarities between His creations, such as chimps and humans, bear His signature.

Platypus

Platypuses are a combination of reptile, bird and mammal. They're duck-billed, beaver-tailed, otter-footed and egg-laying aquatic animals. They sweat milk, have venomous spurs and are covered with waterproof fur. They're one of only two mammals that lays eggs, instead of giving birth to live babies—the echidna is the other.

While demonstrating similar design, the mishmashed platypus also demonstrates our Designer's sense of humour.

They share over eighty per cent of their genes with humans, mice, dogs and chickens.

Strangely, Evolutionism believers think the platypus proves Evolutionism. It's not transitional. It's completely fully-formed. All fossils are identical to living specimens.

Biblical Roots of Science

IT'S amusing when Evolutionism believers refer to science in an apparent attempt to discredit the Bible. Without a Biblical worldview, there cannot be modern science. Remember, we previously discussed that Evolutionism's creation story is that of an uncaused, random explosion/expansion of 'nothing', producing 'everything'. There's no order, no structure, no design. Or, as Richard Dawkins himself puts it, "No design, no purpose, nothing but pitiless indifference."

In a chaotic, erratic environment such as that, established laws aren't possible. Therefore, repeatable experiments couldn't work. Repeating the same experiment would only ever produce random, differing outcomes. Nothing could ever be proved. Thoughts could only ever be irrational, random explosions of chemicals inside someone's mind. Instead of rising in the east, one day the sun would rise in the north, west, or not at all. Navigating by celestial bodies would be impossible. Attempting to boil an egg would be an exercise in frustration, as the boiling point of water would perpetually fluctuate.

Scientific Method

Science means 'knowledge', obtained from the scientific method pioneered by Galileo, a devout Christian and 'Father of modern science'. The scientific method requires theories to be:

1. Testable (experimentation).
2. Observable.
3. Repeatable.

The scientific method necessitates an orderly, structured universe created by a rational, intelligent, Supreme Being, which provides an environment for consistent, unchanging laws.

Due to men believing the Bible and knowing the universe was created, they realised there must be laws that govern this Creation. They went in search of these laws. This search came to be known as, 'science'. Prominent forefathers of modern science were Bible believers. Science historians have credited the Judeo-Christian worldview as being instrumental in the creation and establishment of science in the West. Thank God for science—literally.

Although Egyptians, Chinese, Greeks, Indians and Arabs had some vestiges of science, it quickly dissipated. If modern science had originated from these cultures, it would've been expected. After all, look at the amazing pyramids of Egypt. The Chinese invented gunpowder and the compass. Arabs invented the crank, eventually leading to the development of bicycles and cars. Aristotle, a Greek philosopher, was considered the father of Natural History. This was concerned with observation, rather than with experimentation. Indians have been credited with advanced agricultural innovations.

Instead of science arising from these advanced cultures, science was birthed from the Christian environment of Europe during the 1600s.

Unlike Christian cultures, these civilisations denied the reality of an orderly universe governed by natural laws. Instead, they believed in an angry, random, chaotic universe, at whim to conflicting emotions of numerous gods who they believed governed nature. They didn't investigate natural laws as, unlike Bible believers, they didn't believe there were any. As the Judeo-Christian worldview spread, it eradicated Pagan beliefs about the universe which had hindered science's development. Pagans believe the Creation itself is a god, commonly referred to and revered by Atheists and Evolutionism believers as, 'Mother Nature'.

"Sometimes people ask if religion and science are not opposed to one another. They are: in the sense that the thumb and fingers of my hands are opposed to one another. It is an opposition by means of which anything can be grasped." (Sir William Bragg, winner of the Noble Prize for Physics 1915)

Sir Isaac Newton

"Mathematical physicist Stephen Hawking said Newton was a 'Colossus without parallel in the history of science'." (Charles E. Hummel, 'The Faith Behind the Famous: Isaac Newton', christianhistoryinstitute.org) Newton often wrote papers refuting Atheism, while simultaneously defending Scripture, "In the absence of any other proof, the thumb alone would convince me of God's existence." (Sir Isaac Newton)

My logic meter explodes whenever Evolutionism believers attempt to imply that with Science and God, it is one or the other. They're not mutually exclusive. You simply cannot have one without the other. Newton invested more hours into theology than into science, yet became one of the leading mathematicians and scientists in Europe, proving nature was governed by mathematical laws. Laws require a Law-giver.

Tipping Point

THIS book of my testimony is two books in one. Or more accurately, two parts, in much the same way the Bible is comprised of the Old and New Testaments.

Interestingly, the Jews' Bible is only comprised of the Old Testament. It's not uncommon for many Christians to only read the New Testament. Do you recall my grade four religion teacher telling me the Old Testament was obsolete? Some 'Bibles' only contain the New Testament.

As with the Biblical Old and New Testaments, both parts of this book stand alone, though are undeniably linked. While the first part of my book deals more with doctrinal matters, this upcoming second part deals with Creation vs Evolutionism. This debate is at the crux of the big questions in life—Why are we here? What happens after death? Is there a God?

I encourage you to read part two with an open mind. Question everything, including your own beliefs, ensuring to leave emotions by the wayside. Do your own research.

Part Two

The New 'Testimony'

Everyone Is Religious

TIME, and time again, I'll hear someone proclaim, "I'm not religious."

Those with a superior, pious tone, believe they're saying, "I'm intelligent, I believe in science, I'm too clever to be deceived by fanciful fairy tales."

"Everyone is religious," I state calmly.

They're quick to reiterate, emphatically reassuring me they don't believe in any religion.

"Yes, you do. It's like this, either way, regardless of what you believe, you only have two choices." I pause, looking them in the eye. "Either you believe a Supreme Intelligent Being created the universe and everything in it; or an explosion/expansion of 'nothing', caused by 'nothing', for 'no reason', produced 'everything'. There are no other possibilities—it's either purposeful Creation or mindless accident. Both beliefs are religious, as their foundations are based on faith. However, Intelligent Design is in harmony with the scientific method, whereas Darwinian Evolution isn't. In fact, science proves it's impossible. It's unscientific, it couldn't happen. It didn't happen."

Evolutionism's Creation Story

Once upon a time, billions of years ago, there was 'nothing'—then it exploded/expanded. Rocks miraculously appeared and were rained on, producing a primordial soup. Pond scum formed, which was struck by lightning, creating 'Frank, the Frankensteinian First cell'. This was Evolutionism's 'immaculate conception'. Frank was the ancestor of all plant, animal and human life forms. Creation has Adam in the Garden of Eden. Evolutionism has Frank in the primordial soup.

Frank evolved into 'Bazza, the Bacteria'. "For the first half of geological time our ancestors were bacteria." (Richard Dawkins)

Evolutionism decrees that over 'millions of years', bacteria evolved into worms, which evolved into fish. Some fish decide to evolve lungs and feet, abandon the ocean and evolve into dinosaurs. 'Millions of years' pass and dinosaurs are killed by an asteroid. However, some are resurrected from the dead and evolve into birds. Meanwhile, the remaining fish have evolved into wombats, elephants, mice, kangaroos, giraffes and apes.

Long ages pass once more, or 'deep time', as they love to say and some of those apes are now humans. Mind you, some of the worms in the primordial soup, instead of evolving into fish, decided to evolve into prawns, crabs and lobsters. 'Millions of years' later, these crawled out of the primordial soup and evolved into insects. Despite all of this, some bacteria, worms and fish decided to stop evolving and remain as they were.

As ridiculous as that sounds, it's the premise of Evolutionism. The difference being, they ring bells, sound whistles, throw smoke screens and just-so-stories into the mix, along with pious-sounding words, such as 'peer-reviewed', 'studies show', 'experts agree', and 'scientists say'. I've just stripped their fluff away, leaving their bare-boned beliefs.

Evolutionism believers become enraged when you summarise their creation story, "You just don't understand evolution!" The truth is, those of us who aren't devout Darwinian disciples understand their doctrines far better than they do, which is a sound reason for not believing Evolutionism.

"We are all cousins. Your family tree includes not just obvious cousins like chimpanzees and monkeys but also mice, buffaloes, iguanas, wallabies, snails, dandelions, golden eagles, mushrooms, whales, wombats, and bacteria. All are our cousins. Every last one of them." (Richard Dawkins, *The Magic of Reality: How We Know What's Really True*)

They believe all things are descended from a single original lifeform, hence Dawkins' use of the word 'cousins'. This alleged original life form emerged from primordial soup, following the alleged Big Bang/Bloat.

Are you a believer of Evolutionism? If so, heed the words of your High Priest:

"A delusion is something that people believe in despite a total lack of evidence," and, "When one person suffers from a delusion, it is called insanity. When many people suffer from a delusion it is called Religion." (Richard Dawkins, *The God Delusion*)

Big Bang/Bloat

This theory, which was once an established 'fact', started being discarded by the scientific community years ago.

Essentially, they're claiming, "Once upon a time there was nothing. Then, one day, for no reason, 'nothing' exploded/expanded, producing everything, including space, time, matter, energy, a finely tuned universe, natural laws, consciousness, intelligence, knowledge, truth, logic, emotions, morality, and 'life', itself.

Amazing! Explosions aren't renowned for creating order, they're better known for creating disorder, chaos. What's even more remarkable, they play semantics, claiming it wasn't 'nothing' that exploded/expanded, it was a 'singularity'. It's amusing when you press them for a definition of this so-called, singularity. You always end up back with, 'nothing'. It's all they ever do—talk in circles.

"A singularity refers to a place in the universe where our laws of physics simply break down. These are called singularities." (livescience.com)

If you break the laws of physics, you're not proving the universe created itself, and everything in it, you have gone outside of science and are deferring to the supernatural.

"Aliens Did It"

Invariably, in defiance of primordial soup dogma, the assertion life came from aliens, arises.

"Okay," I ask slowly, "and where did those aliens come from?"

"Other aliens!" Exclaimed triumphantly, as if they believed they had a water-tight case.

"… Okay, and where did those aliens come from?" They're about to say, "Other aliens." I speak first, "And where did those aliens come from … and so on?"

Occasionally, some cockiness will return. "Well, who created God?"

Pausing for emphasis, "Nobody."

There's that stunned-mullet look again, "He can't come from nowhere!"

Shaking my head, "Our Creator is eternal, having always existed. The scientific law you're alluding to, is one of the scientific laws He put in place to govern His physical Creation. As such, He's not bound by the very laws He created. He's independent of them."

While they mistakenly insist our Creator must come from something, they refuse to grasp their creation story claims they arose from an uncaused, explosion/expansion of 'nothing'.

Spontaneous Generation (Abiogenesis)

"The belief that life on Earth arose spontaneously from non-living matter, is simply a matter of faith in strict reductionism and is based entirely on ideology." (Hubert P. Yockey, evolutionist, PhD physicist, 1992, *Information Theory and Molecular Biology*, p. 284, Cambridge University Press, UK)

Big Bangers/Bloaters have to account for the existence of life. The majority mistakenly believe this has nothing to do with Evolutionism. It has everything to do with it. Those who understand the absurdity of abiogenesis attempt to distance their religion from it.

Evolutionism High Priest PZ Myers, associate professor of biology at the University of Minnesota Morris, admits, "I know many people like to recite the mantra that abiogenesis is not evolution, but it's a cop-out." (Vincent Torley, 2014, 'PZ Myers: "Abiogenesis is not evolution" is a cop-out,' uncommondescent.com)

If you believe evolutionism's doctrine, 'life is chemistry', you cannot insist evolution is isolated from the question of how life originated. Regardless, laws of physics and chemistry do not permit life to arise from non-life.

Abiogenesis was widely accepted by the scientific community at the same time Charles Darwin penned Evolutionism's 'Holy Scriptures', *On the Origin of Species*. It's the belief non-living matter can produce living organisms. After all, flies were observed to have evolved from maggots, and maggots had been seen to evolve from decomposing meat. Fleas appeared to have evolved from dust. Mice were observed to have evolved from damp wheat. Following heavy rain, large numbers of frogs, beetles and worms suddenly appeared. Obviously, they'd evolved from mud.

You think I'm joking, don't you? I'm not. These beliefs were considered scientific facts for 2,000 years.

Aristotle

Aristotle, ancient Greek philosopher and scientist, believed oysters had evolved from slime, barnacles evolved from rock crevices and scallops evolved from sand.

Louis Pasteur

Following the publication of Darwin's book, Louis Pasteur a French chemist and microbiologist, conducted experiments proving fermentation and disease were caused by microorganisms and initiated the process of pasteurisation. If you've wondered what pasteurised milk meant, you should now have a pretty good idea. His experiments confirmed the existence of microscopic germs, resulting in hand-washing becoming an accepted medical practice.

Most significantly, using the scientific method, Pasteur proved life cannot arise from non-living matter. Evolutionism demands it can. Intelligent Designers don't have this problem. Life ensues from our Creator, who is eternal. While science cannot disprove the Intelligent Designers' claim, it does disprove Evolutionism's claim. We admit our beliefs are based on faith; they refuse to admit theirs are too.

"Spontaneous generation was scientifically disproved 100 years ago by Louis Pasteur, Spallanzani, Reddy and others. That leads us scientifically to only one possible conclusion—that life arose as a supernatural creative act of God ... I will not accept that philosophically because **I do not want to believe in God. Therefore, I choose to believe in that which I know is scientifically impossible, spontaneous generation arising to evolution.**" (George Wald, 'The Origin of Life,' 1954, *Scientific American*, scientificamerican.com)

Contrast that blatant admission with this one:

"The more I study nature, the more I stand amazed at the work of the Creator. Science brings men nearer to God." (Louis Pasteur)

Darwin penned his book at a time when the scientific community believed mice evolved from sawdust or damp wheat, and flies evolved from rotting meat. Five years after the publication of *Origin of Species*, Pasteur's experiments destroyed that belief. Or should have, as abiogenesis is foundational to Evolutionism dogma—the religious belief that life can arise from non-living matter.

Everything required for life can be found within a dead body. If Evolutionism was true, why aren't the dead rising from their graves? How could pond scum suddenly spring to life after being struck by a bolt of lightning? If anything, lightning strikes take life, not give it.

In the Beginning

"It comes as a surprise to most people to hear that there is abundant evidence that the entire human race came from two people just a few thousand years ago (Adam and Eve), that there was a serious population crash (bottleneck) in the recent past (at the time of the Flood), and that there was a single dispersal of people across the world after that (the Tower of Babel). It surprises them even more to learn that much of this evidence comes from evolutionary scientists. In fact, an abundant testimony to biblical history has been uncovered by modern geneticists." (Dr Robert W. Carter, 'Adam, Eve and Noah vs Modern Genetics,' 2010, creation.com website)

You've heard the mythical Big Bang/Bloat creation story, now you'll hear the historical account of the Creation of our home. Incidentally, we've adopted the name of our home from the Bible—Earth.

Science says everything in the universe consists of just four elements: Time, Energy, Space and Matter. What does the very first verse of the Bible say? The same thing:

"In the beginning (time), God (energy), created the heaven (space), and the earth (matter)." Gen 1:1

How could Atheists possibly explain this, if not inspired by our Creator? Coincidence? Really? While it may seem like an interesting observation, it's much more than that. Think about what you've just read. Yet, you'll still have dullards claim the Bible was 'written' by 'illiterate' goat-herders.

Science has discovered all elements which make up the human body are found in the dust of the earth.

"And the Lord God formed man of the dust of the ground, and breathed into his nostrils the breath of life; and man became a living soul." Gen 2:7

You'll notice, life arose from life, our living, eternal Creator. Evolutionism states life can arise from non-living matter. Science says it can't.

"And the Lord God said, It is not good that the man should be alone; I will make him an help meet for him. And out of the ground the Lord God formed every beast of the field, and every fowl of the air; and brought them unto Adam to see what he would call them: and whatsoever Adam called every living creature, that was the name thereof. And Adam gave names to all cattle, and to the fowl of the air, and to every beast of the field; but for Adam there was not found an help meet for him. And the Lord God caused a deep sleep to fall upon Adam, and he slept: and he took one of his ribs, and closed up the flesh instead thereof." Gen 2:18–21

"So God created man in his own image, in the image of God created he him; male and female created he them." Gen 1:27

Memorial To Creation

Following the six days of Creation, came a Sabbath rest:

"And on the seventh day God ended his work which he had made; and he rested on the seventh day from all his work which he had made. And God blessed the seventh day, and sanctified it." Gen 2:2–3

For this reason, when we observe the seventh-day Sabbath, resting from our labours, we're following the example of our Creator. It's a holy day, a weekly memorial to His Creation.

Spare Ribs

If carefully removed, the rib is the only bone in the human body that will grow back. How do you suppose alleged 'illiterate goatherders from thousands of years ago' knew that?

First Marriage

"And the rib, which the Lord God had taken from man, made he a woman, and brought her unto the man. And Adam said, This is now bone of my bones, and flesh of my flesh: she shall be called Woman, because she was taken out of Man. Therefore shall a man leave his father and his mother, and shall cleave unto his wife: and they shall be one flesh." Gen 2:22–24

That ceremony in the Garden of Eden was the marriage of our direct ancestors, Adam and Eve.

It astounds me that I have to say this—There are only two genders, male, and female. If a man wants to pretend, he's a woman, that's up to him. If he wants us to pretend he's a woman, that's up to us. Painting stripes on a cow doesn't make it a zebra, just like putting makeup and a dress on a man, doesn't make him a woman. Yahshua affirms the validity of Genesis, Creation, two genders and Marriage:

"But from the beginning of the creation God made them male and female. For this cause shall a man leave his father and mother, and cleave to his wife; And they twain shall be one flesh: so then they are no more twain, but one flesh. What therefore God hath joined together, let not man put asunder." Mark 10:6–9

Since God created marriage, He gets to define it. Marriage is a God-ordained, covenant relationship between one man with one woman. No more, no less. Anything other than this is not a marriage. It astounds me the number of people who profess to not believe in the Bible, yet still demand to participate in the Biblical act of marriage.

You may declare a hammer is no longer a hammer, that it is now a screwdriver. Regardless, it does not change the fact that it's still a hammer. You may get people to agree with you. It still doesn't change the fact. You may, in your anger and frustration, hold a gun to someone's head and demand they say the hammer is not a hammer, but a screwdriver. Still, that does not change the fact that a hammer is still a hammer and not a screwdriver.

Likewise, marriage, no matter what anyone says, will always be, one man with one woman. God's Law is higher than man's law. He's the final authority. For far too many, they'll realise the truth of this when it's too late. Do not be one of them.

Where Did Cain Get His Wife?

Ignoramuses allude to the verses regarding the births of Cain and Abel, ignorantly implying the Bible is false, as the brothers couldn't have fathered children by themselves:

"Adam knew Eve his wife; and she conceived, and bare Cain, and said, I have gotten a man from the Lord. And she again bare his brother Abel." Gen 4:1–2

They stop reading, believing they've destroyed the Bible's authenticity. They then evangelise their assumptions all over the internet. Devout Darwinian disciples lap it up, oblivious to what's recorded in the very next chapter:

"And the days of Adam after he had begotten Seth were eight hundred years: and he begat sons and daughters." Gen 5:4

There you have it!

Encountering a woman who gave 'Cain's wife' as her reason for not believing the Bible. I asked, "If I was able to show you, using the Bible, that your assumption is wrong, would you be willing to reconsider your belief in the Bible's integrity?"

You already know the answer.

While there are some who are ignorant on this subject, I've encountered several who know the truth, yet still propagate the lie. While 'bearing false witness' is sinful under Judeo-Christian Law, it's considered a virtue in Atheistic religions.

Objective or Subjective Truth?

Subjective truth is a truth based on a person's emotions, opinions, feelings or perspective. Whereas, objective truth is the opposite, based on natural laws. At Creation, physical (scientific) laws, were put in place to govern His physical Creation, while spiritual Laws (Ten Commandments), were put in place to govern His spiritual Creation—us. These laws are what's known loosely as 'morality'. The Ten Commandments are foundational to all Western law.

Ancient Knowledge

Evolutionism teaches life starts out simple, becoming complex over time. The Bible and the Second Law of Thermodynamics state the opposite. Everything in nature is wearing out, breaking down. Believers of Evolutionism are left gasping for breath like an 'evolving' fish out of water, trying to explain how glorified apes built the pyramids and other ancient structures.

Aware that their creation story is pure nonsense, when pressed for an explanation they'll say with a straight face, "Aliens did it." They're forced to assume the technology came from another world. Hence, their belief in little green men with rubber pyjamas in flying machines. On the other hand, history and common sense say otherwise. The Bible indicates we were created perfect, intelligent, and over the centuries, we've lost knowledge.

Man is a designed, created, living, replicating, complex machine with the breath of life and a soul:

"And the LORD God formed man of the dust of the ground, and breathed into his nostrils the breath of life; and man became a living soul." Gen 2:7

Our Creator who designed and created everything, designed us in His image:

"Let us make man in our image, after our likeness." Gen 1:26

Accordingly, we were created intelligent, with language, an extensive vocabulary and wisdom:

"And out of the ground the Lord God formed every beast of the field, and every fowl of the air; and brought them unto Adam to see what he would call them: and whatsoever Adam called every living creature, that was the name thereof. And Adam gave names to all cattle, and to the fowl of the air, and to every beast of the field." Gen 2:19–20

Before the flood, man lived for long ages:

"And all the days that Adam lived were nine hundred and thirty years: and he died. And Seth lived an hundred and five years, and begat Enos: And Seth lived after he begat Enos eight hundred and seven years, and begat sons and daughters: And all the days of Seth were nine hundred and twelve years: and he died. And Enos lived ninety years, and begat Cainan: And Enos lived after he begat Cainan eight hundred and fifteen years, and begat sons and daughters: And all the days of Enos were nine hundred and five years: and he died." Gen 5:5–11

Upon the culmination of the flood, lifespans dropped:

"And the Lord said, My spirit shall not always strive with man, for that he also is flesh: yet his days shall be an hundred and twenty years." Gen 6:3

We started out complex and knowledgeable. Over time, this knowledge was lost. Especially a lot of the accumulated knowledge before the flood. Imagine being apprenticed to someone who'd mastered a trade over hundreds of years;

"She also bare Tubalcain, an instructer of every artificer in brass and iron." Gen 4:22

Or perfected playing an instrument for hundreds of years:

"And his brother's name was Jubal: he was the father of all such as handle the harp and organ." Gen 4:21

Apart from being musicians and metalworkers, early humans were builders;

"And Cain knew his wife; and she conceived, and bare Enoch: and he builded a city, and called the name of the city, after the name of his son, Enoch." Gen 4:17

And farmers:

"And Abel was a keeper of sheep, but Cain was a tiller of the ground." Gen 4:2

Self-repairing cement was used by the Romans, leading to their structures surviving for many hundreds of years. Some of their concrete has lasted over 2,000 years.

Computer technology was discovered in a sunken shipwreck off the coast of Greece which occurred well over 2,000 years ago, before the birth of Christ. 'Antikythera Mechanism' has several gears so intricate some of the teeth are one millimetre in height. You could use it to accurately calculate the sun and moon's position twenty years from now.

Are you aware of the Incan stone constructions with their obscure edges cut on a knife's edge and placed together so tightly, you cannot even slide a piece of paper between the two stones? What's even more remarkable, they do not use any mortar. It's been suggested they had stone-softening technology.

Where Did All of the Races Come From?

From the same place all of the languages came from, the Tower of Babel.

Fossils demonstrate there was an explosion of lifeforms, complex and full-formed—the Cambrian explosion. There was also a language explosion. Seemingly out of nowhere, complex languages arose across the earth 4,000 years ago. Since that time, languages have been 'de-evolving'.

Tower of Babel

Man decided to build a tower to reach Heaven 4,000 years ago:

"And the whole earth was of one language, and of one speech. And they said, Go to, let us build us a city and a tower, whose top may reach unto heaven; and let us make us a name, lest we be scattered abroad upon the face of the whole earth." Gen 11:1–4

"And the Lord came down to see the city and the tower, which the children of men builded." Gen 11:5

The Creator realised that united, they could do all they intended. To prevent this, He confounded their language. From one language, there were now several:

"And the Lord said, Behold, the people is one, and they have all one language; and this they begin to do: and now nothing will be restrained from them, which they have imagined to do. Go to, let us go down, and there confound their language, that they may not understand one another's speech. So the Lord scattered them abroad from thence upon the face of all the earth: and they left off to build the city. Therefore is the name of it called Babel; because the Lord did there confound the language of all the earth: and from thence did the Lord scatter them abroad upon the face of all the earth." Gen 11:6–9

Suddenly, people found they were no longer being understood, nor could they understand others. They began gravitating to those they could understand, and those who could understand them, since they spoke a similar language. These groups of people migrated away from the area, staying within their language groups.

It's interesting how a variety of complex languages suddenly seems to explode across the world, oral and written, around that time in history, seemingly out of nowhere.

Within time, certain dominant traits within their particular gene pools became apparent within their populations, such as short stature, dark skin, wiry hair, and various eye shapes, producing features we categorise as 'races'.

Black or White?

No human is 'black', or 'white'. All of us are a shade of brown, from the lightest skinned—to the darkest. Melanin is a bodily substance that determines the shade of our skin. The more you have, coupled with exposure to sunlight, the darker you will be. Evolutionism believers use darker skin shades to deceitfully infer closer hereditary to apes, thereby propagating racism.

Blood From a Stone

Evolutionism insists you can get blood from a stone. And not just blood, but hearts, lungs, bones, teeth, brains and eyes—you just have to add two things, imagination and the mythical 'millions of years'.

Intelligent Designers believe all breeds of dogs arose from an original dog kind aboard the Ark. They possessed all of the genetic information required to facilitate the variety of dog breeds today. Atheists believe dogs originated from 'rain on a rock'.

You know that sound an Evolutionism believer makes when he's trying to evangelise? It's called babbling. It's derived from the historical event of the Tower of Babel.

Bait-and-Switch

"EVOLUTION is a religion. This was true of evolution in the beginning, and it is true of evolution still today." (Michael Ruse, Evolutionism High Priest)

Believers are somewhat tolerable about debates, providing you don't insist they state 'evolution's' definition up front. They won't tolerate any inclination against their sacred cow, that of the 'millions of years' doctrine.

When using the word 'evolution', it's important to know there are six meanings attributed to this word, formulated by Kent Hovind, American minister.

1. **Cosmic Evolution:** The origin of time, space, and matter from 'nothing' in the alleged Big Bang/Bloat.
2. **Chemical Evolution:** All elements evolved from hydrogen.
3. **Stellar Evolution:** The origin of stars and planets.
4. **Organic Evolution:** The origin of life.
5. **Macroevolution:** Animals change from one kind of animal into another.
6. **Microevolution:** Variations within the particular animal kind.

Of these six definitions, only one passes the criteria for the scientific method—microevolution. In that, it must be observable, testable, and repeatable. The remaining five are science fiction, fantasy.

When people talk about 'evolution', they're predominantly referring to the fifth type, 'macroevolution'. This entails dinosaurs evolving into birds, apes evolving into humans and whales evolving into bears. When you tell them 'evolution' is anti-science, they'll point to microevolution, variety within an animal kind, such as the 400 varieties that make up the dog kind. Or, they'll imply the variety of differently-shaped finch beaks 'prove' finches evolved from primordial soup. In other words, according to their beliefs, the great diversity within the dog 'kind', coupled with finch beaks slightly altering shape, 'proves' dinosaurs evolved into birds, apes evolved into humans and whales evolved into bears.

Bait-and-Switch

This trick, utilised by deceptive, manipulating salesmen is also employed by Evolutionism believers. They'll claim 'evolution' is true, deceitfully inferring that all six definitions are true. They become furious when you point out that *micro*evolution and *macro*evolution are separate and that only microevolution is true. This truth demolishes their house of cards. Further, they try to distance 'evolution' from the remaining definitions. Especially 'organic evolution'—the origin of life. Deep down, they know science, logic and common sense doesn't allow life from non-living matter.

I'll ask them to provide just one example of observable Darwinian Evolutionism, stipulating it must be observable, as per the scientific method. Also stipulated, proof presented must *not* be proof of the Bible. Yet, every single time they inadvertently and undeniably provide proof for the Bible—plants and animals producing after their kind:

"God made the beast of the earth after his kind, and cattle after their kind, and every thing that creepeth upon the earth after his kind: and God saw that it was good." Gen 1:25

Genesis implies dogs evolve from dogs, never from horses, cats or wombats. Grapevines will always bear grapes, never pineapples, watermelons or bananas. Microevolution is Biblical and scientific, as it can be observed.

This is in harmony with the scientific method. You can test the claim. You observe dogs giving birth to dogs and no matter how many times you repeat this observation, that's all you'll ever see. Use the scientific method against macroevolution and it falls apart. For example, Darwinian evolution insists fish evolved into whales, which later evolved into bears. Then, some bears decided to evolve back into whales. This process occurred over 'millions of years', of course. This foundational dogma of Evolutionism is pure fantasy.

Bacteria Evolution?

Invariably, they'll offer 'bacteria' as an alleged proof of Darwinian evolution.

"What have the bacteria become?" I inquire.

Usually, I'll receive a surprised look, before they answer in a tone that suggests *I'm* the idiot, "Bacteria!"

Patiently, I explain, "Bacteria, evolving into bacteria, is *not* Darwinian evolutionism, it is micro, *not* macro, evolution." Once again, I've been presented with Biblical evidence—plants and animals producing after their kind:

"And the earth brought forth grass, and herb yielding seed after his kind, and the tree yielding fruit, whose seed was in itself, after his kind: and God saw that it was good." Gen 1:12

"And God said, 'Let the land produce living creatures according to their kinds: the livestock, the creatures that move along the ground, and the wild animals, each according to its kind'. And it was so." Gen 1:24

When a believer offers bacteria as proof of Evolutionism, they're offering proof of the Bible, despite being explicitly told not to. What's more concerning, once I patiently spell it out for them, they still don't get it. It's as if they've turned off their brain. Proof for

Darwinian Evolution would be on the scale of a dog evolving into a horse, mouse, cat, or any creature, other than a dog.

Those for whom the pin drops, may suggest the fanciful Evolutionism doctrine of dinosaurs evolving into birds, "The closest living relatives of Tyrannosaurus rex are birds such as chickens and ostriches, according to research published today in Science." (Hugh Powell, 'T. Rex Linked to Chickens, Ostriches,' 2008, *Smithsonian Magazine*)

It seems they don't understand the concept of 'observable', as demanded by the scientific method. Since a dinosaur cannot be observed evolving into a bird, we're forced to believe by faith—blind faith.

"Faith is the great cop-out, the great excuse to evade the need to think and evaluate evidence. Faith is the belief in spite of, even perhaps because of, the lack of evidence." (Richard Dawkins)

Dawkins Admits He's Deluded

"Evolution has been observed. It's just that it hasn't been observed while it's happening" and "Faith is belief without evidence and reason; coincidentally that's also the definition of delusion." (Richard Dawkins)

What's even more remarkable about bacteria being continually offered as proof for Darwinian Evolution, its believers claim bacteria were the geneses of all life forms, eventually evolving into dinosaurs, humans, mushrooms, wombats, daffodils, mice, pelicans and giraffes, while at the same time, remaining as bacteria.

Bacteria produce a new generation every thirty minutes. Imagine that! A new generation, every thirty minutes, for an alleged two billion years, yet it's still bacteria! Where's the evolution? Proponents of Evolutionism claim that over 2 billion years, bacteria has evolved into bacteria, yet, within the same timeframe, bacteria has allegedly also evolved into man. They call this nonsense 'science', and teach it to our children.

Unproved and Unprovable

"Evolution is unproved and unprovable. We believe it only because the only alternative is special creation, and that is unthinkable."— Sir Arthur Keith. He wrote the forward to the 100th anniversary edition of Darwin's *Origin of Species*. He was a conspirator in the Piltdown Man hoax, "Sir Arthur Keith, famous British palaeontologist, spent more than five years piecing together the fragments of what he called a 'remarkable' discovery." (PBS: A Science Odyssey, People and Discoveries, 1953, 'Piltdown Man is revealed as fake,' pbs.org)

Galapagos Islands

On one of these islands, Darwin witnessed a population of birds, reptiles and plants differing slightly from those on the mainland. These differed again, on neighbouring islands. While he saw variety amongst kinds of animals, he was blinded to the fact any particular 'animal kind' stayed within the boundaries of that particular animal kind. For example, tortoises with a domed-shell or saddle-shell, were still tortoises.

Darwin's Finches

Another observation became a revered doctrine I'm sure you've heard of; that of 'finch beaks'. Grade eight science class introduced me to this dogma. Darwin observed Galapagos Island finches had differently shaped beaks to mainland finches. Believers insinuate finch beaks changing shape, proves humans would've been able to evolve from fish—over 'millions of years', of course.

What did the finch evolve into? Nothing, it stayed as a finch. It didn't evolve into a sparrow, toucan or eagle. Let alone, a horse, kangaroo, cat or back into a dinosaur, as per Evolutionism dogma.

Pigeon Evolution

Darwin attempted time and time again, to make pigeons breed into another kind of bird. Requiring new generations quickly, to test his beliefs, he chose pigeons since they breed well in captivity.

Pigeons with different coloured feathers were all he managed to produce. Some were brown, some white. Some had shorter beaks, some had longer legs. They were still pigeons. Intending to prove Evolutionism, he inadvertently proved the Bible.

"And God created great whales, and every living creature that moveth, which the waters brought forth abundantly, after their kind, and every winged fowl after his kind." Gen 1:21

Pigeon breeding was a craze across the world at the time. With all the breeding, all those generations, even incorporating human influence and engineering, no other type of bird was produced; let alone, animal. It stayed as a pigeon.

Darwin reluctantly concurred with scientists—all varieties of pigeons descended from the rock pigeon. These may be the original type of pigeon which contained genetic material to account for all variations within the entire population of any subsequent generation.

Pathetic Proofs

Over the years, devout atheists have sent me what they perceive to be conclusive proof for Darwinian evolution. By doing so, they prove they don't understand their own dogma. They'll point to dogs who escape to the wild becoming more wolf-like. *Yeah, so what?* Wolves, coyotes, dingoes, Chihuahuas and Rottweilers are all dogs. They haven't become a different kind of animal, despite the extreme variety within the dog kind. That is microevolution, not macroevolution. It's not Darwinian evolution.

Another example are cats. Persians, silver tabbies, lions, tortoise-shells, panthers, jaguars, cheetahs, pumas, leopards, and tigers are all cats. Blind Freddy can see that. Evolutionism believers can't.

Here's another pearler, "Elephants are evolving without tusks, to avoid being killed by ivory poachers." Evolutionism believers are so busy trying to force square pegs into round holes, that they cannot see the wood, for the trees. Firstly, losing the ability to develop tusks is a *loss* of information. It's the complete opposite of what their religious beliefs demand. Secondly, all that's happened is that the ability to grow tusks is being removed from the elephant gene pool. 'Mutant' elephants, unable to grow tusks aren't being killed. Therefore, their mutant genes are becoming dominant.

A similar fate is befalling fish. Due to laws banning the taking of undersized fish, genes enabling large sizes are being continually removed from the gene pool. Some populations, such as the Arctic cod, are now continually undersized. (David Catchpoole, 'Smaller fish to fry', *Creation Magazine*, 30(2):48–49, 2008, creation.com)

Brass Tacks

Despite the incredible variety within the dog kind, dogs are still dogs. Some Chihuahuas are smaller than cats, making them look more like a cat than a dog, when compared with Great Danes and Rottweilers. Yet, it's apparent they're still dogs. Despite the intensive breeding they've been subjected to, dogs have always been, and always will be, dogs. This is *micro*evolution. They'll never evolve into a different kind of animal, such as a giraffe, wombat or horse—*macro*evolution.

*Micro*evolution is the name for adaptation, the vast variety contained within an animal kind. Genesis describes it as 'producing after its kind'. This Biblical claim passes the scientific method, in that it can be scrutinised with testable, repeatable, and observable experiments.

Try that with Evolutionism's claims of *macro*evolution. In that, apes evolve into humans, dinosaurs evolve into birds, or crustaceans evolve into insects. Are you aware of any experiments that are testable, repeatable or observable, that prove these claims? Of course not!

Atheists will *bait* you with *micro*evolution, and try to *switch* it as *macro*evolution. They claim that there is no distinction between the two, that they are one and the same. That the great variety within the dog kind '*micro*evolution', which we can observe, proves that crabs can evolve into bees '*macro*evolution', provided we throw enough magical 'millions of years' at it.

Dogs look similar to cats—four legs, a tail, canine teeth, fur and three sets of eyelids. They can also have similar mannerisms. They like to lie in morning sun, or play with their owners. They have an acute sense of smell, night vision capabilities and both can be trained. Do you think this 'proves' cats evolved from dogs? If not, why not?

After all, Evolutionism believers apply the same logic to apes and humans. They love to emphasise the point that apes and humans have an opposable thumb. *Yeah, so?* Koalas have opposable thumbs. According to Evolutionism logic, that's proof humans evolved from koalas. What's more likely? Common ancestry, or common design?

*Macro*evolution, the engine room for Evolutionism, is a religious doctrine, believed by faith. Evolutionism and Atheism are religions, as you'll discover, in the next chapters.

DNA Death Shot

"DNA is like a computer program but far, far more advanced than any software ever created." (Bill Gates)

Really, Bill? Who was the Creator?

You can't make new proteins without DNA. Yet you can't make new DNA without proteins. The 'chicken-egg' conundrum is rife throughout Evolutionism. DNA is a code, a language. Who do you think developed this language? An Intelligent Designer/Creator, or an uncaused explosion/expansion of 'nothing'?

DNA is essentially an incredibly detailed recipe book, an instructional manual. Depending on the creature required, there are instructions on how to build scales, feathers, teeth, wings, fur, tails, etc. There's also specific information for details such as colouring and length of fur or hair. How can you possibly account for this, without an Intelligent Designer? Do you really believe this was accidental, the result of blind chance? Producing this information is one thing, but you also require the information to be interpreted, and then followed, accurately.

"I'm fascinated by the idea that genetics is digital. A gene is a long sequence of coded letters, like computer information. Modern biology is becoming very much a branch of information technology." (Eryn Brown, 'Q&A: Richard Dawkins discusses evolution, religion and his fans', *Los Angeles Times*, 30 November 2013)

Scientists have discovered limits within DNA. There's code within it, prohibiting the development of one kind of animal into another. Darwinian Evolution is impossible for this reason alone.

Evolutionism

EVOLUTIONISM believers define 'evolution' as simply, 'change over time'. They claim this degenerative process, entropy, which falls under the Second Law of Thermodynamics, moves organisms from simple to complex.

They mistakenly believe things breaking down, wearing out, moving toward disorder, accelerates improvements and modifications forward.

In other words, their dogma says entropy and Evolutionism can mean the same thing. Therefore, when things such as cars break down, wear and rust out, crumble and disintegrate, this is 'evolution'. It's also 'evolution' when paint peels from your house and fades from your car. They'll say those things aren't living. Therefore, Evolutionism doesn't apply to them. Well, they also claim 'rain on the rocks' became alive, eventually evolving into dogs, dinosaurs, fish and humans.

Besides, they have no problem labelling elephants losing the ability to grow tusks as 'evolution'. This is degenerative; it's a loss of genetic information. Their doctrine states that elephants chose to lose the ability to generate tusks, thereby sparing them from poachers. While this is a beautiful sentiment, it's not true. All that's happened is that the excessive killing of tusked-elephants is reducing their genetic pool. Mutations corrupt the dwindling gene pool, destroying information required for tusk development. It's the complete opposite of what Evolutionism believers so fervently want to believe.

Science shows DNA is lost in each and every generation from chemicals, mutations, radiation and genetic entropy. Evolutionism teaches the opposite, that new information is gained in every generation, becoming more complex. Hence the belief that fish evolved into humans, and dinosaurs into birds. If 'evolution' was true, reading glasses, facelifts, wigs, hearing aids and false teeth wouldn't exist. Your health would improve, as would your mental faculties over the years, as you continued to 'evolve'. Atheists would have you believe this inevitable, degenerative 'change over time' is 'evolution'. The magical yellow brick road bacteria strolled along, before morphing into fish, then apes, before finally into humans.

Evolutionism Doctrines:

1. **Big Bang:** Evolutionism's creation story. The belief the universe and everything in it arose from an explosion of 'nothing'. However, many are now claiming their previous 'fact' was wrong. The new 'fact' is, everything 'expanded' from 'nothing'. Perhaps they should call it the **Big Bloat**.
2. **Abiogenesis:** The unscientific, religious belief life can arise from non-living matter. Such as, 'flies evolve from rotting meat'. It's Evolutionism's 'immaculate conception'. Frank the Frankensteinian first cell was conceived in primordial soup by Father Time and Mother Nature, with the assistance of Evolutionism's holy spirit, Lady Luck.
3. **Out of Africa:** The belief two humans, male and female, evolved from apes, in Africa.
4. **Punctuated Equilibrium:** Evolution happens so *fast;* it cannot be observed.
5. **Stasis:** Evolution happens so *slowly*; it cannot be observed.
6. ♪ **'Millions of Years'** ♪: This mantra is applied to rocks, rock layers, geological formations and fossils. Any evidence presented which refutes this doctrine is considered the gravest

sin, blasphemy to the highest degree. When uttering their sacred scripture ♪ 'millions of years' ♪ it must be done so with an awed, reverent tone.

7. **"Evolution is a fact!":** The mantra parroted when a believer is presented with science. "Evolution is not a fact. It doesn't even qualify as a theory or hypothesis. It is a metaphysical research program, and is not really testable science." (Karl Popper, Philosopher of Science)
8. **Hydrogen:** "A colourless, odourless gas which, given enough time, turns into people." (Edward R. Harrison, *Cosmology: The Science of the Universe*)
9. **Singularity:** "A singularity" is the answer provided when asked, "What exploded/expanded during the alleged Big Bang/Bloat?" Yes, it's a bit vague, isn't it? Here's a real answer: "Places in the universe where laws of physics break down and mathematics misbehave. When theories predict a singularity, scientists know the theory has been extended beyond its applicability." (livescience.com)

Missing Links

'Missing links', otherwise known as 'transitional fossils', demonstrate plants and animals appeared fully formed and functional, and have remained unchanged.

Darwin admitted fossils should provide "innumerable transitional links," admitting the lack of transitionals as, "The gravest objection which can be urged against my theory." He believed at the time of writing, over 150 years ago, they'd be discovered in future years. Well, here we are, and they're still missing.

This fact is confirmed by Dr Colin Patterson, senior palaeontologist at the British Museum of Natural History. "I fully agree with your comments on the lack of direct illustration of evolutionary transitions in my book. If I knew of any, fossil or living, I would certainly have included them... I will lay it on the line, There is not one such fossil for which one might make a watertight argument." (Gary Bates, 2008, 'That quote!—about the missing transitional

fossils: Embarrassed evolutionists try to "muddy the waters",'
Creation Ministries International, Creation.com)

Evolutionism believing Harvard palaeontologist, Stephen Jay Gould, wrote, "The extreme rarity of transitional forms in the fossil record persists as the trade secret of Palaeontology."

Think about what you've just read. It's not Intelligent Designers making the claims. It's Evolutionism believers, including the father of Evolutionism, Darwin, himself. They're trying to distance themselves from this embarrassing fact by conjuring up other terms, such as 'MRCA', 'Most Recent Common Ancestor'. Or, 'LCA', 'Last Common Ancestor'. A rose, by any other name, is still a rose ...

Piltdown Man and Bird

Early in the twentieth century, two men attached an ape's jawbone to a human skull, presenting it as a 'missing link' between apes and humans. The Piltdown Man fraud would reign for forty years, converting many to Evolutionism.

There was a Piltdown Bird, Archaeoraptor, an alleged transitional link between dinosaurs and birds. All they'd done was glue parts of different fossils together.

Nebraska Man

Apart from deliberate frauds, there have been fanciful mistakes that have advanced Evolutionism, such as Nebraska Man. An ape man and woman had been drawn from a solitary tooth. It was later discovered this tooth had arisen from an extinct pig. Still, this convenient mistake remained in textbooks including mine, for seventy years despite knowledge it was false.

There've been modern contenders to fill the gap of the missing, alleged link between apes and humans. Found in Africa, Australians would be familiar with Lucy, or Australopithecus, meaning 'southern ape'.

All proposed missing links between apes and humans, if not discovered as being fraudulent, have either been reclassified as either fully human, or fully simian. There are no intermediates. Neanderthal Man was fully human, Piltdown Man was a hoax, Java Man was an ape, Peking Man was a monkey, Lucy was a chimp, and Nebraska Man was a pig's tooth. Yet, they're presented as proof for Evolutionism.

'Origin of Species'

This is the oft-forgotten full title of Evolutionism's Bible, penned by Charles Darwin: *On the Origin of Species by Means of Natural Selection, or the Preservation of Favoured Races in the Struggle for Life.*

Racism

What do you think Darwin meant when he said, "favoured races?"

Hitler got it, "I have the right to exterminate an inferior race that breed like the vermin."

Where do you think he obtained his ethnic cleansing ideas from? Since lying isn't admonished within the Atheist worldview, they claim Hitler was Christian. Perhaps they're too stupid to realise Hitler was exterminating Jews, not worshipping them. Nothing Hitler did was objectively wrong, if Evolutionism and Atheism are true.

Evolutionism's founder was racist. It's a racist religion. Picture their drawings of a black ape magically morphing into a human. Notice how the depictions become visibly whiter and more 'human'. How is that not a racist philosophy? Answer the question logically.

Evolutionism teaches dark-skinned people are sub-human, less-evolved and more ape-like, than superior, more evolved white-skinned people. Contrast that with the Bible which declares all men were created equal, in our Creator's image. Believers fly into a rage when you point this out.

"At some future period, not very distant as measured by centuries, the civilised races of man will almost certainly exterminate, and replace the savage races throughout the world," and "Civilised man should not allow inferior populations to breed like dogs," (Charles Darwin, *Descent of Man*, 1871)

Thomas Huxley, known as 'Darwin's bulldog' admired Darwin, often defending his religious doctrines, "No rational man, cognizant of the facts, believes that the average negro is the equal, still less the superior, of the white man." (Henry M. Morris Ph.D., 'Evolution and Modern Racism,' 1973, ICR, Institute for Creation Research, icr.org)

"Huxley, a prominent advocate of Darwin's theory of natural selection, promoted the racist view that black people had inferior capabilities compared with white people." (Philip Ball, 'Imperialism's long shadow: the UK universities grappling with a colonial past,' 2022, nature.com)

Aboriginal Apes

Australian Aboriginal AFL player Adam Goodes was called an ape by a 13-year-old girl in 2013. Fuelled by the media, cries of racism swept the country. All Evolutionism believers jumping on the racism high-horse are hypocrites, every last one of them. According to Evolutionism dogma, it's not racism, it's science. To end racism, stop teaching the religion of Evolutionism and teach the truth of Genesis:

"God created man in his own image." Gen 1:27

Stolen Generation

The 'Stolen Generation' refers to Australia's dark past where Aboriginal children were taken from their families and given to white families. They were attempting to 'breed out the black'. Their motivation? The teachings of Charles Darwin, to advance the 'favoured races'. Aborigines were shackled in chains like dogs.

They were massacred, their heads boiled and the most primitive, ape-like skulls were sent to museums across the world, to prove Evolutionism.

"It is actually on record in the history of Mackay, Queensland, that one overseas collector made a request to the trooper that he shoot a native boy to furnish a complete exhibit of an Australian aboriginal skeleton, skin and skull." (*The Sydney Morning Herald*, 31 January 1955, p. 2)

There's nothing wrong with this, if Atheism/Evolutionism is true—nothing. Do you believe in Evolutionism? Are you an Atheist?

Slavery

Slavery is another word thrown around by dullards, drunk on their own perceived sense of self-righteousness and willful ignorance. The Bible says we are brothers and sisters, one family. Evolutionism, on the other hand, states man evolved from apes. Beasts of burden, if you will. If it's not slavery to use an ox to pull a plough, how can it be wrong to use a half-ape?

Biblical slavery was voluntary. People could sell themselves into bondage for a period of time to pay off debts or to provide basic subsistence. Six to seven years was the maximum amount of time this indenture was permitted to be maintained. For many people in the Western world, they are a slave to their jobs, chained by debt.

Slavery is alive and well today, especially with child trafficking. Those throwing the slavery word around are too ignorant to know whites were slaves too. Christian European slaves went to Africa under the Muslims and white slaves also went to America. Let's not forget the Israeli slaves in Egypt and Middle Eastern territories.

Regardless, the black slave trade to America was ended by Christians. Angelina Grimké wrote an extensive anti-slavery newspaper article, 'Appeal to the Christian Woman of the South'. Scripture was sprinkled throughout, with a large emphasis on Genesis. This reinforced the truth all humans were created equal, in our Father's image. Also, that 'blacks' are not semi-evolved apes, as Evolutionism dogma insists.

Amazing Grace

William Wilberforce was an English politician. Owing to his strong Christian beliefs, he knew man wasn't an evolved ape, but was instead made equal in the image of his Creator. He gave his life to ending slavery. He was inspired and encouraged to fight against slavery by former slave trader John Newton, responsible for the deaths of thousands of African souls. Finally finding peace through the forgiveness of sins, Newton expressed his gratitude in a poem, which became the renowned hymn, Amazing Grace.

RSPCA, or 'Royal Society for the Prevention of Cruelty to Animals' was founded by Wilberforce and other Christians.

"And God said, Let us make man in our image, after our likeness: and let them have dominion over the fish of the sea, and over the fowl of the air, and over the cattle, and over all the earth, and over every creeping thing that creepeth upon the earth." Gen 1:26

Where's the Justice?

History teaches Hitler committed suicide toward the end of World War Two. If that's true, he escaped justice. Do you think this is fair? Do you feel anger he escaped judgement? If so, why? What moral standard are you using to make that judgement? Where do you think your sense of justice comes from?

Atheists have no hope of anyone deserving justice, receiving it at death. When someone they're close to dies—that's it, gone forever, no hope of reuniting. Contrast that with the future Resurrection. We have the hope of being reunited with those we care about, in paradise on a restored Earth. We also have the hope that those who escaped justice on Earth, find it at the Great White Throne Judgement. Atheism has neither—it is a hopeless religion.

Columbine High School Massacre

Both shooters at the 1999 school shooting revered the Social Darwinism of Hitler's murderous regime. Like Hitler, they were inspired by the concept of no moral accountability, justified by Evolutionism's teachings. The ringleader wore a shirt boldly proclaiming 'Natural Selection' on the day of the massacre.

Rachel Scott, seventeen, Christian, was killed first, execution style. After wounding her, the gunman approached and levelled a firearm point-blank at her head. Soulless eyes ran over her horrific wounds as he sneered, "Well Rachel, do you still believe in God?"

Rachel held his gaze, "Yes, I do," before closing her eyes, awaiting the final bullet. She didn't wait long.

There were thirteen innocent victims that day. If the Evolutionism believers' plans hadn't gone astray, there would've been well over 2,000.

Eight years later, a student at a Finland high school describing himself as a social Darwinist murdered eight people. Private writings were found declaring, "I am prepared to fight and die for my cause. I, as a natural selector, will eliminate all who I see unfit, disgraces of human race and failures of natural selection." (David Klinghoffer, 'Slouching Toward Columbine: Darwin's Tree of Death,' 2009, Discovery Institute, discovery.org)

Modern Extinctions

How many animals today would've become extinct if not for conservation laws, reservation parks and rangers? Tigers, whales, lions, elephants, rhinoceroses—the list goes on. If these animals had become extinct, say 700 years ago, believers would point to their bones and declare they died 'millions of years' ago. Elephants and rhinoceroses would've likely been declared as dinosaurs— Elephantasaurus and Rhinocerousasaurus, respectively. Any paintings or written accounts of man having lived with these creatures, well, they would've been fakes, obviously. Descriptions of elephants being used as beasts of burden, pulling farm machinery? Not possible, after all, they were killed by an asteroid 'millions of years' ago.

A Copy of a Copy

Back in the day, when copying a video or cassette tape the copied version would be of lesser quality than the original. If you were to then copy the copied tape, the quality would become progressively worse, and so on.

It's no different with humans. Since the creation of the first two humans 6,000 years ago, our quality, so to speak, has been declining. For this reason, once there was finally a base population, incest was made unlawful. The reason being, as a close relative you both may have the same defective gene (mutation), which would severely affect your offspring.

Darwin himself experienced this firsthand with his children's deformities, after marrying his first cousin. Evolutionism-believing geneticists themselves have realised mutations accumulate rapidly, about sixty to one hundred per person, per generation. Their name for it is, 'genetic entropy'. Everything is breaking down in nature. This scientific observation runs counter to Evolutionism dogma which teaches everything evolves forward. Apart from copying errors, other mutations result from damaged cells due to factors such as drug taking, pharmaceuticals, inadequate diets and chemical exposure.

Therefore, humans should've become extinct at least ten times over, according to genetic studies. That is, if you presume we've been here for over 100,000 years, as Evolutionism stipulates.

Science says mutations are detrimental. Evolutionism says they're beneficial. Which do you side with? Science, or Evolutionism.

Cold Light

When asked questions concerning the nature of our Creator, such as "Why did God allow Adam and Eve to sin in the first place?" I'll respond, "I don't know." I'm usually smiling, remembering the frustration I once felt, just like they're experiencing now. "Look," I begin, "I used to wonder about that too, and it used to do my head in, until I came to the realisation His intellect is vastly superior to mine." Motioning around me, "He created all of this! Fireflies, for example, produce cold light, we can't even do that. We always lose some energy in the form of heat. We can't even produce a blade of grass or a speck of dust from nothing, so how in the hell could we possibly understand the very intellect of 'That' which created us?"

"Surely your turning of things upside down shall be esteemed as the potter's clay: for shall the work say of him that made it, He made me not? or shall the thing framed say of him that framed it, He had no understanding?" Isa 29:16

"Shall the clay say to him that fashioneth it, What makest thou? or thy work, He hath no hands?" Isa 45:9

"Nay but, O man, who art thou that repliest against God? Shall the thing formed say to him that formed it, Why hast thou made me thus?" Rom 9:20

Evolutionism believers think the origin of the technology, the structure, the existence, the capabilities and life of a reproducing firefly, arose from an explosion/expansion of nothing, two at the same instant, male and female.

Natural Selection

Mutations and natural selection have never been observed to create new structures. Dawkins himself was stumped when asked to provide just one example of a genetic mutation or evolutionary process, which could be seen to increase information in the genome.

Natural selection, mutation, and random chance produce slight changes only. These processes aren't capable of producing the genetic modifications required to change an organism into a more complex one. Mutations are a fancy way of saying 'mistakes'. In this case, copying mistakes within the DNA code. There's no way, on God's green Earth, copying errors will turn a fish into a human, regardless of how many 'millions of years' you care to throw at it.

"Natural selection eliminates and maybe maintains, but it doesn't create. It doesn't generate anything fundamentally new. Neo-Darwinists say new species emerge when mutations occur and modify an organism ... I believed it, until I looked for evidence." (Lynn Margulis, internationally renowned evolutionary biologist)

David Attenborough

He's famous for television programs showcasing the animal kingdom and is considered learned on the subject. In several ways, he is. Though, in a glaring way, he isn't. Years ago, I'd met a fan of his. As time went by, she told me I'd, "destroyed David Attenborough" for her. Intrigued, I asked for clarification.

She referred back to an initial conversation in front of the idiot box when his program aired. She'd sung his praises whereas I'd dryly remarked, "I can't stand him."

Her jaw hit the floor, "Why not?"

I delivered the deathblow, "You'll always hear him say, 'this animal evolved over millions of years,' but he'll never tell you what it evolved from, or what it's evolving into. He never explains how, or even why, it evolved."

We'd then commenced sitting through a somewhat subdued, tense viewing of his show, peppered with me occasionally asking, at the appropriate times, "Yeah? Really? When? How? Why?"

Several months later, she'd confided she was saddened by this, as up until that point, she'd been fond of his show. She went on to say that every time since, whenever he made his religious claim, "This animal evolved into that animal," all she heard was, "When? How? Why? What from?" Since he failed to back up his claims, it became unbearable for her to watch.

Perhaps if Attenborough started asking himself the same questions, he wouldn't believe his dribble either.

Whales—Evolved Bears

Darwin asserts whales evolved from black bears. "In North America the black bear was seen by Hearne swimming for hours with widely open mouth, thus catching, like a whale, insects in the water. Even in so extreme a case as this, if the supply of insects were constant, and if better adapted competitors did not already exist in the country, I can see no difficulty in a race of bears being rendered, by natural selection, more and more aquatic in their structure and habits, with larger and larger mouths, till a creature was produced as monstrous as a whale." (Charles Darwin, *On the Origin of Species*)

Isn't that amazing? Bears evolved from 'rain on the rocks', which had been zapped by lightning, following the uncaused explosion/expansion of 'nothing'. Their early ancestors were fish. Over 'millions of years', this fish evolved into all animals we see today, as well as into dinosaurs. Anyway, the former fish, the black bear, which eats fish, decided to evolve back into a fish. Not just any 'fish', mind you, this ambitious black bear evolved into a whale.

Remarkably, other black bears stayed as black bears. I suppose it depends on who you talk to. I've been told it was cows that had evolved into whales, not black bears.

Dinosaurs Evolved Into Birds?

I'm not making it up, Evolutionism believers insist birds are evolved dinosaurs.

Roger Benson, Professor of Palaeobiology at the University of Oxford declares, "There's no longer really any doubt that birds are a type of dinosaur." (Shaun Hurrell interviews dinosaur evolution expert Professor Roger Benson, 2021, 'It's official: birds are literally dinosaurs. Here's how we know,' BirdLife International)

However, out of the other side of their mouth, they declare crocodiles aren't dinosaurs. Dinosaur is a modern word, replacing the archaic word, 'dragon'. King James Bible uses the word 'dragon', since it was written before the modern word 'dinosaur' replaced it, less than 200 years ago. It means, 'great and terrible lizard'. Hearing those words, what picture would your mind conjure up? That of a crocodile? Or that of a hummingbird, swan, flamingo, or peacock? Evolutionism states it is the latter.

Crocodiles and dinosaurs are reptiles, which are cold-blooded. Birds are warm-blooded and aren't reptiles. Yet, believers claim that while birds are dinosaurs, crocodiles aren't. Imagine crocodiles or alligators weren't in existence. One day, their fossils (crocasaurus), are found. Do you really think they wouldn't be added to the list of dinosaurs?

How did dinosaurs/dragons miraculously evolve into birds after they'd become extinct from an alleged asteroid strike, 66 million years ago? The problem compounded when scientists found that not only have dinosaur and bird fossils been discovered together, bird remains have been found as part of dinosaurs' stomach contents. Explain that.

I suppose they'd be forced to submit a just-so story resembling something like this, "While dinosaurs became extinct 66 million years ago, some had already evolved into birds. An asteroid strike killed all foliage and dinosaurs, though spared some, such as tortoises and crocodiles. However, while it killed flying dinosaurs, such as the pterodactyl, it spared the dinosaurs which had already evolved into birds. It just killed everything else."

I was talking with an Evolutionism believer who was telling me I was an idiot for dismissing Evolutionism and believing the Bible. Sizing her up, "Well, I just cannot believe dinosaurs evolved into birds."

Her eyes burned with scorn, "Evolutionists don't believe that!"

I calmly explained their ridiculous theory about dinosaur scales becoming frayed, thereby evolving into feathers—over 'millions of years'. Initially bewildered, she shrugged it off, changing the subject.

It never ceases to amaze me that many disciples of Evolutionism don't even know the basic doctrines of their own religion.

Dinosaur Cartoons

In grade eight, a dinosaur chasing a dragonfly was depicted in our textbook. There were fainter replications of the dinosaur slowly evolving with each cumulative depiction of it, chasing the dragonfly. In the last depiction, the dinosaur had fully formed wings, enabling it to catch the dragonfly. It appeared pretty convincing; I could see the gradual changes, not realising it wasn't based on fact. After all, this was 'science', in a textbook at high school, with the magical ingredient of 'millions of years' thrown in. I was receiving an 'education'. In reality, I was receiving an indoctrination.

Funnily enough, many years later I'd see that same artist's illustration again. This time, shooting holes in the nonsense of a dinosaur evolving into a bird, with a caption asking a pertinent question, "During all of those 'millions of years' in which the dinosaur evolved into a bird, why hadn't the dragonfly evolved?" I kicked myself for not asking the same question, all those years ago when I was first exposed to it.

In the same timeframe it allegedly took a dinosaur to evolve into a bird, the dragonfly failed to evolve, at all. Further, there are numerous fossils of the original dinosaur and dragonfly, but no transitional fossils, depicted by the artist.

Whenever a believer is asked why one particular creature didn't evolve, they'll respond, "They didn't need to." They're forced to say this about every creature.

Fruit Flies Destroy Evolutionism

Occasionally, fruit flies are presented as proof of Evolutionism. Although a tremendous amount of intelligence was utilised in an attempt to turn a fruit fly into anything other than a fruit fly, it failed miserably. All it succeeded in doing was producing either dead or deformed specimens.

There are fruit flies encased in amber dated at 44 million years old, that are identical to the fruit flies currently hovering above my bananas. Every ten to twelve days fruit flies have a new generation. So, in other words, after almost one and a half billion generations, over 44 million years, it's still a fruit fly.

Where's the evolution?

Evolutionism Assignment

Detail the alleged evolution of the biological process that changes a caterpillar into a butterfly after it forms a chrysalis. Account for the complete change in its body form and structure, hormones and biochemistry.

It's a similar conundrum for moths. Explain how a plump, soft, legless and sexless creature with chewing mouthparts and intricate glands to manufacture silk, as well as spinners to work with, evolved. How did it *learn* to make a cocoon, let alone, silk? How did that ability evolve? How did it *know* it had to make a cocoon?

After entering the cocoon or chrysalis, the caterpillar disintegrates into sludge, before emerging five to twenty-one days later as a moth or colourful butterfly. It has legs, wings, an exoskeleton and muscles structured for flight along with the knowledge of flight. How did it acquire this knowledge? Moths and butterflies remember their former lives as caterpillars. How?

Male or female sex organs require the creation of glands producing the appropriate sex hormone. A retractable proboscis and a complete overhaul of the digestive tract is required. How did all of this evolve into a systematised process, by cumulative, naturally selected mistakes? We haven't even discussed the sheer elegance, beauty and symmetrical patterns of butterflies. How, and why, did that evolve? In harsh environments, caterpillars remain cocooned for up to three years! How did it acquire this instinct from liquefied caterpillar sludge?

Butterflies and moths begin life as caterpillars, which can't reproduce. Tadpoles become frogs or toads, maggots become flies. Many insects including bees, wasps, fleas and beetles all undergo metamorphosis. How could these processes have evolved?

Forget the chicken and egg. Which came first, the butterfly? The caterpillar? Or, the caterpillar egg? You know the truth if you're open-minded and honest. Our Creator created two butterflies, male, and female, which lay fertilised eggs, producing a caterpillar. The Creation is proof of the Creator, in the same way a painting is proof of the painter. You don't have to see a painter creating a painting, to know there was a painter. The painting itself is evidence of a painter. Yet, an Atheist/Evolutionism believer will deny the existence of a Creator, in much the same way an Atheist fish will deny the existence of water.

Evolutionism teaches all insects are evolved crustaceans. According to them, butterflies are just glorified flying prawns.

Irreducible Complexity

Biological systems with multiple interacting parts can't function if one part is removed. Therefore, they couldn't have evolved by cumulative minor modifications from less complex systems, via natural selection, as demanded by Darwinian Evolution. Biochemistry professor Michael Behe, explains this in detail in his book, *Darwin's Black Box*.

Before we examine biological systems, let's consider an extremely simple mechanical device; that of the mousetrap. It's comprised of six components. The base, hammer, spring, catch, holding bar and bait. Remove any one of these parts and the device is rendered useless; although you may have limited success without bait. An unseen component of this simple device is the element of design behind it. Then too, it requires someone to build it, place it, set it, maintain it, rebait it, dispose of victims and relocate it.

As you read, remember the words of Darwin, "If it could be demonstrated that any complex organ existed, which could not possibly have been formed by numerous, successive, slight modifications, my theory would absolutely break down."

Systems of the human body entail the skeletal, muscular, nervous, endocrine, cardiovascular, lymphatic, respiratory, digestive, urinary, reproductive and integumentary systems. Which of these eleven systems evolved first?

Let's assume the muscular system evolved first. Why would it have evolved cardiac muscle, when there was no heart, blood, or pathways for the blood, namely a system of vessels, arteries, veins, and capillaries? Where would it have obtained the DNA coding for instructions to build such an apparatus? In other words, where did the blueprint for such a detailed system materialise from, and how?

Already problems are mounting. You see, what would you attach muscles to? After all, your skeletal system hadn't evolved yet. Without the protection of a ribcage, your heart and other vital organs are jeopardised. The heart is an organ within the cardiovascular system, although it's largely comprised of muscle and has its own nervous system.

How would you filter poisons from your blood without a urinary system? Perhaps it evolved first? How? Why? The cardiovascular system hasn't evolved yet, remember? There's no blood to filter poisons from.

If blood evolved first, what was the order of its evolution? Red blood cells? White blood cells? Plasma, or platelets? Platelets are responsible for causing clots to stop or prevent bleeding. These are manufactured in bone marrow, as are the red and white blood cells. The problem is, the skeletal system hasn't evolved yet. The famed chicken/egg scenario can be applied to everything. It's an aggressive cancer to Evolutionism dogma.

Perhaps you feel the urinary tract evolved after the cardiovascular system. Well, whichever organism was waiting for this miracle to occur would've died from blood poisoning.

All of these systems have to be encased by the integumentary system. Skin is our largest organ, holding everything together—the wrapping, so to speak. Our hair, nails, glands and skin are our first line of defence against bacteria and ultraviolet rays.

Skin requires nutrients. For this, you need a digestive system. Skin also requires a circulatory system to deliver the nutrients. By the same token, blood requires the skin as a barrier to bacteria and to regulate body temperature.

Blood Clotting

This brings us to another interesting paradox—blood clotting. If it occurs on the inside, it's lethal, unless it clots to arrest internal bleeding. Once this situation is resolved, the clot dissolves. Generally speaking, blood clotting on the inside, is lethal. However, if it doesn't occur outside, it too, is lethal.

Complexity of blood clotting defies Evolutionism. Despite all of the intricate, complex requirements for blood clotting, blood also has to be at the right temperature and pressure. Blood carries oxygen. How can it possibly do this if the respiratory system hasn't evolved yet? Without oxygen, the organism dies.

Let's assume, despite all these insurmountable obstacles and miracles, we did have a living, functioning creature. How, and why, did the reproductive system evolve? Remember too, you'll require male and female components. These opposite components would have to evolve simultaneously, otherwise, reproduction is impossible.

Without even touching on the other systems, surely you can see for yourself the absurdity of the claims of Darwinian Evolution? If not, which system evolved first? How? Why?

Symbiotic Relationships

Besides missing links, another Achilles' heel Darwin admitted to for his wild speculations was symbiotic relationships:

"If it could be proved that any part of the structure of any one species had been formed for the exclusive good of another species, it would annihilate my theory, for such could not have been produced through natural selection." (*The Origin of Species by Means of Natural Selection, or the Preservation of Favoured Races in the Struggle for Life*, 1859, Masterpieces of Science edition, 1958, p. 164)

Sharks spare the life of fish which in return clean their teeth. Crocodiles and birds have a similar arrangement. How could these mutually beneficial arrangements have possibly evolved?

Fungi provide moisture and protection to algae. In return, algae nourish fungi with nutrients, keeping them alive. Fungi consume a quarter of the sugar trees photosynthesise. This sugar fuels fungi as they probe the soil for phosphorus, nitrogen, and other minerals, which are then absorbed and consumed by trees.

Bees pollinate flowers while obtaining nectar for food. Do you believe the process and equipment required for this were merely the result of coincidence? Bees don't pollinate at random. Pollen from one flower won't pollinate a flower of a different species. Flowers, orchards and crops require bees. Simultaneously, bees require nectar. Which evolved first, the bees (pollinators), or the flowers (food source)? How could one possibly exist without the other? How did both manage to evolve simultaneously?

A bee buzzing and hovering is performing a dance instructing other bees on the direction, distance and location of nectar, as well as water sources and potential nesting sites. How did this sophisticated communication evolve?

Ion Idriess

He was an Australian bushman, World War One soldier and prospector. Along with his writings overseas during the war, Ion Idriess's books detail life living alongside Aborigines and travelling remote parts of Australia's top end, Torres Strait Islands and Papua New Guinea. Gallipoli was one of many campaigns he served in. He was also present at Beersheba, witnessing the heroic, magnificent charge of the gallant Australian Light Horse Brigade, which liberated Israel, leading to the fulfilment of a Biblical prophecy. Col Stringer has written a book on this subject, *800 Horsemen: God's History Makers*. I recommend you visit the ANZAC Memorial Centre and adjoining war graves at Beersheba if you're ever in Israel.

Unless you've read Idriess's works, you don't know Australia. Mysterious communication between humans and animals is described, experienced firsthand with recluse bushmen, living in solidarity with Australia's creatures. Remember scoffers ridiculing the notion of man communicating with a serpent in the Garden of Eden? This is due to profound ignorance of the depth of communication between man and beast. Have you heard of a horse whisperer?

Hunting crocodiles with Aborigines, Idriess recounts how once-abundant crocodile numbers would fall, dropping to nothing at all, as the hunters moved from waterhole to waterhole. He surmised crocodiles would telepathically communicate with other crocodiles, over vast distances, warning them of impending danger. Science would later prove him correct. Crocodiles would be encountered miles from a water source, relocating over land. Idriess's horse

Evolutionism

would suddenly rear up, spying crocodiles concealed by grass, during a buffalo hunt.

Plants communicate with each other. Trees have been found with their leaves devoured, whereas subsequent trees of the same species nearby, haven't. Mutilated trees emitted signals to neighbouring counterparts, instructing them to produce bitter-tasting tannins, deterring consumption of its foliage.

Encountered firsthand on several occasions by Idriess, were detailed human mental communications over vast distances, by Torres Strait Islanders and Australian Aborigines. Three languages were utilised by Aborigines; an oral, sign, and telepathic language. The development of which, was encouraged from a young age.

Torres Strait Islanders were known to mummify their dead and Egyptians have hieroglyphs of boomerangs. Egyptian boomerangs are on display at the Egyptian Museum in Cairo. What would be the logical conclusion?

Atheism – a Hopeless Religion

ATHEISTS mistakenly believe Atheism isn't a religion. They believe Buddhism is a religion, although Buddhists don't have any gods or worship deities. Conversely, Atheists worship an Evolutionism Trinity: Father Time, Mother Nature and Lady luck. Their 'Buddha' is Charles Darwin.

Atheism isn't a lack of belief in the existence of God. It's a denial of God, despite the evidence. Below are statements that describe what it is to be an Atheist, or what the religion of Atheism entails. While some may sound insulting, that's unfortunate. No one can logically deny the truth of these statements, especially Atheists themselves:

Atheist Definitions

"A man who believes himself to be an accident" (Francis Thompson); Letting a non-belief in something, define who you are; The belief that non-intelligence created intelligence; The belief that non-belief, isn't a belief; The religious belief in a spontaneous, causeless, purposeless, meaningless, hopeless existence; Believing a series of genetic mutations can turn an ape into a human, or a dinosaur into a bird; The religious belief nothing produced everything; A person who disbelieves or lacks belief in the existence of God or gods (yet, they'll spend a great portion of their time arguing against the existence of the Judeo-Christian

God). Or, as Stephen Colbert says, "The religion devoted to the worship of one's own smug sense of superiority."

Atheist Religion

Atheists adhere to Evolutionism, a religion that requires more faith than all others. This is because while all religions are grounded in faith, science negates Evolutionism's doctrines and dogma.

Atheism is a religion, according to the dictionary: "A philosophical or religious position characterized by disbelief in the existence of a god or any gods. archaic: godlessness especially in conduct: ungodliness, wickedness." (Merriam-Webster's dictionary, webster.com/dictionary/atheism)

"Atheism is a religious worldview because it claims to know something fundamental about reality that hasn't been—or can't be—proven. Like theists, Atheists operate out of a foundational faith or belief that shapes their perceiving, thinking, and living in the world." (Michael Wagenman, 'Is Atheism a Religion?' Columns, 2019, Cross Examination, *Banner*, thebanner.org)

Richard Dawkins hits the nail on the head, "We've all been brought up with the view that religion has some kind of special privileged status. You're not allowed to criticise it." Ironically, there's a group known as, 'Freedom From Religion'. They prosecute schools teaching Intelligent Design. University teachers are expelled at an alarming rate for even suggesting an alternative theory to the religious dogma and doctrines of Evolutionism. Ben Stein has a documentary showcasing this bigoted intolerance, 'Expelled, No Intelligence Allowed'.

You'd think they'd at least teach Evolutionism dogma alongside Intelligent Design, as a critical thinking exercise. Here's why they refuse to allow it, "Darwinian evolution is unscientific, unobservable, unbelievable, but understandable in a world that hates God." (Ray Comfort). It's for this reason alone, Professor

Richard Lewontin insists, "We cannot allow a Divine Foot in the door."

An Important Distinction

Every Atheist is an Evolutionism believer, though not every Evolutionism believer is an Atheist. Take Darwin himself, for example, "I have never been an Atheist in the sense of denying the existence of a God." (Charles Darwin letter to John Fordyce, 7 May 1879, Darwin Correspondence Project, University of Cambridge, darwinproject.ac.uk)

Whenever this publication mentions Atheists, it's referring to 'new Atheists', or 'militant Atheists', the aggressive, intolerant breed, brimming with hate. A large portion of their time is spent evangelising online and in the media. As well as communing and congregating with other Atheists. These are opposed to the old-school Atheists who don't believe in the Judeo-Christian God, yet live their lives with more of a Biblical worldview, than a hopeless, selfish, Atheist worldview.

Atheist 'Morality'?

It baffles me when Atheists attempt to disown their own evil, immoral, racist worldview, to steal from the Biblical worldview and try to pass Biblical morality off as their own. While it's possible to follow the Biblical teachings of, 'Love thy neighbour', and still be an Atheist, to do so, is inconsistent with the Atheist worldview—'jungle law', every man selfishly for himself. That being the case, what is their basis and standard for their morals and ethics, if not a Biblical worldview?

If you admit there is 'evil', by default you admit there is 'good'. You cannot differentiate between the two without a moral law. A moral law requires a Lawgiver, who is moral—God. Yet, Atheists deny the existence of 'evil', 'good', 'morality' and a 'Law-giver'. Even so, a constant theme of their evangelism is how the God they claim doesn't exist, is evil.

Without a moral Law-giver, there cannot be a concept of 'good'. By default, there cannot be a concept of 'evil'. So, unbeknownst to evangelising Atheists, every time they refer to concepts of 'good', 'evil', 'right' and 'wrong', they're establishing the truth of the moral Law-giver, the existence of God.

Atheism Is Anti-Morality

Evolutionism High Priest, Sam Harris, is loyal to his religious beliefs, "There's nothing more natural than rape. Human beings rape, chimpanzees rape, orangutans rape. Rape clearly is part of an evolutionary strategy to get your genes into the next generation" (Sam Harris, *The Religion Report*, ABC Radio National, 20 December 2006). It's likely for this reason he also had this to say, "If I could wave a magic wand and get rid of either rape or religion, I would not hesitate to get rid of religion."

Perhaps Sam Harris is a misogynist, following in the footsteps of the father of Evolutionism, "The chief distinction in the intellectual powers of the two sexes is shown by man attaining to a higher eminence, in whatever he takes up, than woman can attain, whether requiring deep thought, reason or imagination, or merely the use of the senses and hands." He adds, "Thus man has ultimately become superior to woman." (Charles Darwin, 1871, *The Descent of Man*)

Cannibalism

"I can think of no moral objection to eating human road-kill," Richard Dawkins, in an interview with Peter Singer, concerning the possibility of legalising cannibalism. ('Peter Singer, The Genius of Darwin: The Uncut Interviews', 2009, Richard Dawkins Foundation for Reason & Science)

Singer himself is a real piece of work. Not content with the wholesale slaughter of unborn Australian children during the entire nine months of pregnancy, he wants to legalise the murder of children after their birth, up until age three. Or, the 'age of reason,' as he likes to put it. He argues some animals fit under the banner of 'personhood', whereas physically and mentally handicapped children don't, and should be killed.

Dawkins makes this shocking admission to Peter Singer at the start of the above interview, "Peter, I think you must be one of the most moral people in the world."

"Woe unto them that call evil good, and good evil." Isa 5:20

But, credit where credit is due, "I'm a passionate Darwinian when it comes to science, when it comes to explaining the world, but I'm a passionate anti-Darwinian when it comes to morality and politics." (Richard Dawkins, in an article by Gary Bates and Lita Sanders, 'The Bible: the only basis for objective morality,' 2015, Creation Ministries International, creation.com)

Jeffery Dahmer, the Milwaukee Cannibal, proved he's loyal to the doctrines of Atheism, "If a person doesn't think there is a God to be accountable to, then what's the point of trying to modify your behaviour to keep it within acceptable ranges? That's how I thought anyway. I always believed the theory of evolution as truth, that we all just came from the slime. When we, when we died, you know, that was it, there is nothing ..." (Jeffrey Dahmer interview with Stone Phillips, *Dateline,* NBC, 29 November 1994)

He's right. Atheism/Evolutionism is a dangerous, evil, racist religion. Milwaukee Cannibal sums it up succinctly, "I always believed the lie that evolution is truth; the whole theory cheapens life."

Untrustworthy Atheists

Of all religions, it's the adherents of Atheism who are least trusted. Atheists themselves distrust their fellow believers, more so than those of other faiths. It makes sense, especially considering their hatred for commandments such as, "Thou shalt not steal" and "Thou shalt not bare false witness." If you're in a relationship, how about, "Thou shalt not commit adultery?" As for, "Thou shalt not kill," well, there's a strong worldwide link between the religion of Atheism and mass shooters, mass murderers and serial killers. You've just read some examples of this.

Atheist Awakening

"A world governed purely by Atheistic, evolutionary ethics has been shown by history to be a horrible place to live. Most Atheists recognise this and choose to live by the ethical systems of other religions instead." (Daniel Smartt, 'Is Atheism a religion?' 2010, Creation Ministries International, creation.com)

Conscious and Conscience

Not only did consciousness arise from the alleged explosion/expansion of 'nothing', so did conscience. Conscious means to be awake and aware, whereas conscience refers to a sense of right and wrong, an inner moral compass. You don't require man's law to differentiate between right and wrong. Instinctively, you know it's wrong to take something that doesn't belong to you. Where did this instinct come from? Conscience shouldn't exist, if the concepts of good and evil don't exist. These cannot exist, without a moral Law-Giver.

"I will put My law in their minds, and write it on their hearts; and I will be their God, and they shall be My people." Jer 31:33

Fairies, Leprechauns and Unicorns

"Atheists don't hate fairies, leprechauns, or unicorns because they don't exist. It is impossible to hate something that doesn't exist. Atheists hate God because He does exist." (Ray Comfort)

Are you aware of Atheists spending their time online, on the idiot box, on the airways, or in books, evangelising against the flying spaghetti monster, fairies, leprechauns or Batman? Of course not! They know those things don't exist. Are you aware of any Atheists evangelising against Buddha, Zeus, Thor, Apollo, Athena, Krishna, etc.? No, again. Instead, it's a constant onslaught, relentless evangelism against their Creator. They, like Satan, do not care for the counterfeits. They hate and wage war against truth.

Atheist 'Creation Story'

Atheists believe 'nothing' exploded, for no reason, from which arose 'everything'. Life was birthed in Evolutionism's 'immaculate conception', the zapping of pond scum from a bolt of lightning.

"Sometimes when I'm faced with an Atheist, I am tempted to invite him to the greatest gourmet dinner that one could ever serve, and when we have finished eating that magnificent dinner, to ask him if he believes there's a cook." (Former US President, Ronald Raegan)

Evolutionism believers/Atheists have a propensity to be drawn to science fiction and fantasy. It makes sense; after all, that's what their religious beliefs are based on. Dawkins admits, in a brief moment of clarity, "I think looking back to my own childhood, the fact that so many of the stories I read allowed the possibility of frogs turning into princes, whether that has a sort of insidious effect on rationality, I'm not sure. Perhaps it's something for research."(*Washington Times*, 'Edge: The Richard Dawkins Delusion,' 7 November 2008)

Charles Darwin arrived at the same conclusion, "Often a cold shudder has run through me, and I have asked myself whether I may have not devoted myself to a phantasy." (Letter to Charles Lyell, 23 November 1859, Darwin Correspondence Project, University of Cambridge, darwinproject.ac.uk)

Evolutionism's 'Sacred Trinity'

Atheists, by default, are Evolutionism believers, worshiping their sacred Trinity, three gods in one:

Father Time: aka 'millions of years'.
Mother Nature: 'magical sky mummy'.
Lady Luck: aka 'blind chance'—Evolutionism's 'holy spirit' / creative force.

Atheist 'Holy Scriptures'

Darwin produced Atheism's 'Old Testament'; *On the Origin of Species by Means of Natural Selection, or the Preservation of Favoured Races*. Devout Darwinian disciples have penned a 'New*Atheist* Testament'. Evolutionism messiah and gospel writer, Richard Dawkins, is responsible for many books of the 'New*Atheist* Testament'. Scriptures penned by other believers have also been added to their sacred canon.

Atheist Denominations

There are different denominations of Atheists, according to Atheists themselves: activist, anti-theist, non-theist, militant/new (aggressive, modern Atheist), seeker-agnostic, ritual Atheist, hard Atheist, implicit Atheist, explicit Atheist, etc. Some have a strong Atheist faith, some weak.

Atheist Preachers

Evolutionism evangelists are everywhere. Notably on social media, the idiot box, YouTube and Wikipedia. Any opponents of their religion are silenced and removed from schools and universities. Their religion is complete with the equivalent high priests, bishops and cardinals, such as Richard Dawkins, PZ Myers, Christopher Hitchens, Sam Harris, Daniel Dennett, Neil deGrasse Tyson and Bill Nye. These prophets travel the world spreading their '*Bad* News', their message of hopelessness. Unlike with a Judeo-Christian worldview, they do not have the hope of being reunited with loved ones and experiencing eternity in paradise, on a restored, sinless Earth.

Believers attend worldwide seminars and commune online. Even though they profess to fervently believe this life is all they'll ever have, they spend a great percentage of their time trying to win converts, evangelising that there isn't a God, and that they hate Him.

Atheist Religious Symbols

Their symbolic representation of their religion is that of their sacred, fictitious four-legged Darwinian fish emerging from primordial soup. They have another symbol, that of the letter 'A' inside of the atomic whirl, falsely believing their doctrines are grounded in science. This couldn't be further from the truth. Ironically, the atom was discovered by the same Christian who founded atomic physics. (John Dalton)

Atheist Churches

Sunday worship is growing within the Atheist community. At least they're worshipping on the right day, the adversary's day, Sunday. Their goal is to fill the void, the hole which is left when they deny the truth of God's existence.

Burgeoning mega-churches allow Atheists to celebrate their perceived lack of faith. Reminiscent of Catholic church services, offering each other the 'sign of peace' by shaking hands with those near them, Atheists instead high-five one another. A cherished Atheist hymn, 'Lean on me', as opposed to, 'Lean on God', is often sung. Another favourite is 'Here Comes the Sun'. It's fitting, as their religion is a worship of their 'creator Sun', as opposed to our Creator Son. (snippets taken from an article in *The Denver Post*, 'What exactly is an "Atheist mega-church"?' 29 June 2023)

Church assemblies have mantras, such as, 'live better, help often, wonder more' and 'good is great'. Confused? You should be. They borrow teachings from the Biblical worldview and try to force them into the selfish, dog-eat-dog, every man for himself, Atheist worldview.

One church read 'scripture' from Alice In Wonderland, before having a sermon titled, 'Wonder'. Heads were bowed for two minutes. Following the culmination of the sermon, they were encouraged to contemplate the miracle of life, pond scum zapped to life in the primordial soup—Frank, their ancestor. Services are followed by cake and tea. (Brian Wheeler, 'What happens at an Atheist church?' 2013, *BBC News Magazine*, bbc.com)

Florida has a religious Atheist monument alongside the Ten Commandments, outside a courthouse. Amusingly, it includes quotes from Founding Father, Thomas Jefferson, a Christian.

Atheist Prayer—'Our Darwin' (satire)

Our Darwin, who aren't in Heaven,
Evo be thy name.
Thy judgement come,
Thou were damned on Earth,
So shall not go to Heaven.
Give us this day our daily spin,
And forgive us for our computer simulations,
As we ignore those scientific laws that are against us.
And lead us not up the garden path,
But deliver us from *evil*ution.
For thine are the falsehoods, the missing links,
and the just-so stories.
For always and ever,
A man.

Atheist 'Ten Commandments'

These are mind-boggling, to say the least. For example, their second commandment is 'empathy', their eighth commandment is 'forgiveness'. These concepts are Biblical, running counter to a selfish, Atheist worldview. Commandment nine is, 'hope'. (David Sandison, '10 new virtues for atheists: Alain de Botton unveils new manifesto,' 2013, *Independent*, independent.co.uk)

Atheist Pilgrimages

Atheists have pilgrimages to the Galapagos Islands—Atheists' Holy Land. Here was Darwin's inspiration for the Atheist Old Testament—*On the Origin of Species*. Believers can walk in Father

Darwin's footsteps, having their faith strengthened as they see their sacred texts come alive. They'll see many creatures instrumental in the production of his sacred writings.

It's where Darwin observed finch beaks changing shape, thereby leading believers to assume this proves finches eventually evolved from primordial soup.

Atheist Patron Saint

Darwin has been venerated as the Patron Saint of the Galapagos Islands. Statues have been erected in his honour there and around the world, for the worship and adoration of devout Darwinian disciples. Along with Atheist church congregations on Sundays, they even have two 'holy feast days'.

Atheist 'Holy Days'

Atheists desired a solemn day of worship for their deities. It's understandable, as scientists have found our brains have been 'hard-wired' to believe in a deity. "U.S., surveys show 90 per cent of adults believe in some higher power, spiritual force or God with a capital G. Even self-proclaimed atheists have supernatural leanings." (Bridget Alex, 'The Human Brain Evolved to Believe in Gods. How belief in the supernatural makes sense in light of evolution,' 2018, The Crux, *Discover Magazine*, discovermagazine.com)

1. Darwin Day

Atheists have chosen the birthday of the founder of Evolutionism, Charles Darwin, as their sacred day, 12th February. Religious celebrations are conducted around the world on this date. Richard Dawkins sits on the advisory board of this organised religion. This whole fiasco is made even more amusing with the knowledge they already have a special day set aside for them—1st April.

"The fool hath said in his heart, There is no God." Ps 14:1

2. Evolution Day

Another sacred holy day for Atheists is Evolution Day, 24th November, the date Evolutionism's holy scriptures were published by Father Darwin.

Atheist Evolution

Something I've noticed lately when listening to an Atheist debate, they no longer tend to use scientific arguments, preferring instead to use philosophical arguments. Perhaps they're starting to realise not only is science on Creation's side, it negates theirs.

It's laughable when Atheists talk about evil, which often features in their philosophical rants. When they do, ask them to define the concepts of 'right' and 'wrong', 'good' and 'evil'. There's a catch. They cannot defer to a Biblical worldview, only to their Atheist worldview. They cannot do it. It's not possible to define any of those four words without a Biblical worldview.

Famous Atheists:

Being consistent with their dishonest method of substituting frauds and hoaxes to prop up their religious dogma, Atheists falsely claim prominent people are disciples of their religion. They peddle propaganda posters with the sarcastic caption, 'Atheism, good enough for these idiots'. Featured in a collage, are the pictures of those named below. By showing these men, they're implying they were all Atheists. They weren't, only one was. The quotes next to their names are not included on this poster.

Charles Darwin: "I have never been an Atheist."

Thomas Jefferson: "I am a real Christian, that is to say, a disciple of the doctrines of Jesus Christ."

Benjamin Franklin: "I believe in one God, the Creator of the universe."

Carl Sagan: "Atheism is very stupid."

Albert Einstein: "There are good people who say there is no God. But what really makes me angry is that they quote me for the support of such views."

Mark Twain: He attended church and helped build one.

Abraham Lincoln: "In regards to this great Book, I have but to say it is the best gift God has given to man. All the good the Saviour gave to the world was communicated through this Book. But for it we could not know right from wrong."

Ernest Hemmingway: He was an Atheist who believed religion was detrimental to human happiness. He committed suicide, blowing his brains out with a shotgun. Besides Hemmingway, other famous Atheists include Pol Pot of Cambodian Killing Fields fame, Lenin, Trotsky and Stalin.

What About the Fossils?

DURING high school when I'd mentioned something about the truth of Genesis, my mother had asked me this question, implying fossil existence destroyed the Biblical timeline. I had no answer, asking this of myself, many times. Once more I'd felt the erosion of faith. Yet still, there was something there. I couldn't explain it. Instinctively I knew the Bible was true, I just couldn't defend it. Now I can.

The question posed will invariably arise around the same time the dinosaur card is played. Previously, I dreaded the question. Now, I relish it. You see, fossils, their creation and existence, disprove Evolutionism. Ironically, believers continue to play this hand. Ignorant Christians are largely to blame, as they make a few absurd claims, such as:

"God Put Them There"

This is the excuse ignorant Christians provide when this seemingly daunting question is asked. Typically, the person asking is referring to dinosaur fossils. Rather than admitting they don't know, Christians may say God created fossils to test their faith. They've bought the lie dinosaurs lived 'millions of years' ago. Scripture denounces this, claiming all land animals were created on Day Six.

Grade Eight Fossils

There I was in grade eight, sitting beside Ebo. It was my first year of high school, we'd met that year. You'll recall he was predominant in my drowning story, which would occur months later. Interestingly, many years would pass and it would come to light our grandfathers had also been close friends.

An explanation for fossil formation in our textbooks showed a dead fish on the ocean floor. Over time, this fish was covered with layers of sediments and compressed. As you may have guessed, this process took, 'millions of years'. You're about to discover why this explanation is impossible. Your logic and reasoning will reveal this to you.

In some ways, I'd been as stupid as David Attenborough, failing to see the obvious. It would be twenty years and take the exposure to Creation Ministries International before I'd see the light. In hindsight, it was so obvious I should've seen it back in grade eight.

Road-Kill

What does roadkill look like? Is it pristine, or mangled? As days and weeks pass, you'll see it deteriorate, especially due to scavengers and harsh weather conditions. How often have you seen predatory birds scavenging on the roads, inadvertently ending up as road-kill themselves?

While walking through the bush, you'll see a kangaroo leg-bone over here, and maybe a kangaroo skull or tailbone over there, but not much else. Why? Scavengers again—dingoes, foxes, crows, maggots, ants, worms and bacteria. Elements wreak havoc too; blazing sun and driving rain.

Do you see where this is going? Dead fish don't sink to the bottom and stay there, let alone, stay intact. Gasses will cause them to bloat and float, where they're attacked by other fish, or at the very least, break apart. Remains fall to the bottom, but aren't left to rest in peace. Or pieces, as it were. Crabs, lobsters—they have to eat too. How about ocean currents?

Do you now see why Evolutionism's just-so-stories, sold to us through the pages of alleged scientific textbooks, are utter nonsense? Are you starting to catch a glimpse as to how the existence of fossils shoots a massive hole in the 'millions of years' dogma? There's no way an intact fish lies peacefully on the ocean floor, slowly being covered by sediments over 'millions of years'.

How Fossils Are Formed

"The fossilization process takes at least ten thousand years." (Brigit Katz, 'Scientists Baked a "Fossil" in 24 Hours,' 2018, *Smithsonian Magazine*)

You read the above quote regarding the alleged time span required for fossil formation. Darwin would agree, admitting soft-bodied fossils, such as those of jellyfish, could never exist, due to the alleged slow fossilisation process, "No organism wholly soft can be preserved." (*On the Origin of Species,* 6th Edition, 1872, p. 422) Keep in mind, if the 'millions of years' doctrine was true, he'd be right.

He isn't.

Numerous intricate soft-bodied fossils are seen in fossil graveyards across the earth, such as the Burgess Shale in the Canadian Rockies and the Solnhofen Limestone of Germany. Worms, squid, jellyfish and even leaves of plants, footprints, sand ripples and raindrop impressions are fossilised. These fossils negate Evolutionism dogma.

Science proves fossils form quickly. They have to, before the carcass deteriorates, or is disturbed.

Noah's Flood—Fossil Creator

Unique, rare conditions are required for fossil creation. Evolutionism believers state fossils are derived from dead animals. In that, fossilisation begins once they've died. Conversely, science says it's often the fossilisation process itself, which causes death.

Take, for instance, jellyfish fossilised against a rippled sand background. The process couldn't have begun after a dead jellyfish had been washed ashore. Corrosive action of waves would've obliterated it. Not to mention, destructive sun rays, seagulls—you get the picture. These jellyfish must've been living at the point of fossilisation.

Have you seen a fish swallow a smaller fish? It occurs in the blink of an eye. Fish have been fossilised in the middle of this action. Imagine the speed at which fossilisation and subsequent death must've occurred. Imagine too, the sudden depositing of tons of sediment required to preserve this action. It was a sudden, catastrophic event that killed these fish. Similar fossils are found worldwide. These fossils fly in the face of the slothful 'millions of years' doctrine.

Evidence for a worldwide flood is observed across the earth. Once you see the geological formations formed by Noah's Flood you cannot un-see it. You'll recognise it everywhere. Case in point, I'd spent a few days in the canyons of the Blue Mountains, west of Sydney. Paths have been carved into these steep canyon walls. Close to the top, I found myself walking on fossilised ripples. According to Darwin, fossils such as these shouldn't exist.

Noah's Flood is the best explanation for fossils. They must be buried rapidly, protecting them from scavengers and oxygen. They must be buried deeply to ensure adequate protection as well as provide substantial pressure to activate and accelerate fossilisation. Think of the process this way—quickly and deeply. This worldwide flood produced the unique conditions required for fossilisation. No other explanation comes close.

Dead clams open after a few hours. Closed, fossilised clam shells prove they were buried quickly, killed during the fossilisation process. Pressure exerted by tons of sediment prevented the clams from opening, once they'd died. Clams and other marine fossils have been discovered on mountain ranges across the world, including Mt Everest. This is clear evidence for Noah's Flood. It's an open-and-shut case. Watertight, too—puns intended.

Fossils prove animals don't evolve into completely different animals. In the process, they obliterate the 'millions of years' doctrine. What was once unexplainable to me, is now laughable to me—the question, "What about the fossils?" My response, "Exactly!"

Fossil Graveyards

These are precisely what the name suggests. Several enormous fossil beds scattered across the earth contain hundreds of dinosaurs. Try to imagine the vast area such a graveyard would cover. Further, try to imagine the turbulent catastrophic conditions that would've caused hundreds of living dinosaurs to be buried rapidly, in one area, under tons of sediment.

You may be wondering, *How could there have been hundreds of dinosaurs congregated in one area?* Good question. What if they were distributed there by swirling, violent waters, conceivably by tidal wave action, caused by the tearing up of the foundations of the great deep? Subsequent wave action then buried them under tons of sediment. Perhaps this is why revised Evolutionism doctrines now declare that dinosaur fossils were created by said dinosaurs having, 'slipped and fallen into a river'.

Evolutionism-believing 'scientists' have attributed one such fossil graveyard, found in North Dakota USA, to an alleged asteroid that supposedly hit Earth 66 million years ago. Not 60, or 70, or even 65 million years, mind you, but '66' million years. Well now, these fossil graveyards are found across the earth. Why isn't there any mention of asteroids within these colossal graveyards? This fossil graveyard contained a tangled mass of branches, freshwater fish, dinosaurs, (including tyrannosaurus and triceratops), mammals, sea turtles, logs, crocodiles, frogs, snakes, birds, marine ammonites and sharks. Did anything stick out as you read that list, perhaps seem, 'out of place' to you? Many of those creatures shouldn't have existed at the same time as dinosaurs, according to Evolutionism. That's not all, marine creatures were mixed with land animals. How would you explain this, logically?

Feathers and Teeth From Scales?

Remember the Evolutionism claim that 'dinosaurs evolved into birds'? Their just-so story solemnly declares dinosaur scales became frayed, subsequently 'evolving' into feathers. You'd think I'm making it up. I'm not. They're currently abandoning this doctrine, due to the absolute ridiculousness of it. Scrambling to find another just-so story, you can be sure that their new substitute will follow a similar fate, in due time. Then, the cycle will repeat.

Archaeopteryx

There aren't any fossils of dinosaurs 'part-evolved' into birds, only fossils of fully formed dinosaurs and fully formed birds. Yet, dinosaur stomachs have contained birds—So much for birds evolving from dinosaurs. Archaeopteryx is an extinct bird. Evolutionism believers insist it's a transitional link between dinosaurs and birds. It doesn't have frayed scales allegedly on their way to evolving into feathers. It's fully avian.

Go look at a feather under a microscope, read up on its structure. It's moronic to believe they're 'evolved, frayed scales'. Evolutionism also teaches animal and human teeth evolved from our alleged fish ancestors' scales, which had migrated into their mouths. Where are fossils demonstrating scales have become frayed and 'part-evolved' into feathers or teeth?

"New analysis of one of the world's weirdest animals—the sawfish—supports the idea that teeth first appeared when ancient fishes' body scales migrated into their mouths about 400 million years ago." (Daniel Leonard, 'Ancient Sawfish Help to Illuminate Our Teeth's Scaly Origins,' 2022, scientificamerican.com)

We have fossils of feathers, scales and teeth, but nothing in between. Why have scales stopped evolving into feathers? Shouldn't fish have feathers, according to Evolutionism? Fish are constantly grazing coral reefs and barnacles. Why hasn't this caused their scales to 'become frayed and evolve into feathers'?

"Hair, scales, and feathers seem to have very little in common. But these structures appear to have evolved from a single ancestor—a reptile that lived 300 million years ago—according to new research." (Ben Panko, 'Human hair, bird feathers came from reptile scales: New study suggests a common ancestor for all three skin coverings,' 2016, science.org)

Several dinosaur fossils have been found alongside hundreds of mammal fossils, in the Gobi Desert of Central Asia. These fossils have a remarkable, preserved appearance, looking as if they were created recently, as opposed to 'millions of years' ago. In Alberta, Canada, one such graveyard runs for hundreds of kilometres, containing innumerable fossils, many of which, are dinosaurs.

A South African fossil graveyard, The Karoo Formation, contains billions of fossils. Don't get hung up on the number, you're probably thinking it's outlandish. On the contrary, it's quite conservative. How did so many animals become pushed into one area? What was it that caused them to be buried quickly, with tons of debris, concentrated over a vast area?

Desert Whales

Eighty whales, as well as several other fossilised marine animals in a Chilean desert, were discovered in 2011. Naturally, those who'd succumbed to Evolutionism struggled to come up with a plausible, logical conclusion as to how this may have occurred.

A logical explanation is they were swimming over the sunken landmass at the culmination of the worldwide flood, becoming stranded as floodwaters drained from the earth.

Missing Links

'Transitional fossils' and 'missing links' are different terms for the same thing. They don't exist. These are in-betweens, the non-existent fossil 'stepping-stones' between apes and humans, cats and dogs, or dinosaurs and birds. Darwin declared the lack of transitional fossils as, "The most obvious and gravest objection which can be urged against my theory." He expected they'd be unearthed in due time. Well, 200 years have passed. We have advanced technology and sophisticated digging equipment, yet those alleged missing links are still missing.

Living Fossils?

Sounds like an oxymoron, doesn't it? This is the common occurrence where a living creature or plant is found, identical to creatures or plants found in rocks dated as being 'millions of years' old. Take, for example, the coelacanth fish. This is our forefather, according to Evolutionism's family tree.

Coelacanth Fish

These are ugly, primitive-looking. Evolutionism maintains their fossils have been scientifically dated at over 410 million years. Due to their numerous odd-looking fins, 'science' informs us they were predecessors to man, declaring these fins magically evolved into arms and legs. Yes, these fish are our ancestors, we're their descendants, "It's science," they allege.

It was taught they died out 70 million years ago. That doctrine was shattered when they were discovered swimming off the coast of Africa in the seventies, and later, off the coast of Indonesia, identical to fossilised coelacanths. Evolutionism believers are content with labelling it a living fossil, then merrily carrying on their way. Don't do that. Stop, ask yourself a few questions (unrhetorical):

1. What animal were they before they evolved into coelacanth fish?
2. Why was there no evolution in 410 million years?
3. If science was wrong in declaring the coelacanth fish as our direct ancestor, what else are they currently wrong about, concerning origins?

Considering then that coelacanths didn't evolve, it stands to reason their environment, food source and predators didn't evolve either. So, you have to ask, "Just what *did* evolve?"

After all, an alleged minimum of 410 million years has passed, and not only is it still a fish, it's still a coelacanth. You'd think at the very least it may have sprouted a leg, a hand, feathers, wing or beak. So much for them having evolved into humans.

According to Evolutionism dogma, coelacanth were around for 200 million years before the dinosaurs. Dinosaurs evolved from these fish too, remember?

"There is nothing new about humans and all other vertebrates having evolved from fish." (University of Copenhagen, Faculty of Science, 'We're more like primitive fishes than once believed, new research shows,' 2021, sciencedaily.com)

How is it that the fish scales didn't evolve into feathers, but the dinosaurs' scales did? To bring the point home, how did an alleged asteroid, which allegedly killed all of the dinosaurs, have no impact (pun intended), on the coelacanth fish?

Don't misunderstand, it's not just coelacanth fish that are living fossils, it's everything—koalas, snakes, sharks, bees, horseshoe crabs, dragonflies, platypuses, aardvarks, anything and everything.

Stop and think about what you've just read.

Stasis

Evolutionism believers have a word for the existence of living fossils—'stasis', as in, 'stays' the same. This is a fancy way of saying, "No evolution, is proof of evolution." Or, as they like to word it, "It didn't evolve, because it didn't have to." This is one of their just-so stories to explain away missing links.

Punctuated Equilibrium

Another ambitious attempt to explain away missing links is—'punctuated equilibrium'. This just-so story surmises evolution occurred rapidly, leaving no fossil evidence. This doctrine alone runs counter to Evolutionism dogma:

'Natura non facit saltum', is Latin for, 'Nature doesn't jump'. Darwin used this statement several times in his Origins book: "Natural selection acts solely by accumulating slight, successive, favourable variations, it can produce no great or sudden modification; it can act only by very short and slow steps. Hence the canon of 'Natura non facit saltum'." (Charles Darwin, *On the Origin of Species*)

As with stasis, punctuated equilibrium is another fancy way of saying, "No evolution is proof of evolution."

An example of punctuated equilibrium is their mythical doctrine of the first bird evolving from a reptilian egg. This doctrine contradicts Darwinian Evolution, which stipulates slow and gradual change.

Dawkins sums it up this way, "Evolution has been observed. It's just that it hasn't been observed while it's happening." Ponder what you've just read. Attempt to reconcile it in your mind. You're probably scratching your head, thinking it's a printing error. It's not. It's delusion, imagination and unwavering faith flying in the face of science, logic and common sense.

Cambrian Explosion

Also known as the 'Biological Big Bang', the 'Cambrian explosion' is the Evolutionism believer's way of endeavouring to disguise the truth of Genesis. It's a time when they believe most of the major groups of animals first appear as fossils. Owing to the relatively short period over which the diversity of lifeforms appears (jumps into existence), it's called the Cambrian Explosion.

Yes, animals appeared abruptly and fully formed (Genesis), in the earliest fossils, and stayed that way. Evolutionism believers slap fancy, contradictory labels on this fact—'stasis' and 'punctuated equilibrium'—claiming it as proof for their religion.

In summary, once you boil away their jargon and fancy word salads, they have two excuses for non-existent transitional fossils:

1. Evolution happened too fast.
2. Evolution happened too slowly.

If science alone hasn't proven to you that fossils refute Evolutionism, surely logic and common sense have. If not, you're either a moron or you're too emotionally attached. Harsh, but true. You can get angry, you probably will. Regardless, that doesn't change the fact. Yes, you've been living a lie—Choose now to live in truth instead. I'm not here to tickle your ears—go to a Christian counterfeit church if that's what you're looking for. If you want truth, read the Bible from an unbiased, unassuming position.

♪ Millions of Years ♪

LESS than 250 years ago the world's scientific community believed in a Biblical timeline, with earth's geographical features being formed during the catastrophic conditions of Noah's Flood. Geologist Charles Lyell set out to destroy this belief and conjured up the mythical notion of 'millions of years'. It's a case of the blind leading the blind, since Darwin swallowed this nonsense hook, line and sinker.

Unfortunately, Christians have been swayed by unrelenting Evolutionism propaganda of 'millions of years' dogma. They attempt to force it into the Six Days of Creation, claiming days could be extended periods of time, even durations of millions of years. They'll defer to the verse, "One day is with the Lord as a thousand years, and a thousand years as one day." 2 Peter 3:8

Plants were created on Day Three. The sun and moon were created on Day Four. Do you think plants would've survived 1,000 years without the sun, let alone, 'millions of years'? Logically, the Creation account is referring to twenty-four-hour periods. Stop bending the knee to this false doctrine.

Although we've already referenced the mythical concept of 'millions of years' several times, there are many things to keep in mind. Many, if not all, say it devoid of thought. When uttered, it's said with a mystical, musical, reverence. It's almost as if they've momentarily placed themselves into a trance, regressing into a state of brief hypnosis. Those being preached to, appear to enter a stupor themselves. It's declared similarly to a counterfeit Christian preacher saying, "Jeeezzzzzzzz—US!" Likewise, the Evolutionism believer vocalises 'millions of years' with a deep sense of awe and reverence. You can almost envision them casting magic pixie dust into the air as they proclaim their sacred mantra.

Driving up the Kuranda Range in Cairns (my backyard, mind you), with an ex-relative, he pointed to buckled, cross-bedded layers, which we've previously established as proof of Noah's Flood. Smugly he informed me, "They're 'millions of years' old."

Really? And how do you know that? How do you know they aren't thousands of years old? Tens of thousands of years old? Or, hundreds of thousands of years old? No, it's always the cliché, 'millions of years'. To say otherwise is considered blasphemy.

Next time you hear someone proclaim 'millions of years', ask them, or at least yourself, "How do you know? How many 'millions of years'? 10 million? 16 million? 100 million? 110 million? Are you sure it's millions? Why not hundreds of thousands of years? Why not tens of thousands? Why not thousands?"

Dinosaur Blood

Unfossilised dinosaur bones complete with red blood cells are another nail in the coffin of 'millions of years'. You'll read about this in the 'Dragons or Dinosaurs?' chapter.

Carbon-14 Dating

Invariably, the sacred cow of C-14 is mentioned. It's believed with a faith so devout; it'd put the faith of many professed Christians to shame. The problem is, C-14 is flawed. It's garbage, especially when used to produce the ages Evolutionism dogma demands.

It's an old horse continually flogged by believers, due in part to them not understanding the dogma they're pushing. Carbon dating offers strong evidence for a young Earth. You see, C-14 cannot provide anywhere near the ages they claim it does. By its very nature, C-14 dating can only give a maximum age of 50,000 years.

C-14 utilises radioactive decay rate to determine ages. The half-life, instrumental for calculations, is approximately 5,700 years. Therefore C-14 is only somewhat useful for dating fossils that are allegedly up to 50,000 years old. You'll quickly discover this yourself when you look into it. Despite this, radiocarbon has been discovered in fossils alleged to be 'millions of years' old. Those ages can't be correct, not even close.

"Living things take carbon from atmospheric CO_2, which contains radioactive carbon-14. Carbon-14 undergoes radioactive decay, with half its atoms disappearing roughly every 6,000 years. No detectable carbon-14 should survive from 76m years ago, but the bones were full of it." (Nicholas R. Longrich, 'Dinosaur bones: Hidden life revealed inside them,' *The Conversation*, 2019, phys.org)

Besides, calculations are based on assumptions about the past. As a result, they're far from accurate. Further, results are hampered by other factors. For example, extra water in the environment, past and present, can distort readings. Consider the watery state the entire Earth was in a few thousand years ago.

Shells from living snails have been carbon dated as being 27,000 years old. Believers refuse to budge, however, as 'millions of years' is the shifting sands upon which Evolutionism's house of cards is built upon.

Those adamant on the virtues of C-14, rarely know much about it. If they did, and so long as they weren't prone to lying, they'd never suggest that C-14 was proof for 'millions of years'. Whenever the C-14 card is played, ask them what it is and the process that leads to the conclusion for a date. Hardly anyone will be able to explain it.

The Bible is the inspired word of our Creator. Therefore, whatever it teaches is true, including its commentary on Earth's age. The

Bible is clear, Creation occurred only 6000, to 10,000 years ago. This is demonstrated by the genealogies of Genesis 5, 11, and other Biblical information.

Darwin's Fantasy

Many people including Christians, still dogmatically say Earth looks old, because we've been conditioned to see it as old. We've all seen photos and videos of Grand Canyon, with the claim that each layer of sediment is 'millions of years' old. Charles Lyell is responsible for this as he purposefully sought to develop a system of geology, 'to free the science from Moses'. He wasn't looking for truth, he was looking to establish an agenda. Until this time, scientists had believed Earth was 6,000 years old.

Lyell had first put the 'millions of years' myth into Darwin's head, inspiring him to make evidence conform to the new, 'millions of years' assumption. Darwin would later divulge his deepest fear, which modern science has since proven, in his following letter to Lyell, "Thinking of the many cases of men pursuing an illusion for years, often & often a cold shudder has run through me and I have asked myself whether I may not have devoted my life to a phantasy." (Letter to Charles Lyell, 23 November 1859, Darwin Correspondence Project, University of Cambridge, darwinproject.ac.uk)

Polystrate Fossils

The existence of polystrate fossils, alone, destroys the fanciful notion of 'millions of years'. Large canyons have been observed to form from a lot of water, over minimal time. Then factor in the polystrate fossils and marine fossils contained within them. Further, there's no visible evidence of erosion within the alleged millions of years separating each layer. Besides, Noah's Flood is the only explanation for the initial deposit of Grand Canyon sediments anyway, before the canyon was carved.

Soft Rocks

Not convinced? Have you ever seen rocks bend? You may have seen rock formations that appear as though they have. The layers are bent, buckled, twisted and cross-bedded. How is this even remotely possible, according to the doctrines of 'millions of years'?

No doubt you'll try to explain it away. Perhaps you'll say there was a mudflow and while it was still soft, earthquakes or other factors caused sediments to bend, before finally hardening into rock. There's an insurmountable obstacle with that belief—the claim there are 'millions of years' between layers. Observable evidence shows this claim is simply not possible. After the first buckled, curved, twisted layer solidified, you'd need the next layer to conform to the same unique, distorted shape, having the same process repeat (layer, 'millions of years', layer), and so on. If you want to claim buckled layers don't require 'millions of years' separating them, why claim unbuckled layers such as Grand Canyon, do?

If you suspend your belief in layers of rock being separated by the mythical 'millions of years', and say it was an earthquake or similar that formed the layers quickly; then how can it be said that layers in Grand Canyon also weren't laid rapidly? Especially as several pieces of evidence, logic, and common sense suggest it's the most logical conclusion.

Keep in mind, we're talking about sedimentary rocks. Evolutionism believers say they take 'millions of years' to form. Across the earth, rock layers are observed which are bent and folded at radical angles without fracturing. When you see these warped, buckled, sedimentary landscapes, realise you're likely seeing evidence of Noah's Flood. These soft, pliable layers were buckled and cross-bedded during the catastrophic conditions of the breaking up of the foundations of the great deep at the outset of the flood. Then the sodden earth was raised at the culmination of the flood, where the layers bake and harden in the sun. Keep this in mind when you're out and about. You'll start seeing it everywhere.

Dragons or Dinosaurs?

TWENTY years ago, I was doing a study in Brisbane with Seventh-day Adventists. The facilitator visited one day with a pamphlet that had been placed in his letterbox. It was an invitation to hear Gary Bates from Creation Ministries International speak about dinosaurs aboard the Ark. He said he'd go if I went.

With my arms crossed, I sat up the back believing it would be some fanciful, Christian nonsense, grasping at straws, attempting to explain away the existence of dinosaurs. *After all, everyone knew these creatures were prehistoric. They weren't living today; the Bible didn't make any mention of them. Besides, they were huge, there's no way they would've fit aboard the Ark. Even if they had, they would've eaten the animals.*

I don't recall much from the presentation, other than it made a lot of sense. Cognitive dissonance had impaired the process of my understanding. As with most kids, I'd loved dinosaurs and spent numerous hours reading about them. Suddenly, I was being subjected to compelling evidence I'd been sold a lie.

Since that time, I've attended several Creation Ministries seminars, taking my children and friends. All who attend cannot deny the information they're presented with makes sense.

Dragons

Dragon legends are found in every culture across the earth. Ignoramuses mock the word 'dragon' in the Bible. It's an archaic word, replaced less than 200 years ago by the modern word, 'dinosaur', which translated, means 'great and terrible lizard'. Crocodiles fit that description, don't they? How about monitor lizards? The idea of men having lived with dragons/dinosaurs is mocked, yet we're living with them now.

The only difference between dinosaurs, crocodiles, monitor lizards or tortoises, is the mythical ingredient of 'millions of years'. Most dinosaurs are extinct. Animals go extinct all the time.

Marco Polo

There are countless depictions and descriptions of man living with dragons/dinosaurs. Marco Polo records he encountered dragons while exploring Asia. Read about it yourself in his book, *The Travels of Marco Polo*. Many are opposed to this truth as it refutes the religious doctrine of 'millions of years'. Deniers say he's encountering a crocodile. Really? Do you think Marco Polo, world traveller, is unfamiliar with a crocodile? He describes dragons in detail, saying they abide in caves or caverns on land and have three claws on the forefeet—crocodiles have five.

Bunyip

Australian Aborigines described the legendry 'bunyip' to a sketcher in the early days of English settlement. The resulting picture was that of a duck-billed dinosaur. There's a carving of a stegosaurus dinosaur on a temple in Cambodia, lost to the jungle for over 900 years. I've seen this depiction firsthand.

Biblical Sauropod Dinosaur

"Behold now behemoth, which I made with thee; he eateth grass as an ox. Lo now, his strength is in his loins, and his force is in the navel of his belly. He moveth his tail like a cedar: the sinews of his stones are wrapped together. His bones are as strong pieces of brass; his bones are like bars of iron. He is the chief of the ways of God: he that made him can make his sword to approach unto him. Surely the mountains bring him forth food, where all the beasts of the field play. He lieth under the shady trees, in the covert of the reed, and fens. The shady trees cover him with their shadow; the willows of the brook compass him about. Behold, he drinketh up a river, and hasteth not: he trusteth that he can draw up Jordan into his mouth. He taketh it with his eyes: his nose pierceth through snares." Job 40:15–24

This creature is dismissed by Evolutionism believers as either a hippopotamus or rhinoceros. Picture the tail of both creatures. Does this description fit, 'He moveth his tail like a cedar'? Of course not, though it does fit the description of a dinosaur's tail.

'His nose pierceth through snares'—this seems to suggest capturing this creature was possible, and then tethered via a hole in its nose, similar to a bull.

Hunted Into Extinction

Evolutionism declares, "Sixty million years ago, an asteroid killed the dinosaurs." Even though believers also claim, "Dinosaurs evolved into birds." Noah's Flood would've killed the majority of dinosaurs. Offspring of those aboard the Ark were likely hunted into extinction.

Most, anyway. As established, crocodiles are still living with man. Back when it was legal to shoot these man-eaters, it was feared they may become extinct, as is the current case with Chinese alligators and Philippine crocodiles. Across the world, several types of crocodiles have been classified as critically endangered. Since the shooting of crocodiles was outlawed in Australia, they've grown to plague proportions.

By the way, let's address the pious, ignorant claim, "They were here before us." They weren't. They were created on the same day as man. Further, humans were given dominion over the animals, not the other way around:

"And God said, Let us make man in our image, after our likeness: and let them have dominion over the fish of the sea, and over the fowl of the air, and over the cattle, and over all the earth, and over every creeping thing that creepeth upon the earth." Gen 1:26

Wild tiger populations have decreased by over ninety-five per cent in the last 100 years—hunted into near-extinction. Bali tigers went extinct in the 50s. In less than 200 hundred years, Australians have eliminated the Tasmanian tiger and the toolache wallaby. Overseas, several species have gone extinct, such as the Western black rhino.

Species of dolphins, zebras, hippopotamuses, peacocks and giraffes, to name a few, are in danger of extinction.

Crocodiles and Paedophiles

Another nonsensical claim, again by the same unthinking mob, regards the culling of crocodiles, "Leave them alone, they're in their natural environment!"

Is that so? Well, a paedophile loitering around a schoolyard or a playground is also in his or her, natural environment. According to your logic, the paedophile should be left alone also. Don't forget, as an Evolutionism believer, you think humans are animals. According to your logic, crocodiles and paedophiles cannot be held accountable. After all, they're only doing what comes naturally, they were 'born that way'. Their actions aren't the result of reason and thought, they are the result of random explosions of chemicals inside their brains. If you were to remove all emotion from your thinking, logically, you'd have to agree on this point. In both environments, the paedophile and the crocodile are predators, threats to those who are in their natural environments.

Dragons or Dinosaurs?

Leviathan

Perhaps legends of knights fighting dragons are based on factual events. Yes, fire-breathing ones too. Why not? After all, there are passage ways in dinosaur skulls that scientists are unable to account for. Who's to say these weren't the result of engineering to produce a fiery explosion? After all, contemplate the bombardier beetle. They have two chemicals stored separately. When threatened, they mix the chemicals, instantly directing a scalding chemical explosion at their predators. How could this possibly have evolved without the beetle blowing itself to smithereens?

Who's to say similar engineering wasn't devised with the creation of some dinosaurs too? Here's a description of Leviathan:

"Out of his mouth go burning lamps, and sparks of fire leap out. Out of his nostrils goeth smoke, as out of a seething pot or caldron. His breath kindleth coals, and a flame goeth out of his mouth."
Job 41:19–21

Winton

This town in outback Queensland, Australia, is famous for two things. Firstly, it's connected with the Great Shearer's Strike of the 1890s, inspiring bush poet Banjo Paterson to pen 'Waltzing Matilda'. This song was performed in public for the first time there.

'Matilda' was another word for your 'swag', or 'bed roll'. Waltzing, is a form of dancing. 'Waltzing Matilda' was to walk with your swag, as you searched along dusty roads for employment. You may be wondering, *What has this to do with the title of this book?*

Simply put, "Context." I have a personal interest in history, as does Gospel writer, Luke. Since he was also a medical doctor, he often included both historical and medical themes in his writings. It's this human tendency which adds to the authenticity of the Scriptures, once you study them.

Winton's second claim to fame?—The legendary fossilised 'Dinosaur Stampede'.

Fossilised Dinosaur Stampede

Reading the alleged explanation for the creation and preservation of these dinosaur footprints was painful. Several contradictions, opinions and just-so stories peppered it. One of them admitted rain would destroy footprints, then turned around and said rain caused the footprints to fill with sediment. So, in other words, rain destroyed the footprints, but also filled the 'destroyed footprints', with sediment, 'preserving them'.

They say this occurred 95 'million years' ago. That's the problem with visiting various historical or geographical sites. We're constantly told 'this and that' occurred, 'millions of years' ago. It's bad enough seeing it written on a sign or printed in literature. However, hearing someone say it, makes me want to throw up in my mouth.

Believers insist the fossilised stampede preserves evidence of herbivore dinosaurs fleeing a larger, carnivorous dinosaur. Instead, extensive study and comparison of fossilised trackways have established the alleged carnivorous dinosaur was an herbivore also.

Besides, it's been discovered the dinosaurs ran in water, rapidly rising water. Or in other words, floodwaters. Many tracks had large spacing between their steps, relative to the size of the dinosaur, inferring the dinosaurs were being taken with the current. Most tracks headed northeast, suggesting the current was in that direction. However, the alleged meat-eating dinosaur was headed south, and not swimming.

Researchers have since altered their just-so story, now claiming the tracks were made over days or weeks. They don't seem to realise this new opinion of theirs seriously undermines their explanation for the preservation (fossilisation), of the stampede in the first place.

The irony is, while presenting the dinosaur stampede as proof of Evolutionism, on the contrary, science demonstrates that it's proof of Noah's Flood, instead.

Chinese Star Signs

The dragon is one of the twelve Chinese zodiac animals. The remaining animals are: rat, ox, tiger, rabbit, snake, horse, goat, monkey, rooster, dog, and pig. Do you really believe that they'd have eleven real animals, and one mythical animal?

Unfossilised Dinosaur Bones

Another area where science confounds Evolutionism is the discovery of red blood cells inside dinosaur bones. Scientist Mary Schweitzer from Montana State University discovered part of a tyrannosaurus rex bone had not fossilised. That alone should tell any thinking person it could not be 'millions of years' old. (Carl Wieland, 'Sensational dinosaur blood report!' *Creation* 19(4):42–43, 1997, creation.com)

Believing in 'millions of years', she 'knew' they couldn't be red blood cells—the test must be wrong. For this reason, Mary tested it a total of seventeen times. The result was unwavering, they were red blood cells. Rather than change her beliefs to align with the scientific method, the plan was to discover how red blood cells could last for 'millions of years'. They can't. What you'll hear them claim is that the specimen was 'contaminated'. This is utter rubbish. They think they can wave science away by throwing out a dismissive, faulty complaint. It's an incredibly weak argument and they know it. That aside, scientists now go completely out of the way to eradicate any possible accusation of contamination, before testing bones.

Dinosaur bones complete with soft, stretchy material and red blood cells continue to be found. They cannot be 'millions of years' old, not even tens of thousands of years old.

While suppressed, there is growing evidence of dinosaurs/dragons having lived with man. The Bible mentions them, as does a renowned explorer. Ancient legends describe encounters with them. Ancient artefacts and paintings bear their resemblance. Science continues to find their unfossilised bones. While some try to sell us on the idea that crocodiles aren't dinosaurs, what do your eyes tell you?

Fool's Gold

THIS term is used in the context of something spoken or written, which someone foolishly perceives to be a brilliant argument. Unbeknownst to these fools, drunk on their ignorance, their words have no value. They are worthless, vain babblings. Bible opponents parrot Fool's Gold, even when they know it's false. Here's a common one, possibly one you've used yourself:

Fool: "Religion causes all wars"
One afternoon I was with my young children in Orange, a country town in New South Wales. Radio DJs were ridiculing the Bible, as they often do. These people worship celebrities and often talk crude, immature, meaningless and trivial garbage, day in and day out. It's almost as if a job requirement is to first have half of your brain removed.

Brain-dead people were ringing in with their take on how they believed religion was the cause of all wars. Naturally, the idiot DJs lapped it up. Praying to God (not literally), that the station would answer my call, I jumped on the phone. They did.

Telling them I was ringing about religion being the cause of all wars, they enthusiastically murmured their agreement. The trap was set, "Which religion caused World War One?"

Radio silence (pun intended). "Which religion caused World War Two?"

There were uncomfortable mutterings. How dare I go on their airways and demolish their arguments! Especially when their arguments were opposed to the Bible! Any minute now, they'd hang up. For this reason, when they tried talking over me, I talked over them, "What about Vietnam? Korea? Falklands War? Malayan Emergency? Boer War One and Two? Boxer Rebellion?" My children grinned, listening to the live exchange. Reeling from the onslaught, the DJs couldn't take the embarrassment of their propaganda being annihilated in front of a huge, live audience. They abruptly ended the call.

Fool: "Hitler was a Christian."
This causes my brain to stop, trying to determine if they're ignorant, incredibly stupid, or both. I remind them, "Yahshua was a Jew." If the penny doesn't drop, and often it doesn't, I help them further, "Hitler killed Jews, he didn't worship them."

Fool: "There's no evidence for God!" (a)
"Even the concept of evidence is evidence for God, since evidence presupposes truth and knowledge, and you can't account for that, without God."

Fool: "There's no evidence for God!" (b)
"What would *you* consider *acceptable* as evidence for God?"

Fool: "I don't believe the Bible because it's full of contradictions."
"People don't reject the Bible based on erroneous claims it contradicts itself. They reject the Bible because it contradicts how they live."—E. Paul Hovey

Fool: "Why the Bible and not the Quran?"
"Did Mohammed claim to be God on Earth? Did he rise from the dead?"

Fool: "Religion is used to control people"
What's the first thing a dictator does when he comes to power? He bans the Bible. If the Bible was about control, far from banning

it, he should be enforcing its reading. Bible-believing men are uncontrollable. Here's why, in a nutshell:

"Fear not them which kill the body, but are not able to kill the soul: but rather fear him which is able to destroy both soul and body in hell." Matt 10:28

Bible believers know our time on Earth is a dress rehearsal, an audition. It's not all about our life here and now. It's how we live it, so that following the Resurrection of the Dead, we're granted eternal life on a restored Earth, rather than perish forever in the Lake of Fire.

Fool: "Atheism is not a belief. It is the rejection of an unproven assertion."
"Do you believe that?"

Fool: "Where did God come from/Who created God?"
This is asked once they realise the undeniable truth, 'something' cannot come from 'nothing'. Which, by itself, nullifies Evolutionism's creation story. They fail to realise our Creator is eternal, outside of time. He has no beginning, or ending. Things only require a beginning if they exist within the boundaries of time. He, in fact, created 'time'.

A fool asking this question it telling you they do not understand the meaning of 'eternal'.

Fool: "If God made the universe, then who made God?"
"If the cook cooked the burger, who cooked the cook?"

Fool: "Why would a loving God burn people in Hell for eternity?"
"Eternal torment isn't biblical. But, let me ask you, do you feel those who escaped justice on Earth, deserve to escape justice forever? Do you think it's fair for someone to rape and murder and just pass unpunished into nothingness, rather than face judgement?"

Fool: "You don't need religion to have morals. If you can't determine right from wrong, you lack empathy and common sense, not religion."
"Define the concepts of good and evil, right and wrong, from a purely Atheistic, dog-eat-dog, survival of the fittest, jungle law, every man for himself, worldview. You can't, without deferring to the Biblical worldview." Try it, and see.

Fool: "Why do bad things happen to good people?"
"That only happened once. He was innocent and volunteered in your place, so that good things could happen to bad people."

Fool: "There are 3,000 gods. What makes you think yours is the right one?" (a)
"Your question."

The fool is bewildered, "What do you mean?" He believed his question to be gold. After all, those he associates with believe it to be gold.

Two of the largest world religions believe in the Biblical God—Christians and Jews. Atheists also claim the Judeo-Christian God and Islam God, are one and the same. They're not attacking God so much, as they're attacking His Son. After all, it's Christianity that is constantly ridiculed, not Islam or Judaism. They'd be better off asking, "There are 3,000 gods, what makes you think the Christian god is the right one?"

They aren't concerned with Jews, and they wouldn't dare criticise Islam, but it's open slather on Christians. There's no need to attack the counterfeits; they're leading people away from the truth. Why go after the red herrings? Why aren't they opposed to the flying spaghetti monster? Because they know it isn't real. They're only interested in attacking the truth.

Hollywood Blasphemy

Who does Hollywood continually mock? Hindus? Buddhists? Evolutionism believers? Muslims? Of course not, they only attack Christians. Hollywood loves to violate the Third Commandment:

"Thou shalt not take the name of the Lord thy God in vain; for the Lord will not hold him guiltless that taketh his name in vain." Ex 20:7

Seduced By Satan

How many times do you hear 'Jesus Christ' uttered in a derogatory manner? For an industry that despises truth, they reference Him often. This sustained, concentrated attack isn't surprising. The adversary isn't concerned with counterfeits; Satan is only opposed to truth so you'll see hatred spewed at anything representative of God. Can you guess why?

"Wherein in time past ye walked according to the course of this world, according to the *prince of the power of the air*, the spirit that now worketh in the children of disobedience." Eph 2:2

There you have it! Satan owns the airways. He uses it to spew hate.

Fool: "There are 3,000 gods. What makes you think yours is the right one?" (b)

Let's turn the question around, "You claim there are 3,000 gods, so why do you only attack, criticise and mock the Christian God?"

The answer to the fool's question lies within their question. Atheists attack one God, and then have the audacity to ask you how you know you're worshipping the right one.

Evolutionism believers will claim they attack people of all religions. They don't. Buddhists or Hindus aren't attacked. Aboriginal Australians and Native Americans worship other gods, though Atheists won't attack them. Charles Darwin, the founder of Evolutionism isn't attacked, though they do turn on some of their High Priests: Richard Dawkins, Christopher Hitchens, PZ Myers, Neil deGrasse Tyson, Bill Nye and Sam Harris, to name a few. They don't often openly attack Evolutionism dogma either. It's always the Judeo-Christian God who is singled out for ridicule.

Fool: "There are 3,000 gods. What makes you think yours is the right one?" (c)
"I would ask you the same question."

After the fool recovers from his initial shock, he or she will launch into a false, pious claim about only believing in science. I point out the blatantly obvious, they believe in a trinity, three gods in one:

Father Time ('millions of years'), Mother Nature (creative force) and Lady Luck (holy spirit).

So, believers of Evolutionism, the shoe is on the other foot. Tell us why you believe your gods are the real ones.

Fool: "There are 3,000 gods. What makes you think yours is the right one?" (d)
The Bible is a collection of sixty-six verified historical documents, harmonious in theme, despite having forty different writers comprising three different languages, across three continents, over 3,000 years.

They're recorded by writers of occupations including: fisherman, king, shepherd, tax collector, musician, military commander, prince, tentmaker and medical doctor. It was written during exile, and also from behind prison bars. It comprises numerous styles, including memoir, law, biography, autobiography, parable, allegory and historical narrative. Yet it reads as if there was only one Author. Eyewitnesses recorded supernatural events during the lifetime of other eyewitnesses, which accurately fulfilled specific prophecies. They testify their writings are of Divine origin. This statement was formulated from a similar commentary, penned by Voddie Baucham, American pastor, author, and educator.

Fool: "Why are unicorns in the Bible?"
Unicorns in the Bible is an excellent example of 'Fools' Gold'.

Unicorns are a type of rhinoceros. 'Unicorn', in the 1828 version of the Noah Webster Dictionary says, "An animal with one horn; the Monoceros. This name is often applied to the Rhinoceros." It stipulates the word 'unicorn' is derived from the Latin word 'unicornis'. Unus 'one', and cornu, 'horn'.

Fools unwilling to let go of their perceived gold may say a rhinoceros has two horns, not one. Suit yourself; this is what's listed under rhinoceros in the same dictionary, "A genus of quadrupeds of two species, one of which, the unicorn, has a single horn growing almost erect from the nose. There's another species with two horns, the bicornis."

When you look up 'unicorn', it says 'rhinoceros'. When you look up 'rhinoceros', it says 'unicorn'. This dictionary is 200 years old. The King James Bible was printed 400 years ago.

Fool: "What came first, the chicken or the egg?"
This question is asked by someone attempting to be funny, deflect, appear wise, or a combination thereof. They'll often use it when erroneously claiming we can never know anything for sure.

"Our Creator created the chicken, which laid the egg." Then I ask them what they believe. They'll often say the egg. They believe birds/chickens evolved from dinosaurs, and they feel this nonsense is more plausible if this alleged new creature emerges from a shell. Remind them that dinosaurs came from eggs themselves. Then ask them, "What came first, the dinosaur, or the dinosaur egg?" Whatever they answer with, ask, "How?"

Once they say, "The egg," ask them if it was fertilised. If they claim it was, ask, "How?" Also ask, "Where did the new DNA coding to make chicken feathers, instead of scales, come from?"

Fool: "What about the dinosaurs?" (a)
Pause for effect, "… What about them …?"

The fool is bewildered by the fact you don't have an ashen-looking face, aren't stammering, and haven't tried changing the subject. Turn the tables, "What did dinosaurs evolve from?"

Fool: "What about the dinosaurs?" (b)
"Exactly!"

"Huh?" The fool is blindsided.

"How do you get dinosaurs from an explosion/expansion of nothing?"

Fool: "What about the fossils?" (a)
"I'm surprised you'd bring that up. Fossils are testimony to Creation, Noah's Flood, and spell death for the '♪ millions of years ♪' mantra."

Remember the phenomenon of what Evolutionism believers call, 'living fossils'. This is where fossilised animals appear abruptly, fully formed and stay that way for 'millions of years', identical to modern creatures. So, where's the evolution?

Fool: "What about the fossils?" (b)
"Yes, the alleged transitional fossils are still missing, so where are they?" Allow them to stumble around, then state the obvious, "They're missing, because they never existed."

Fool: "What about the fossils?" (c)
"What about them?" This is enough to rattle them, as it's not the response they'd been eagerly anticipating. Ask them how fossils are created, then tell them the specific and rare conditions required for fossil formation.

Fool: "You only believe in God because you were institutionalised by Western culture and education. As a result, you no longer have a choice of religious belief as an adult."
"As a child, I was indoctrinated as a Catholic, then in high school as an Evolutionism believer. As an adult, I did my own research and arrived at the only truthful, logical, scientific conclusion."

It's predominantly Westerners who make the accusation. If there was any truth to their ridiculous statement, everyone growing up under Western culture and education would believe in God.

Fool: "Why would Jesus be white, in a Middle Eastern country?"
"He wasn't." Sometimes I prefer to ask, "What makes you think He was?"

Those depictions you see are artists' interpretations, not portrait paintings or photos. Having been born and raised in the Middle East with parents of Middle Eastern heritage, Yahshua would have similar features. In Asian countries, Yahshua is depicted with Asian features. It's an extremely poor argument, used to sway people incapable of independent thought.

Others state the Bible is wrong as they've seen a picture of Adam and Eve, with belly buttons. They imply it's proof they couldn't have been created. How does it not occur to these feeble-minded simpletons it's an artist's rendition, not a photo?

Yahshua is depicted as having feminine features, weak stature, long hair and meek personality. He was a carpenter. He didn't use power tools. As for being meek, he went berserk in the temple, flipping tables:

"And Jesus went into the temple of God, and cast out all them that sold and bought in the temple, and overthrew the tables of the moneychangers, and the seats of them that sold doves, and said unto them, It is written, My house shall be called the house of prayer; but ye have made it a den of thieves." Matt 21:12–13

Then, there's this. Here you have a crowd, incensed, baying for Yahshua's blood, intent on throwing Him off a cliff:

"And all they in the synagogue, when they heard these things, were filled with wrath, and rose up, and thrust him out of the city, and led him unto the brow of the hill whereon their city was built, that they might cast him down headlong. But he passing through the midst of them went his way." Luke 4:28–30

I can assure you, Yahshua was certainly not meek. This occurred at Mt. Precipice in Nazareth. From the summit, you can see Megiddo, where the Battle of Armageddon will be fought. As for having long hair:

"Doth not even nature itself teach you, that, if a man have long hair, it is a shame unto him? 1 Cor 11:14

Fool: "How did Jesus find people in the Middle East called Matthew, Mark, Luke and John?"
"… You're reading an English translation …"

Other pieces of Fools Gold include, "Where did Cain get his wife?' and "Where did all of the races come from?" These have been covered in the 'In the Beginning' chapter.

I Can't Come to Bed Yet—
Someone Is Wrong on the
Internet

ANYONE who has debated militant Atheists knows they dispute observations made of their religion. They'll laugh at the fact all varieties of dogs descended from an original dog pair aboard the Ark. When you point out they believe all dogs descended from fish, from evolved 'rain on the rocks', following an explosion/expansion of 'nothing', they become incensed, throwing a tantrum, "You just don't understand evolution!" Or, "That's not how evolution works!"

I tell them, "If you really understood Evolutionism, you wouldn't believe it either."

To verify my claims on what militant Atheists believed, I decided to go online and capture interactions with these creatures. By doing so, I was presented with a startling realisation, *I've witnessed their evangelism evolve!* I then posted my observation online:

"It amazes me how Evolutionism believers today constantly argue from a philosophical point of view. About ten years ago, they at least tried to make scientific arguments. I suppose they just became sick of Intelligent Designers disproving their religion with science."

After I'd posted my statement in an Atheist forum, they refused to publish my comment and sent a warning. I continue to see this style of Atheist evangelising. They profess to align with science, though continually offer philosophical arguments. Others have noticed this shift also. Here's 'Justine's' observation: "Almost every argument in here seems to be arguing that God doesn't exist because of some moral reason. I find this really bizarre."

I found a transcript of a debate I had with an Evolutionism believer, (CP), ten years previously:

PE: CP, seeing as you say you want to talk science, let's! Do you believe that a man can rise from the dead, after three days?

CP: No, that doesn't seem possible, based on our understanding of biology. Do you have reasons why you think it might be?

PE: Why can't that be possible? What 'scientific evidence' do you have to make that claim?

CP: Well, within minutes cells start to decay. Neurons are some of the first to go. Essentially your body's cells explode, irreparably. After a few minutes of actual death, it's irreversible. The structures necessary for life no longer exist.

PE: So, in other words, you're admitting that it's 'scientifically impossible' for 'non-life' to become 'life'. Therefore, according to your beliefs and science, the origin of life is NOT a NATURAL occurrence, but a SUPERNATURAL occurrence, just like Genesis records.

If CP had said that life can arise from non-life, I'd have told him it would make the Resurrection scientifically possible.

Those were the good ol' days, when believers attempted to use science to support their claims. Today, all I see are philosophical arguments.

~~Science~~ Imagination

On an Atheist page, someone had posted a sarcastic, misconstrued statement, attempting to ridicule theology. Reuben showed agreement to the post with his comment, "Fairy tales."

Nick had also chimed in, "Sounds like a fairy tale."

It was time to make them aware they were no better than the kettle calling the pot, 'black'. "How do you explain the explosion/expansion of 'nothing', caused by 'nothing', for 'no reason', producing 'everything', including, space, time, matter, energy, a finely tuned universe, natural laws, consciousness, intelligence, knowledge, truth, logic, emotions, morality, and 'life', itself?

Nick's knowledgeable answer, "Imagination."

Strangely enough, I've encountered this answer several times. Though again, for people who have a propensity for science fiction and fantasy, why should we expect anything less? After all, an Evolutionism High Priest gave the same answer, "You know, the problem with those who are unable to see evolution, I think, is they don't have imaginations." Gail E. Kennedy, PhD, Associate Professor, Anthropology, UCLA, from the video, *Evolution vs God*, Living Waters Publication.

Nick found an ally in Dianne, who was responding to his claim of theology being a fairy tale with, "Exactly what it is." I then asked her the same question I'd asked Nick.

May God bless her soul. Her answer was innocent, sincere, "Maybe ask someone with a science degree. They could explain it better than me." She wasn't a militant Atheist. She was an innocent victim who'd swallowed the lie that she was essentially pond scum that had been zapped by lightning.

Hopefully, I could make her see she was special, created by her Heavenly Father, in His image, "Dianne, you have common sense and logic. As such, you know you cannot get something from nothing, let alone, everything from nothing. Why do you cling to a belief you know to be false? Ask yourself, honestly, is it because you don't want to accept the possibility of a Creator? You don't want the moral accountability?"

Dianne's response demonstrated she'd been taken for a ride, "It's because I trust in science. What it tells me makes sense. What you tell me doesn't."

I hoped I could break through the years of Evolutionism indoctrination, and relentless propaganda she, and all of us, had been bombarded with, "Dianne, you say you trust in science, but science says you CANNOT get something from nothing. You know that, your logic and common sense tell you that, so what's REALLY going on? Consider this. Don't answer it on here. Ask yourself this question:

Which is more likely?

1. A Supreme Intelligent Being, created the universe and everything in it, putting in place laws to govern both the physical and spiritual Creations.

Or

2. An explosion/expansion of 'nothing', caused by 'nothing', for 'no reason', produced 'everything'. Including space, time, matter, energy, a finely tuned universe, natural laws, consciousness, intelligence, knowledge, truth, logic, emotions, morality, and 'life', itself.

Unfortunately, some of the smug Atheist attitudes had infiltrated a portion of Dianne's heart, "Sorry, I don't have enough crayons."

Oh, you want to throw a punch? WWJD—What Would Jesus Do? He wasn't a doormat. Among other things, He went ape in the temple, flipping tables. So, if you want to throw a punch, you'd better be prepared to take one, "Then stop eating them! But in all seriousness, read back over our interaction and think on it. Good night."

Dianne has a sense of humour! I cracked her shell, "Ha ha ha why are you even in this group?"

Two Evolutionism believers were harassing a Christian online, so I asked them the same question I'd posed to Dianne. It blows my mind that they were willing to admit, in front of others, that they believed the second option. I'd then asked both of them to show me one experiment, just one, where 'something', could come from 'nothing'. They gave me silence.

It's amazing how devout Darwinian disciples lay their logic, brains, common sense, integrity, honesty and self-worth by the wayside, declaring option two is most likely.

There's a militant Atheist who posts several of his religious posts every day. He's certainly not backward in coming forward with his beliefs. Due to his devotion to Atheism and his propensity to be constantly online, I asked him the same question I'd asked above. No response. I continued this over several weeks, each time receiving the same response, silence.

During another interaction, Carmel made this claim, "Time is a man-made construct as is science and space. Energy is, each individual, we are energy therefore we are God. The use of the Bible by organised religions is one of many attempts to distract from our own power by giving our energy and power away to others, i.e., an external God." She too, was asked the same question.

Her answer demonstrates how people will sacrifice logic and common sense, for the sake of their religious beliefs, "Neither."

"There are no other options. None. If you feel there is, let's hear it."

While Carmel responded to other commenters, my request went unanswered. Days later I offered another opportunity for redemption, "I'd really like you to back up your claim. If you can provide a third option, we'd love to hear it." Days passed, all I received was silence.

On yet another page, an Atheist claimed the Bible contained no factual evidence about the universe. Kimberley showed her ignorance as she voiced her approval, "I find it incredible that an all-powerful, all-knowing, ever-present being can only communicate through an old book full of factual errors."

It was time to get straight to the point, "Kimberley, how do you explain the explosion/expansion of 'nothing', caused by 'nothing', for 'no reason', producing 'everything', including space, time, matter, energy, a finely tuned universe, natural laws, consciousness, intelligence, knowledge, truth, logic, emotions, morality, and 'life', itself?"

Although Kimberley and I had a small interaction, I cannot re-tell it word for word, as she deleted her replies to my questions. She did this, as I'd blasted holes in all the religious dogma she'd spouted. I believe her last comment was something about a 'magical sky daddy', or some other babble. Atheists rarely seem to use science in debates, probably because they know their religion doesn't have a leg to stand on. She may have been falsely implying Evolutionism doesn't have deities.

Kimberley was given a lesson on her religion, "There's an Evolutionism Trinity—Father Time, Mother Nature and Evolutionism's holy spirit, Lady Luck. Your beliefs are just that—beliefs. In fact, the scientific method says 'something from nothing' is impossible. Are you at least honest and intelligent enough to agree your beliefs are grounded in faith, and are therefore, religious?"

Radio silence. Hopefully, she'd gone away to think. If so, I pray the interaction will play on her mind and allow her to see through her delusions and finally come to learn the truth.

When asked about Evolutionism's creation story, Reuben had this piece of 'scientific knowledge' to contribute, "It was merely a freak occurrence. The chance of it happening again the same way is completely and utterly nonsensical."

I was dumbfounded. Are they really that stupid? I held his feet to the fire, "Show me an experiment where you can get something from nothing. Do you expect us to believe Evolutionism's creation story on faith alone?" As it was with Kimberley, so it was with Reuben—radio silence.

Ten years ago, I had a militant Atheist insist the universe arose from 'fuzz balls'. I've just heard today of their latest alleged creative force, 'quantum foam'. The names change, the nonsense doesn't. Faith possessed by militant Atheists would put any Christian to shame.

Atheist Conspiracies

In another interaction, I posed the following question, "What's everyone's go-to conspiracy theory to explain away the empty tomb?"

- "I am going to walk down a line that nobody is going to like. He was drugged on the cross and he slept it off in the tomb, just like Lazarus, which was a test of the drug. The men dressed in white in the tomb were Essenes. Most of the aftermath was myth-making. Jesus went to India where he was eventually buried."—James
- "Prove it was empty. It's a Bible claim. If it was empty, it's evidence of an empty tomb. That's it. Grow up."—Lee
- "Dogs ate the body."—Mike
- "He wasn't dead when they took him down. Sabbath was coming, he was sleeping it off."—Steph

I couldn't believe what I was reading, was Steph really that stupid? I had to know, "Do you really believe Roman executioners don't know when someone is dead?" There was no reply.

Militant Atheist Suddenly Realises God Is Real

An online debate was instigated by a militant Atheist asking this question, "How to persuade a Christian to become an atheist?"—then answering it himself, "Create doubts!"

'NS' Had this to say, "There's nothing you can do if they don't prioritise truth over comfort in their beliefs."

Obviously, the irony of his comment dragged me off the sidelines and into the fray. Here's a transcript of the ensuing dialogue:

PE: Show us an experiment where you can get something from nothing. We'll wait.

NS: Why? That has nothing to do with this post or my comment.

PE: It has everything to do with it. It is the Evolutionism believers' creation story.

NS: Have you actually asked an Atheist if they believed that?

PE: They believe it, by default. They don't want to admit it, as they don't want to lose their religion.

NS: That's a no. It's amazing what you can learn if you test your hypotheses.

PE: Sorry, either purposeful design and Creation, or accidental, uncaused, explosion/expansion of nothing.

NS: That's a false dichotomy.

PE: Oh, really? Then you should have *no* trouble providing a third option. Let's hear it. Thanking you in advance.

NS: Other true dichotomies would be: Designed/not designed; Intended/unintended; Naturally occurring/artificial; Caused by a god/not caused by a god. [*Hopefully, you can see the contradictions between his suggestions and the argument he thinks he's making. He's saying the same thing as me, just in different words*]. And here's the big one: I know what caused the universe to exist/I don't know what caused the universe to exist. I don't happen to know or pretend to know. What do you think?

PE: All you postulated falls into the two positions I stated. You haven't provided a third option. You can't, it's simply not possible.

NS: Given that something exists, there are only two possibilities; something *can* come from nothing, or there was always something. Only the second one makes sense to me. What do you think?

PE: Yes, you nailed it. Our Creator tells us He is eternal.

Following this comment, NS vanished.

Evolutionism's High Priests

Richard Dawkins

This bloke is a walking contradiction. According to Dawkins, the cell has, "**all of the characteristics of highly advanced, specially designed equipment**." But then, out of the other side of his mouth, he says, "The universe we observe has precisely the properties we should expect if there is, at bottom, **no design, no purpose, no evil, no good**, nothing but blind, pitiless indifference." (Richard Dawkins, *River Out of Eden: A Darwinian View of Life*)

You're probably thinking, *That makes no sense.* You're right. But then, he turns around again and says that there *is* evident design. "Biology is the study of complicated things that have the appearance of having been **designed with a purpose**." So, Dawkins, which is it? Designed, or not designed? Purpose, or no purpose? Evil, or no evil? Good, or no good?

Richard Dawkins says 'evil' doesn't exist, and God doesn't exist, Yet, he constantly implies God is evil. It's as if he speaks with a forked tongue.

"If you want to do **evil**, science provides the most powerful weapons to do **evil**; but equally, if you want to do **good**, science puts into your hands the most powerful tools to do so." (Richard Dawkins, The Richard Dimbleby Lecture: 'Science, Delusion and the Appetite for Wonder,' 1996, BBC1)

Did you notice in his above statement his acknowledgment of 'good' and 'evil', even though he'd previously claimed they both don't exist?

"A double minded man is unstable in all his ways." James 1:8

Once more Dawkins denies the existence of 'good' and 'evil':

"Good and evil—**I don't believe that there is hanging out there, anywhere, something called good and something called evil.**" Dawkins is on a roll, "If it is solely an evolutionary convenience, **there is really no such thing as good or evil.**"

Here are other statements Dawkins has made: "And **from this flows much evil**; I had always been scrupulously careful to avoid the smallest suggestion of infant indoctrination, which I think is ultimately **responsible for much of the evil in the world**; Religion is the root of quite **a lot of evil**; The Roman Catholic Church is a disgusting institution, the second most **evil religion** in the world; Faith is one of the world's **great evils**; Technology can be used for **evil purposes**." (All quotes taken from AZ Quotes.com)

Contrast Dawkins' belief the universe wasn't designed, with the Father of String Theory—Leonard Susskind, "Our own universe is an extraordinary place that appears to be fantastically **well-designed** for our own existence. This specialness is not something that we can attribute to lucky accidents, which is far too unlikely. The apparent coincidences cry out for an explanation." (Jonathan Kirsch, 'The universe in a nutshell,' *Los Angeles Times*, 15 January 2006)

The Anthropic Principle refers to the miraculous fine-tuning of the universe to support life. Physicists and cosmologists have likened the parameters and laws of the universe being akin to a large switchboard with fifty dials. Each dial may be turned infinitely, in either direction. Yet, they're each in precisely the right setting to support life. If just one setting was slightly off, consequences would be lethal. There are approximately 400 'at the same time' requirements, for the possibility of life on Earth. Where, how, did this 'switchboard' evolve? Who, 'What', set those fifty dials at the precise settings, necessary to support life?

"Physicist Paul Davies asserts that, 'There is now broad agreement among physicists and cosmologists that the Universe is in several respects 'fine-tuned' for life. It is fine-tuned for the building blocks and environments that life requires.'" Paul recounts astronomer and mathematician Sir Fred Hoyle at Cambridge University saying, "A common sense interpretation of the facts suggests that a super-intellect has monkeyed with physics, as well as chemistry and biology." (gcarkner, 'Is it a Fine-tuned Universe?' 2013, ubcgcu.org)

Dawkins v Pell

Below is a transcript of a portion of the Australian Broadcasting Commission's *Q&A* program hosted by Tony Jones, on the 9th of April 2012, between Evolutionism high Priest Richard Dawkins and the late Catholic Cardinal, George Pell. Witness for yourself, the incredible delusion of Evolutionism's most cherished high priest:

During the program, Pell states the blatantly obvious, "Something CAN'T come from nothing!"

Dawkins ignorantly admonishes him, "Something CAN come from nothing, and that's what physicists are now telling us!"

It appears Dawkins doesn't understand the meaning of 'nothing,' confusing it with 'something', "Of course, it's counterintuitive you can get something from nothing. Of course, **common sense doesn't allow you to get something from nothing**, that's why it's interesting. It's got to be interesting in order to give rise to the universe, at all. **Something** pretty mysterious had to give rise to the origin of the universe."

Dawkins continues, "The 'nothing', that Lawrence Krauss is talking about, whether or not it's what a naïve person would conceive as 'nothing' or what a sophisticated physicist would consider to be 'nothing', it is going to be something much, much simpler, than a creative intelligence. You can dispute what's meant by 'nothing', but whatever it is, it's very, very simple."

At that point, everyone in attendance laughs. Dawkins, oblivious to the nonsense tumbling from his own mouth is baffled, "Why is that funny?"

George Pell responds, "Well I think it's a bit funny trying to define 'nothing'." The crowd erupts with laughter and clapping. Dawkins, oblivious to the nonsense he spouted, sits there, looking like a stunned mullet that has just emerged from primordial soup, wondering how it can now possibly breathe without lungs.

There are several things to keep in mind. Firstly, earlier in the debate Dawkins admitted, "Common sense doesn't allow you to get something from nothing."

Secondly, in an interview with physicist Lawrence Krauss, Dawkins admiringly tells him what he finds "stunningly exciting," (from reading his book), is the revelation that "nothing," is, "literally nothing." (Richard Dawkins and Lawrence Krauss, *Something From Nothing?* 2012, Shirley Films, ANU TV)

For the record, Krauss admits he's not really talking about 'nothing'. As He says himself, "By nothing, I don't mean nothing. Nothing, isn't nothing, anymore, in physics." (Lawrence Krauss, *A Universe from Nothing*, AAI 2009, Shirley Films, Richard Dawkins Foundation for Reason & Science)

Thirdly, Dawkins only ever debates soft targets, as in this case, a Catholic clergyman. He refuses to formally debate Intelligent Designers, since he knows Evolutionism's dogma and doctrines would be decimated under scientific scrutiny. Yet, incredibly, when in front of an extremely uninformed person on the subject, he still manages to appear the fool.

During the interview, he says, "'What is the purpose of the universe?' is a silly question." Yet, in one of his books, he says,

"Intelligent life on a planet comes of age when it first works out the reason for its own existence." (Richard Dawkins, *The Selfish Gene*)

Something From Nothing

Dawkins has defied the scientific method, common sense and logic several times with his religious belief, "You can get something, from nothing."

"The fact that life evolved out of nearly nothing, some ten billion years after the universe evolved out of **literally nothing**, is a fact so staggering that I would be mad to attempt words to do it justice." (Richard Dawkins, *The Ancestor's Tale: A Pilgrimage to the Dawn of Evolution*)

Yet, in another interview Dawkins makes this admission, "There could be **literally nothing**, from which then, something suddenly springs, and, I mean, it is very hard to grasp, and I certainly can't grasp it." (Richard Dawkins and Lawrence Krauss, *Something From Nothing?* 2012, Shirley Films, ANU TV)

Here are his words, again:

1. "Common sense doesn't allow you to get something from nothing."
2. "There could be literally nothing, from which then, something suddenly springs."

Have you ever wondered what a dictionary definition may be for someone who lacks common sense?: "A **simpleton** is an **idiot** —a person **without much common sense** or intelligence." (vocabulary.com)

Keep in mind, Dawkins just said that 'something' could jump from 'literally nothing'. Darwin says, "Nature doesn't jump." They contradict each other.

Dawkins & Hawking

They both know the truth, but choose to deny it, constantly contradicting themselves. You've just seen Dawkins contradict himself. Now, you're going to see him do it again—he can't help himself. Here's Dawkins from his book, *The Blind Watchmaker*: "The essence of life is **statistical improbability** on a colossal scale. Whatever is the explanation for life, therefore, **it cannot be by chance**." He is right. Just like a stopped clock can be right twice a day, so too, can Dawkins. Yes, life cannot arise by chance. The only logical explanation is intelligent, purposeful, Creation. He even alludes to this truth, then contradicts himself, as evidenced earlier:

1. "Without a doubt, the modern machinery of the cell, the replication of DNA and protein synthesis, it has all the characteristics of a **highly advanced, specially designed** equipment." (Richard Dawkins, *The Blind Watchmaker*)
2. "The universe we observe has precisely the properties we should expect if there is, at bottom, **no design, no purpose**." (Richard Dawkins, *River Out of Eden: A Darwinian View of Life*)
3. "Before Darwin came along, it seemed absurd to imagine that the **beauty**, **complexity**, the **purposefulness** of the living world, could possibly have come into being, without, a **Designer**." (Richard Dawkins, 'Humanists UK,' The Darwin Day Lecture, 2019)

See if you can spot one of several instances where Stephen Hawking contradicts both himself, and Dawkins:

"**No one created the universe** and no one directs our fate. This leads me to a profound realization that there probably is no Heaven and no afterlife either. We have this one life to appreciate **the grand design of the universe** and for that, I am extremely grateful."

Did you catch it?

Hawking contradicts himself again:

1. "I believe the simplest explanation is, **there is no God**."
2. "You cannot understand the glories of the universe without believing **there is some Supreme Power behind it**." (Stephen Hawking, 'Stephen Hawking Quotes – 40 quotes by a brilliant scientist,' *The Wealthy Niche*, thewealthyniche.com)

Dawkins Is a Coward

Lastly, as evidenced by his televised debate in Australia, Dawkins is *not* opposed to debating Evolutionism v Intelligent Design. The uncomfortable truth for him and all of his disciples is, he's a coward. He only goes after soft targets, running and cowering from a real fight. His interview with Pell proves it.

Expelled: No Intelligence Allowed

Expelled: No Intelligence Allowed is a 2008 documentary produced by Ben Stein. It highlights the agenda in America whereby teachers and lecturers are being fired for even suggesting an alternative to Evolutionism. Dawkins' interview is quite entertaining. While I encourage everyone to view the ninety minute presentation in its entirety, here's a snippet; talking about Evolutionism's creation story:

Ben Stein gets to the point, "Well how did it get created?"

Dawkins is uncomfortable, "Well, um, by a very slow process."

Stein persists to the crux of the matter, "Well how did it start?"

Dawkins begins to mix a word salad, "Nobody knows how it started. We know the kind of event that it must have been, the sort of event that must have happened for the origin of life."

"What was that?" Stein is not letting go.

Dawkins counters with another just-so story, "It was the origin of the first self-replicating molecule."

"Right, and how did that happen?" Stein holds Dawkins' feet to the fire.

Dawkins feels the pain, "I told you; we don't know."

"So, you have no idea how it started?" Stein seeks clarification.

Dawkins squirms in his seat, which is beginning to feel like a furnace. "No, no, nor has anybody."

Stein turns up the heat, "What do you think is the possibility that Intelligent Design might turn out to be the answer to some issues in genetics or in Darwinian evolution?"

Dawkins sweats bullets, side-steps the question and serves up another just so, word salad. "Well, it could come about in the following way. It could be that at some earlier time, somewhere in the universe, a, civilisation, evolved, by, probably some kind of Darwinian means to a very high level of technology, and designed a form of life that they seeded onto, perhaps this planet. Now that is a possibility and an intriguing, possibility and I suppose you might find evidence for that if you look at the, um, at the details of biochemistry, molecular biology, you might find a signature of some sort of designer. Um, and that designer could well be a higher intelligence, from elsewhere, in the universe."

Ben, noticing that Dawkins dropped his guard, steps in for the knockout punch. Dawkins, panicking, realising he's just put his foot in his mouth, talks over the top of him. He hastens into damage control, "But that higher intelligence would itself, have to have come about, by some, explicable, or ultimately explicable process. **It couldn't have just jumped into existence spontaneously, that's the point.**"

Ben points out in a voiceover, "Professor Dawkins was not against Intelligent Design, just certain types of designers, such as, 'God'." Or more specifically, the One True God, the God of the Judeo-Christian Bible.

Let's compare Dawkins' last comment to Ben Stein, with two of his previous comments:

1. "Common sense doesn't allow you to get something from nothing."
2. "There could be literally nothing, from which then, something suddenly springs."
3. "It couldn't have just jumped into existence spontaneously, that's the point."

Fuzzy Words

Whenever an Evolutionism believer is preaching, watch for 'fuzzy words'. It's also in their literature. For example, I'll now list the words and phrases from Dawkins' previous assertions, in the order he says them in:

"Something pretty mysterious; Whatever it is, it's very, very simple; There could be literally nothing, from which then something, suddenly springs; Must have been; Must have happened; It could come about; It could be that; Probably; Perhaps; Probably; Some kind of Darwinian means; Perhaps; That is a possibility; I suppose; You might find evidence; You might find a signature; Could well be."

Another Believer in the Hot Seat

Michael Ruse, another Evolutionism High Priest, was interviewed also. Again, Stein hits hard, "How did we get from an inorganic world, to the world of the cell?"

Are you ready for an intellectual, word-for-word scientific reply, from a world authority on Evolutionism? Here it is, in Michael Ruse's own words, "Well, one popular theory is that it might have started off on the backs of crystals. Molecules piggy-backed on the back of crystals forming and that this led to more and more complex; but of course, the nice thing about crystals is that every now and then you get mistakes, mutations, and that this opens the way for natural selection."

Stein isn't deterred by nonsense; he refuses to chase the absurd red herring. He wants science, "But, but, at one point, there was, not, a living thing …"

Ruse nervously touches his nose, as he'd been doing repeatedly. A speaker will do this if he, or she, is feeling uncomfortable. This is the behaviour of someone lying. The same way children will cover their mouth after telling a lie, "Among the most common signs of lying is the nose touch." ('Signs of Lying in Body Language,' *Psychologia*, psychologia.co)

Responding to Stein, following the touching of his nose, Ruse's voice cracks as he utters a weak, high-pitched, "Yeah," as he shuts his eyes. He wishes he wasn't there, that a gaping hole would instantly swallow him. Perhaps, in this brief period of time, where he visually shuts reality out, he's fulfilled his fantasy.

"Well, that's just the—I've just told you! I don't see any reason why you shouldn't go from, very simple, to more and more complex." He attempts to fake a pass, tries to side-step the uncomfortable question.

Stein is relentless, "I don't either, I don't either, but, I don't know how you get from mud, to a living cell. That's my question."

"Yes, well I've told you!" Ruse is incredibly flustered.

Stein wants to be clear. He presses for clarification, "One more time."

Ruse laughs nervously and surrenders, "One more time."

"On the backs of crystals?" enquires Stein.

Nervous laughter as Ruse realises how ridiculous Evolutionism sounds, "On the backs of crystals is at least one hypothesis, yes."

"So, so that's your theory and you think that is more likely and less farfetched than an Intelligent Designer?" Stein sets the record straight.

Ruse is unwillingly beaten into submission, "I think it is."

That's the best these Evolutionism High Priests can come up with? How can any of this nonsense possibly be considered science? "Anyone ... anyone?"

Dawkins Is Stumped

In another famous interview, courtesy of Creation Ministries International, Richard Dawkins is utterly stumped when asked to provide just one example of Darwinian Evolution. This brief video clip is aptly titled, *Richard Dawkins Stumped*. It's been transcribed with the permission of CMI.

CMI: "Professor Dawkins, can you give an example of a genetic mutation or an evolutionary process, which can be seen to increase the information in the genome?"

Dawkins stumped, stares silently at the ceiling for a few seconds. Taking a breath, as if about to answer, he then turns his head to the side, lost for words. Frowning, he opens his mouth, blinking, before biting his lower lip. Dumbstruck, he holds up an open hand in defeat, stammering, "Can you just stop there?"

Unfortunately, the interviewer obliges, allowing him to be 'saved by the bell'. Why? It was an interview. It was a basic question, foundational to the doctrines and dogma of Evolutionism. He should've been able to cite example after example for hours. When the interview resumes, Dawkins is seen head down, deep in thought. Looking up to resume his interview, you'd be forgiven for thinking he had an ironclad example, or at the very least, one example. If you thought this, you'd be sorely mistaken.

Dawkins: "There's a popular misunderstanding of evolution, which says that, ah, fish turned into reptiles, and reptiles turned into mammals, and, and so, somehow, we ought to be able to look around the world today and look at our ancestors, we ought to be able to see the intermediates between fish and reptiles, and between reptiles and mammals, we ought to be able to see fish, kind of, on the way to becoming, reptiles. But of course, that's not the way it is at all. Fish are modern animals. They are just as modern as we are. They're descended, from ancestors, which we're descended from. Way back 300 million years ago there would have been an ancestor, which was the ancestor of modern fish, and, the ancestor of, uh, of, modern, modern humans [at this point you can see he's struggling himself with the absurdity of the words falling from his mouth], and that ancestor, if you could have been there then, you could have seen the first steps, towards a fish, uh, say coming out onto the land and becoming, um, becoming something like an amphibian. But that was a long time ago. You wouldn't expect to see that today. And so, ah, quite a lot of the misunderstanding of evolution, I suppose, I suppose, stems from the fact that people are looking at modern animals, and thinking that Darwin had said we're descended from them. Well, we're not. We're not descended from, from, modern fish, we're not descended from modern monkeys, we're not descended from modern apes. They are modern animals just as we are. They're our cousins, they're not our ancestors."

Hopefully, you noticed that amongst his ridiculous word salad, he'd neglected to answer the question. This was despite the passing of time he was asked the question, up until the time he was ready to resume the interview. Then, despite all of that, he still failed to provide a single evidence for Darwinian Evolution. Did you notice 'fuzzy words'? If not, read it again.

Evolutionism dogma insists we're descended from fish. Evolutionism High Priest, PZ Myers, PhD, Associate Professor, Biology, University of Minnesota Morris, admits it in an interview with Ray Comfort:

Professor Myers: "Human beings are still fish."

Ray Comfort: "Human beings are still fish?"

Professor Myers: "Why yes, of course they are!"

Evolution vs. God, from Living Waters Ministry. Watch the entire video. It's less than forty minutes duration.

Choke On This

Militant Atheists have complained that CMI misrepresented what occurred during the 'Dawkins Stumped' interview, via disingenuous editing. These accusations appear to have been instigated by Dawkins' claims himself. This is hardly surprising. It's typical behaviour when their doctrinal shortcomings have been succinctly exposed for all to see. On the other hand, Creation Ministries International is constantly under attack from evangelical militant Atheists, spewing hatred. CMI has integrity, going to great lengths to ensure the accuracy and truthfulness of all they publish.

Yes, there was some editing done, some favourable editing toward Richard Dawkins. **CMI shortened Dawkins's stumped pause from a full nineteen seconds, to only eleven seconds, almost halving it!** If you have any doubt whatsoever, as to the truth being disclosed here, type 'creation.com/choke' into your web browser and read the full disclosure.

15 Questions for Evolutionists

1. How did life originate?
Evolutionist Professor Paul Davies admitted, "Nobody knows how a mixture of lifeless chemicals spontaneously organized themselves into the first living cell."[1] Andrew Knoll, professor of biology, Harvard, said, "we don't really know how life originated on this planet".[2] A minimal cell needs several hundred proteins. Even if every atom in the universe were an experiment with all the correct amino acids present for every possible molecular vibration in the supposed evolutionary age of the universe, not even one average-sized functional protein would form. So how did life with hundreds of proteins originate just by chemistry without intelligent design?

2. How did the DNA code originate?
The code is a sophisticated language system with letters and words where the meaning of the words is unrelated to the chemical properties of the letters—just as the information on this page is not a product of the chemical properties of the ink (or pixels on a screen). What other coding system has existed without intelligent design? How did the DNA coding system arise without it being created?

3. How could mutations—accidental copying mistakes (DNA 'letters' exchanged, deleted or added, genes duplicated,

chromosome inversions, etc.)—**create the huge volumes of information in the DNA of living things?**
How could such errors create 3 billion letters of DNA information to change a microbe into a microbiologist? There is information for how to make proteins but also for controlling their use—much like a cookbook contains the ingredients as well as the instructions for how and when to use them. One without the other is useless. See: Meta-information: An impossible conundrum for evolution. Mutations are known for their destructive effects, including over 1,000 human diseases such as hemophilia. Rarely are they even helpful. But how can scrambling existing DNA information create a new biochemical pathway or nano-machines with many components, to make 'goo-to-you' evolution possible? E.g., How did a 32-component rotary motor like ATP synthase (which produces the energy currency, ATP, for all life), or robots like kinesin (a 'postman' delivering parcels inside cells) originate?

4. **Why is natural selection, a principle recognized by creationists, taught as 'evolution', as if it explains the origin of the diversity of life?**
By definition it is a selective process (selecting from already existing information), so is not a creative process. It might explain the survival of the fittest (why certain genes benefit creatures more in certain environments), but not the arrival of the fittest (where the genes and creatures came from in the first place). The death of individuals not adapted to an environment and the survival of those that are suited does not explain the origin of the traits that make an organism adapted to an environment. E.g., how do minor back-and-forth variations in finch beaks explain the origin of beaks or finches? How does natural selection explain goo-to-you evolution?

5. **How did new biochemical pathways, which involve multiple enzymes working together in sequence, originate?**
Every pathway and nano-machine requires multiple protein/enzyme components to work. How did lucky accidents create

even one of the components, let alone 10 or 20 or 30 at the same time, often in a necessary programmed sequence? Evolutionary biochemist Franklin Harold wrote, "we must concede that there are presently no detailed Darwinian accounts of the evolution of any biochemical or cellular system, only a variety of wishful speculations."[3]

6. Living things look like they were designed, so how do evolutionists know that they were not designed?

Richard Dawkins wrote, "biology is the study of complicated things that have the appearance of having been designed with a purpose."[4] Francis Crick, the co-discoverer of the double helix structure of DNA, wrote, "Biologists must constantly keep in mind that what they see was not designed, but rather evolved."[5] The problem for evolutionists is that living things show too much design. Who objects when an archaeologist says that pottery points to human design? Yet if someone attributes the design in living things to a designer, that is not acceptable. Why should science be restricted to naturalistic causes rather than logical causes?

7. How did multi-cellular life originate?

How did cells adapted to individual survival 'learn' to cooperate and specialize (including undergoing programmed cell death) to create complex plants and animals?

8. How did sex originate?

Asexual reproduction gives up to twice as much reproductive success ('fitness') for the same resources as sexual reproduction, so how could the latter ever gain enough advantage to be selected? And how could mere physics and chemistry invent the complementary apparatuses needed at the same time (non-intelligent processes cannot plan for future coordination of male and female organs).

9. **Why are the (expected) countless millions of transitional fossils missing?**
Darwin noted the problem and it still remains. The evolutionary family trees in textbooks are based on imagination, not fossil evidence. Famous Harvard paleontologist (and evolutionist), Stephen Jay Gould, wrote, "The extreme rarity of transitional forms in the fossil record persists as the trade secret of paleontology."[6] Other evolutionist fossil experts also acknowledge the problem.

10. **How do 'living fossils' remain unchanged over supposed hundreds of millions of years, if evolution has changed worms into humans in the same time frame?**
Professor Gould wrote, "the maintenance of stability within species must be considered as a major evolutionary problem."[7]

11. **How did blind chemistry create mind/intelligence, meaning, altruism and morality?**
If everything evolved, and we invented God, as per evolutionary teaching, what purpose or meaning is there to human life? Should students be learning nihilism (life is meaningless) in science classes?

12. **Why is evolutionary 'just-so' story-telling tolerated?**
Evolutionists often use flexible story-telling to 'explain' observations contrary to evolutionary theory. NAS(USA) member Dr Philip Skell wrote, "Darwinian explanations for such things are often too supple: Natural selection makes humans self-centered and aggressive—except when it makes them altruistic and peaceable. Or natural selection produces virile men who eagerly spread their seed—except when it prefers men who are faithful protectors and providers. When an explanation is so supple that it can explain any behavior, it is difficult to test it experimentally, much less use it as a catalyst for scientific discovery."[8]

13. **Where are the scientific breakthroughs due to evolution?**
    Dr Marc Kirschner, chair of the Department of Systems Biology, Harvard Medical School, stated: "In fact, over the last 100 years, almost all of biology has proceeded independent of evolution, except evolutionary biology itself. Molecular biology, biochemistry, physiology, have not taken evolution into account at all."[9] Dr Skell wrote, "It is our knowledge of how these organisms actually operate, not speculations about how they may have arisen millions of years ago, that is essential to doctors, veterinarians, farmers …."[10] Evolution actually hinders medical discovery.[11] Then why do schools and universities teach evolution so dogmatically, stealing time from experimental biology that so benefits humankind?

14. **Science involves experimenting to figure out how things work; how they operate. Why is evolution, a theory about history, taught as if it is the same as this operational science?**
    You cannot do experiments, or even observe what happened, in the past. Asked if evolution has been observed, Richard Dawkins said, "Evolution has been observed. It's just that it hasn't been observed while it's happening."[12]

15. **Why is a fundamentally religious idea, a dogmatic belief system that fails to explain the evidence, taught in science classes?**
    Karl Popper, famous philosopher of science, said "Darwinism is not a testable scientific theory, but a metaphysical [religious] research programme …."[13] Michael Ruse, evolutionist science philosopher admitted, "Evolution is a religion. This was true of evolution in the beginning, and it is true of evolution still today."[14] If "you can't teach religion in science classes", why is evolution taught?

References
1. Davies, Paul, Australian Centre for Astrobiology, Sydney, New Scientist 179(2403):32, 2003.
2. Knoll, Andrew H., PBS Nova interview, How Did Life Begin? 1 July 2004.

3. Harold, Franklin M. (Prof. Emeritus Biochemistry, Colorado State University) The way of the cell: molecules, organisms and the order of life, Oxford University Press, New York, 2001, p. 205.
4. Dawkins, R., The Blind Watchmaker, W.W. Norton & Company, New York, p. 1, 1986.
5. Crick, F., What mad pursuit: a Personal View of Scientific Discovery, Sloan Foundation Science, London, 1988, p. 138.
6. Gould, Stephen Jay, Evolution's erratic pace, Natural History 86(5):14, May 1977.
7. Gould, S.J. and Eldredge, N., Punctuated equilibrium comes of age. Nature 366:223–224, 1993.
8. Skell, P.S., Why Do We Invoke Darwin? Evolutionary theory contributes little to experimental biology, The Scientist 19(16):10, 2005.
9. As quoted in the Boston Globe, 23 October 2005.
10. Skell, P.S., The Dangers of Overselling Evolution; Focusing on Darwin and his theory doesn't further scientific progress, Forbes magazine, 23 Feb 2009; http://www.forbes.com/2009/02/23/evolution-creation-debate-biology-opinions-contributors_darwin.html.
11. E.g. Krehbel, M., Railroad wants monkey off its back, Creation 16(4):20–22, 1994; creation.com/monkey_back.
12. pbs.org/moyers/journal/archives/dawkins_now.html, 3 December 2004, accessed 4 May 2022.
13. Popper, K., Unended Quest, Fontana, Collins, Glasgow, p. 151, 1976.
14. Ruse, M., How evolution became a religion: creationists correct? National Post, pp. B1, B3, B7, 13 May 2000.

Copied with permission of Creation Ministries International, Brisbane, Australia.

Wanted Dead, in Israel

IN a way, it's a miracle you're reading this. I was meant to leave Israel in a wooden box. At 2:30 a.m. one morning I couldn't sleep, feeling drawn to arise and walk through the Valley of the Shadow of Death to view the sunrise from the Mount of Olives. While there, my uncle in Melbourne and I talked on the phone for close to an hour. Finally, it was time for him to go, "Uncle Peter, wait! There's something I have to tell you!"

Twenty-one years ago, I'd received a prophetic revelation regarding a family member. I'd kept it to myself. Due to conversations I heard from others at the time, I realised they'd subconsciously picked up on it. Still, I kept my silence. Over the years, I revealed it to a few family members and close friends; including this particular uncle. Unfortunately, due to the privacy of others, I won't reveal it within these pages.

I told my uncle that months before my sojourn to Israel, I'd been sensing that my death was imminent; the catalyst for the commencement of my premonition from twenty-one years previous. During my time in Israel, I felt I'd possibly be killed there, and told my uncle so. Strangely, later that day I was with a Dutch acquaintance, Shirley, inside the walled city of Old Jerusalem. At the end of the day, as we rose from our seats to begin the fifteen-minute walk to the outside via Damascus Gate, a strong sense of foreboding engulfed me. This was similar to the premonition I had before I'd drowned. Somehow, my friend had sensed something amiss. While I was on high alert, scanning my environment as we walked, Shirley turned to me with a concerned expression, "Are you alright?"

"No."

"What's wrong?"

"Just keep walking, I'll tell you once we're outside."

At that point, I'd been visiting Old Jerusalem for a week. You'd often see people filming with cameras and phones, but today I saw what looked like a news camera. A bloke in a suit was talking to a smartly dressed woman, both with their backs to me. As I passed a few metres behind them, amongst the bustle, they both stopped their movements and turned as one, looking at me, with inquisitive expressions.

Noticing, Shirley stopped, wearing a frown, "What's going on?"

I was well aware of the fact terrorists love to have their actions televised, "Just keep walking. Hurry up, we have to get out of here." Minutes later, I spied a similar camera. All I could think about was being able to say goodbye to my children and family. As I walked, I racked my brains, wondering who I could count on to carry out my wishes, in the event of my untimely death. Veria would be ideal. I began making mental notes to pass on to her.

Once outside, I told Shirley I'd had an extremely unnerving premonition. Unperturbed, she brushed it off, "Oh well, you're outside now."

She's not getting it. We said goodbye and I crossed the road to my hostel. Once in my room, I put a vague message online, "Are any of my Australian friends awake?" It was 2:30 a.m. in Australia. Two minutes later, Veria in Townsville sent me a message, "What's up?" She told me she'd awoken from a deep sleep with the feeling that something was wrong, and to check Messenger—something she'll never do when waking up in the middle of the night. I couldn't believe it! What are the chances!?

Leaving Israel in a Wooden Box

There was no time to waste. I quickly told her of the event from twenty-one years ago, what had just occurred, and what I required her to do. She was given contact information, messages and instructions for my parents, my children, and my landlord. The premonition hadn't abated. It was awful. It felt as if every second was precious. As I hurriedly imparted information, I 'felt' a mocking voice, "You'll be leaving Israel in a wooden box!"

Oh great, I've got less than a week to live. Veria was attempting to ally my concerns. "No, Veria. It's going to happen; I'll be dead within a week. You have to do as I ask." I'd been on edge for a couple of hours, jumpy, complaining of hunger. I was annoyed that I was going to die in a foreign country, "I have to eat. I'm going downstairs to get something." As I said it, the mocking voice returned, "What's the point?—you'll be dead within twenty-four hours!"

Ah damn it! This sucks! Bugger it, I don't care anymore, I have to eat something. Resignedly, I ventured downstairs to possibly meet my fate. I was staying in East Jerusalem, a bustling Arab locality directly across from the Damascus Gate entrance into Old Jerusalem. This was a couple of hundred metres from the 'Garden Tomb', a site where the Jewish Messiah, Yahshua, is believed to have been crucified and buried. The way all of them looked at me, their eyes seemed sorrowful, curious, knowing, As I looked at them, my eyes asked, "Is it you?"

Returning to my room I rang Veria, "I'm due to move into Old Jerusalem tomorrow. I've already paid a week in advance. If this feeling is still here in the morning, I'm going to forfeit my accommodation and get the hell out of Jerusalem!"

Hanging up the phone, still jittery and highly-strung, I found time for personal reflection, *This doesn't make sense—my book isn't finished yet!* From that moment, the premonition abated.

"You're Living on Borrowed Time"

Touching down in Sydney was surreal. I made it home, outside of a wooden box! It felt as if I'd cheated death—for a time. Over the next two weeks, seemingly out of nowhere, three times I heard this sneering message, "You're living on borrowed time." I'm happy to say, It's been close to a year and I haven't heard from that sinister entity since.

There's a spiritual battle being waged around us, all of us, whether we're aware of it, or not.

The Last Stand

THE Bible is true. Yes, there are parts I don't agree with, like, or understand. However, this doesn't make it untrue. You don't like His rules? Take it up with Him. They're not my rules. I'm in the same boat as you.

You'll never get one kind of animal to 'evolve' into a completely different kind of animal, regardless of how many magical 'millions of years' you care to throw at it. Let's just say, hypothetically, that you could. Well now, you've just added Intelligent Design to the process—human engineering. Then, you're left explaining how animals came from an explosion of 'nothing'.

Lessons From Titanic

Don't mock God:

"Not even God himself could sink this ship." (Employee of the White Star Line, at the launch of the *Titanic*, 31 May 1911, American Originals, National Archives and Records Administration)

"I remember when the Titanic sank in 1912, it was the ship that was supposed to be unsinkable. The only thing it ever did was sink. When it took off from England, all kinds of passengers were aboard—millionaires, celebrities, people of moderate means, and poor folks down in the steerage. But a few hours later when they put the list in the Cunard office in New York, it carried only two categories—lost and saved." (Vance Havner, AZQuotes.com)

So too shall it be at the Resurrection and Judgement—Lost, or Saved. Choose wisely.

This Is My Take on It

For whatever reason, God decided to create Earth, fill it with fascinating creatures then proceeded to create two humans, male and female, in His image, after His likeness.

Typically, humans have empathy, creativity, a sense of humour, a sense of justice, a desire to have children, etc. These traits are reflected in the Scriptures—like father, like son; or daughter.

Earth was perfect, until sin entered and corrupted that which had been created 'good'. "Why?" you ask. I don't know. I can't stand it when someone doesn't know an answer, they'll make one up. Often, when asking a question, I'll instruct the person to answer with either, "Yes," "No," or "I don't know." After receiving an "I don't know" answer, I'll thank them for not making something up.

Either way, the Creation was corrupted with the arrival of sin. Suddenly, Adam and Eve were aware of their nakedness. Concepts and reality of death and decay had now infiltrated the Creation, a previously foreign concept.

Everything had to be restored back to the original Creation. A 'factory reset', if you will. There was the problem of justice, however. The Law had been broken; justice had to be served.

A plan was devised for Yahshua to live on Earth as a man, though lead a sinless life. As an innocent man, His death would be atonement for our punishment. In other words, rather than having the sentence of 'punishment by death' placed on us, we could opt for Yahshua's sacrificial death to be a substitute for our deaths.

There's a catch. This was a huge price. Yahweh's Son would be falsely accused, charged, mocked, tortured and horribly executed, in our place. His Son was innocent, we are not. Yet His Son received the death penalty. If we live our lives not acknowledging the price that was paid for the atonement of our sins, then we're not deserving of it:

"I said therefore unto you, that ye shall die in your sins: for if ye believe not that I am he, ye shall die in your sins." John 8:24

Yahweh paid a price too, exemplified by Abraham and his son Isaac. Why should Yahshua step in and take our punishment if we've lived a life of indifference toward His sacrifice? Worse, if our life centred around denying His existence and deriding Him with swear words.

"Whosoever therefore shall confess me before men, him will I confess also before my Father which is in heaven. But whosoever shall deny me before men, him will I also deny before my Father which is in heaven." Matt 10:32–33

If Yahshua intercedes on our behalf, we'll be accepted into Heaven. Earth will be restored back to its original Creation. Yahshua will be King over Earth, ruling from New Jerusalem. There'll be no more death and suffering:

"And I saw a new heaven and a new earth: for the first heaven and the first earth were passed away; and there was no more sea. And I John saw the holy city, new Jerusalem, coming down from God out of heaven, prepared as a bride adorned for her husband. And I heard a great voice out of heaven saying, Behold, the tabernacle of God is with men, and he will dwell with them, and they shall be his people, and God himself shall be with them, and be their God. And God shall wipe away all tears from their eyes; and there shall be no more death, neither sorrow, nor crying, neither shall there be any more pain: for the former things are passed away. And he that sat upon the throne said, Behold, I make all things new. And he said unto me, Write: for these words are true and faithful." Rev 21:1–5

If we're found not deserving of atonement, we'll be tossed into the Lake of Fire for the second death, soul death. We shall be burnt up and be no more:

"He that overcometh shall inherit all things; and I will be his God, and he shall be my son. But the fearful, and unbelieving, and the abominable, and murderers, and whoremongers, and sorcerers, and idolaters, and all liars, shall have their part in the lake which burneth with fire and brimstone: which is the second death." Rev 21:7–8

The Bible truly is our Creator's word for His Creation. If we choose not to believe, we are without excuse:

"Because that which may be known of God is manifest in them; for God hath shewed it unto them. For the invisible things of him from the creation of the world are clearly seen, being understood by the things that are made, even his eternal power and Godhead; so that they are without excuse." Rom 1:19–20

If Evolutionism is true, how would you decide right from wrong? What's the standard you would use, to judge by? Do you let the majority, or the government, decide? Without God, objective morality, the distinguishing of right and wrong, and good and evil, is reduced to individual, personal opinions, not matters of objective reality. By default, slavery, paedophilia, murder, rape, apartheid, holocausts, etc., couldn't be forbidden. It would come down to this nonsensical claim, 'Whatever is true for you'.

If humans are just animals, as Evolutionism dogma declares, why don't we apply survival of the fittest to them? If a lion kills a zebra, it's not murder. So, if humans are just a kind of animal, how can murder be objectively wrong? This is why you have Evolutionism-believing Peter Singer wanting to legalise the killing of physically and mentally handicapped children. If that wasn't bad enough, you have Evolutionism High Priest, Richard Dawkins, telling Singer, "Peter, I think you must be one of the most moral people in the world."

Yahshua Was a Jew

He observed the holy days, food laws and commandments. They were His, after all. His followers did likewise. They attended and preached in Synagogues. Their Bible was the Old Testament. Yahshua was the Jewish Messiah their Scriptures proclaimed:

"In those days came John the Baptist, preaching in the wilderness of Judaea, And saying, Repent ye: for the kingdom of heaven is at hand. For this is he that was spoken of by the prophet Esaias, saying, The voice of one crying in the wilderness, Prepare ye the way of the Lord, make his paths straight." Matt 3:1-3

Here's what's interesting about this. Most Jews do not accept Yahshua as their Messiah. Then, you have Catholics and Protestants who claim to be followers of the Jewish Messiah, but aren't. The vast majority worship on the wrong day and think Yahshua was joking when He said:

"If ye love me, keep my commandments." John 14:15

As for His holy days, they're not observed, in defiance of His command and example. Instead, Pagan gods and their associated feasts are celebrated.

This isn't a game. We're playing Russian Roulette with our lives. If you speak English, burn any Bible version you have and get yourself the Holy Bible, the KJB.

Hard Truth

The Bible, Jews, Judaism and Christianity have withstood all eradication attempts. The Bible is God's word. It's written within a historical theme, stating specific and verifiable events, names, places and dates.

We were created. There is an option for eternal life in a restored 'Heaven' on Earth. Or, damnation and soul annihilation in the Lake of Fire. It's our choice. "If something is true, no amount of wishful thinking will change it." (Richard Dawkins)

During high school, our mathematics textbooks revealed the answers in their back pages. 'Revelation', the last Book of the Bible, also contains answers. Significant of these is, "In the end, God wins."

So, ask yourself, do you want to be a loser, or a winner? Will you choose smoking, or non-smoking? Lost, or saved?

Am I therefore become your enemy, because I tell you the truth?" Gal 4:16

So be it.

Evolutionism, with all of its fanciful doctrines, is a joke. The institution of the Roman Catholic Church is satanic. Roots from this church have spread into protestant groups, some more so than others.

Have you ever wondered, "What's the meaning of life?" If you have, that's your conscience telling you Evolutionism is a fairy tale. If the universe and everything in it, including yourself, exists due to some random, unguided, explosion/expansion of 'nothing', then life wouldn't have a purpose. The fact that you ask yourself this question means you know, deep down, Evolutionism isn't true.

Would you like to know the meaning of life? It's really quite simple —'To know God'.

'It Is Finished'

This has been a tough read. Congratulations on making it to the end. For some reading this, it'll be as if I've just poured holy water on the Devil. For those who are currently seething, before you spew your hate, keep this in mind:

"Blessed are ye, when men shall revile you, and persecute you, and shall say all manner of evil against you falsely, for my sake." Matt 5:11

Thank you.

"It is finished." John 19:30

www.ingramcontent.com/pod-product-compliance
Lightning Source LLC
Chambersburg PA
CBHW031230290426
44109CB00012B/234